JAN & DEAN ARCHIVES
VOLUME 2

Dean Torrence at Kittyhawk Graphics with unissued Deadman's Curve Soundtrack album cover

FOREWORD

Have a Bitchen Summer

That's what Dean wrote to me in 1977 or 1978 on the front of a 1960s Jan & Dean tourbook (it's reproduced later in this volume). I wasn't there at the time he did it: my parents were vacationing in California and I had given them Dean's Kittyhawk studio address which he used on the post card cover he designed for the Beach Boys Live In London U.S. issue LP. Beach Boys fans know all sorts of important trivia like that.

Being the great parents that they were, my mom and dad drove up and down Sunset Boulevard until they found the address, knocked on the door and miraculously, Dean was there.

By all accounts he was incredibly good to my parents, walking them around his studio and letting them take pics to be sent back home to me. He has just finished work on the Almost Summer soundtrack graphics and even sang with Mike and a couple of other musicians on a live appearance promoting it. He also posed for the picture with the album cover he was designing for the soon to be issued Deadman's Curve soundtrack for the TV biopic (which never did get released). Dean even tried calling my house to talk with me, but I was probably in class at the time.

It was one of the most thoughtful gifts my parents ever brought me and an incredibly nice thing for Dean to do for two strangers with a young fanboy at home. I was a fan before, but became something of a freak thereafter.

My mom, by the way, was a real sport and later took me, her (then) underage son to a Philadelphia nightclub where Jan & Dean were appearing. She even had a good time.

So the reason for this personal diatribe? To explain the reason for these books and the huge personal collection I have. We all have a different reason why the music speaks to us or why we become obsessive: that's mine. And YOU gain the benefit since I wanted to archive it all and place it into book format.

Enjoy this second volume of articles, fanzines, photos and other assorted treasures that you may have missed, even if you WERE collecting stuff during their first or second wave of popularity!

Copyright 2013 White Lightning Publications

TORRENCE OF BURIED TREASURES

JAN & DEAN

TORRENCE OF BURIED TREASURES

TORRENCE OF BURIED TREASURES

INTRODUCTION

"TORRENCE OF BERRY'D TREASURES" is an attempt to present in an easily accessible form a variety of archival items associated with JAN & DEAN which have been discovered in that now famous garage high in Bel Air. The greater majority of these items are handwritten lyrics to songs that Jan Berry and/or Dean Torrence either subsequently plied into songs or were in the process of doing so before other interests diverted their attentions. There are also a number of sets of lyrics which progressed no further than the form in which you find them now. Apart from Jan and Dean themselves, a number of these handwritten lyrics were composed by various affiliates including longtime friend Don Altfeld, disc jockey Roger Christian, femme fatale Jill Gibson and confidante Joan Jacobs, to name just a few. The following pages will indeed provide many surprises as well as add just that much more mystery to the "clown princes of rock 'n roll" .... JAN & DEAN.

Special thanks to JAN BERRY, a talent undiminished by fate .....

CONTENTS

```
1 .......... ODDS 'N ENDS
3 .......... ROCK 'N' ROLL STAR AT SINATRA TRIAL (clipping)
4........... JAN & DEAN EXPLAIN THE BIG BEAT (clipping)
5 .......... CROSSING THE BRIDGE (clipping)
            STRICTLY OFF THE RECORD (clipping)
            'DANCE PARTY' BACK AGAIN ON SATURDAY (clipping)
6 .......... WEIRD FILM CRASH (clippings)
8 .......... THE BEAT OF THE MODERN SOUND: WILL IT LAST? (clipping)
9 .......... JAN & DEAN FAN CLUB NEWS SHEET FEBRUARY 1962
10 ......... JAN & DEAN FAN CLUB NEWS SHEET MAY 1962
11 ......... JAN & DEAN FAN CLUB NEWS SHEET MAY 1963
12 ......... HANDWRITTEN LYRICS
78 ......... JAN & DEAN FAN CLUB NEWS SHEET MAY 1963
79 ......... JAN & DEAN FAN CLUB NEWS SHEET AUGUST 1963
80 ......... JAN & DEAN FAN CLUB NEWS SHEET MARCH 1964
81 ......... NOTES FOR HANDWRITTEN LYRICS
89 ......... JAN BERRY'S NON JAN & DEAN SCREEN GEMS COMPOSITIONS
```

TORRENCE OF BURIED TREASURES

ODDS 'N ENDS

In addition to the bulk of the text contained in pages 12 to 77 inclusive, a number of other interesting and mysterious items have come to light. Although physical proof of their existence is at hand, the following resume will detail them.

A DEUCE A GOER	Roger Christian's lyrics. Lead guitar riff.
ANGEL	Music only, no author
BLUE MOON	Music and recorded demo (backing vocals only)
(A) BOY	Music only, no author
BEHAVE	Music only, no author
BAT CAVE	Music and recorded demo (instrumental)
BIG CITY	Music only, no author
CAN'T TIE ME DOWN	Words and music, no author (1.7.64)
CLOSER YOU ARE	Music only, no author
CANARY	Music only, no author (AKA HOT CANARY)
CRYING OUT LOUD	Music only, no author (Designation GLEN CAMPBELL/CAPITOL RECORDS) (ARRANGEMENT: CHARLIE CALELLO)
DEEPER & DEEPER	Music only, no author (AKA ALL THE WAY)
DREAM ROVER	Music only, no author
DON'T YA' JUST KNOW IT!	Music only, no author (circa 1966)
DON'T BREAK MY HEART	Words & Music by Gary Zekley and Don Altfeld
DON'T BREAK MY HEART	Words & Music by Don Altfeld
ELEVENTH MINUTE	Music by Jill Gibson and Don Altfeld (Instrumental demo exists) Track AKA ELEVENTH HOUR, subsequently became WALK ON THE WET SIDE.
ELEPHANT CANDY	Music by Jan Berry
FLOWING DOWN STREAM	Music only, no author. Arrangement by Jan Berry
FAST & ALONE IN MY STINGRAY	Words only, no author
FEEL ALRIGHT	Words & Music, no author
FREE FREE FREE	Music only (rhythm track) No author
(THE) GOLDEN ROSE	Words & Music, no author
GONE TO THE MOON	Music only, no author
GOODBYE BROADWAY	Music only, no author
GLAD ALIVE	Music by Jan Berry, no words
GRASSHOPPER	Music only, no author
HE MADE IT (& THAT'S ALL THAT COUNTS)	Music only, no author
HOT LOOKIN' LADY (TOO HOT)	Words & Music. Full demo exists. Song AKA HOT SHOT, HOT LADY. Various contributors include Gary Snyder, Bill Berry Jr., Jan Berry, Alan Wolfson and Jim Armstrong
HE'S THE GUY FOR ME	Music only, no author
HEARTBREAKER	Music only, no author. Rhythm track recorded April 1st 1966 at Columbia Studios
HUSH-ABYE	Music only, no author
HELPLESSLY	Music only, no author
HOW VERY WONDERFUL	Words & Music by D.Wood
JESTER'S PARTY	Pseudo radio show by Jan Berry & Don Altfeld. Recording exists, circa 1959. Radio KLQW.
JACK STRAW	Music only, no author
JOHN GLENN	Music only, no author

TORRENCE OF BURIED TREASURES

I WILL ALWAYS LOVE YOU	Words & Music by Tony Garcia (30.3.76)
I KNEW IT WOULDN'T LAST	Part words, full music, no author
I'M DYING TO GIVE YOU MY LOVE	Words & Music by Jan Berry and Don Altfeld. Demo record at United Recording Studios.
I'M COMIN' OUT OUT OUT	Words & Music, no author
I DON'T WANNA GO BACK TO SCHOOL	Words & Music, no author
I GUESS YOU KNOW	Words & Music by Goffin-King
IT'S GETTING TOUGHER EVERY NIGHT	Words & Music by Goffin-King
KEY TO YOUR HEART	Music only, no author
KISSABLE SUE	Music only, no author
LONELY BULL	Music only, used as warm-up tune for Jan & Dean's sixties live appearances
LOVE - LOVE IN	Music only, no author
LIKE OLD TIMES	Words & Music by Jan Berry
LONG WAY TO GO	Music only, no author
(THE) LAND OF LOVE	Written by Bodie Chandler (1961)
LOOK OUT	Words & Music, no author
LITTLE SCHOOL GIRL	Music only, no author
LOOK NO MORE	Music only, no author
L.A. TOWN	Music only, no author
LAWRENCE	Music only, no author, used as warm-up for Jan and Dean's sixties live appearances
LIGHT MY FIRE	Music only, no author
MAMA'S GONE SURFIN'	Music only, no author
MISS YOU	Music only, no author
MOVE OVER ROVER	Written by Jack Keller and Cynthia Weil. Arranged by Jan Berry
MARGIE	Music only, no author
MAKE UP YOUR MIND (1961)	Music by Bodie Chandler, Lyrics by Ed McKendry
MYSTERIOUS THINGS ARE HAPPENING	Words & Music by Jan Berry
NICE GUYS FINISH LAST	Written by Barry Mann and Mike Anthony. Demo recorded by The Matadors for Liberty Records.
ONE MINUS ONE	Music by Bob Maughan, Lyrics by Cliff Stephenson
ON A TRIP	Music only, no author
ONLY ME	Lyrics only, no author
PLAY ON BRAVE BULLS	Music only, no author, used as warm-up for Jan and Dean's sixties live appearances
QUASIMODO	Music only, no author
QUEEN OF THE ANGELS	Words & Music, no author
SONG NO. 2	Music only, no author. Arranged by Jan Berry
SHE LOOKS LIKE A GIRL I USED TO KNOW	Words & Music, no author
SHE DIGS IT	Music only, no author
SIDNEY THE SEASICK SURFER	Words & Music, no author
SURFBOARD COWBOY	Words & Music by Harry Owens and Gene Cross
SEE YOU IN THE MORNING	Music only, no author
SUGAR SHACK	Music only, no author
TIME & SPACE	Lyrics only, no author
THAT'S ALL I WANT FROM YOU	Music only, no author
THAT'S THE WAY IT IS	Music only, (AKA SHE'S JUST A HOT SHOE)
TEACH ME HOW	Written by Goffin-King
THOSE EYES	Music only, no author
TWIST TWIST	Music only, no author
TWO STARS	Words & Music, no author

CONTINUED ON PAGE 89

TORRENCE OF BURIED TREASURES

Rock 'n' Roll Star at Sinatra Trial

Rock and roll star Dean Torrence took the witness stand in the Frank Sinatra Jr. kidnap trial today and swore that he took no part in the alleged abduction of the youthful singer and lent no money to finance it.

Torrence, member of the red-hot "Dean and Jan" song team, was called to testify after the court ordered that Sinatra Sr. appear for further testimony Wednesday and young Sinatra be on hand Thursday.

Torrence, whose record album "Surf City" sold more than 800,000 copies, testified that defendant Barry Worthington Keenan was "my best friend". But he denied he was taken into Keenan's confidence on what defense attorneys call a "publicity hoax" kidnaping on Dec. 8.

He testified he had met defendant Joseph Clyde Amsler, but said he never met the third man accused in the federal court trial, John William Irwin.

DIRECT QUESTIONS

Asked on direct examination if he had 'any knowledge prior to Dec. 8 about the kidnaping of Frank Sinatra Jr.," Torrence replied: "No sir, I did not."

Exchanges in the question-and-answer testimony included:

Q.—Did you lend money to defendant Barry Worthington Keenan for the purpose of financing the abduction of Frank Sinatra Jr.

A.—No sir, I didn't.

Q.—Did you discuss it (the kidnaping) with anyone prior to Dec. 8.

A.—No, sir, I did not.

Q.—Did Mr. Keenan give you $25,000 in a paper sack, hand it to you on the lawn, on Dec. 11.

A.—No sir.

Q.—Did Mr. Keenan tell you he went to Tijuana to buy the guns.

A.—No sir.

Torrence admitted he had a joint safety deposit box with Keenan, but said it was all Keenan's idea. He testified that after the three defendants were arrested FBI agents took him to the bank and opened the box.

SAYS HE TOOK NO PART IN ALLEGED KIDNAP
Dean Torrence, right, is shown with Jan Barry

MONEY ENVELOPE

The witness said the FBI took an envelope containing money from the box but he did not know before this time that there was money in the envelope.

Before the trial opened, the FBI said that about $1800 of the $240,000 ransom money paid by the young singer's famous father was in the envelope.

Before Torrence took the stand another friend of Keenan, swim pool service owner Theodore M. Beck, also denied he knew of any plans for the asserted abduction.

MORE MONEY

He said the FBI found an undisclosed amount of money in the closet of his apartment after a visit from Keenan, but denied knowing it had been left there.

Beck, under cross-examination, admitted being acquainted with Torrence. He also testified he was acquainted with Nancy Sinatra, and "went to a party at her home when I was about 15 years old."

Beck said Keenan was "in and out" of the Beck apartment on various occasions. He said Keenan spent the night Dec. 11. The FBI assertedly found the money in the closet Dec. 14.

The return of the Sinatras was assured by a ruling of the Federal Court trial judge, who earlier ordered defense attorneys to show their testimony was needed on "material cause" before defense attempts at a subpoena would be upheld.

Sinarta Jr. now is in Europe on an entertainment tour. The date of his expected return was not immediately disclosed.

Meanwhile, three earlier witnesses testifying near the windup of the prosecution's case produced a colorless court session today that established little other than:

• One witness rented a car to defendant Barry Worthington Keenan the day after young Sinatra allegedly was kidnaped for $240,000 ransom.

• Another rented a motel room to Keenan and another man shortly before the case broke.

• The third received a call that Sinatra was "alive and all right" the morning after the kidnaping.

James V. Schmidt, fleet manager of a car rental service, identified Keenan in court as renting the 1963 auto from the agency at the Beverly Hilton on Dec. 9.

Robert Barton, manager of a motel at 115 S. Fairfax Ave., identified Keenan as the man who rented a room Nov. 21 under the name "Bill Keene." He said Keenan and the other man, registered as "Bob Allen," occupied the room from Nov 21 to Dec. 2.

Barton added that the two men left without paying the bill. He saw Keenan on several occasions during their stay but did not see "Allen," he testified.

William Dahle, sports wire reporter for radio station KMPC, testified he received a call on Dec. 9 informing him that young Sinatra was alive and well. The unknown caller requested him to call Sinatra's parents, he said.

Dahle testified he did not call the Sinatras, but instead notified the FBI.

The Federal prosecutor expects to complete his case tonight or before noon tomorrow.

Then the defense will take its turn and attempt to show that the alleged kidnaping was a "publicity hoax."

Keenan, 23, Joseph C. Amsler, also 23, and John W. Irwin, 42, are named in a six-count indictment covering the alleged abduction of the 20-year-old singer from a Lake Tahoe lodge Dec. 8 and the procuring of the ransom from Frank Sinatra Sr.

Both Sinatra Jr. and his famous father have denied on the witness stand in Federal court under questioning by prosecution and defense that the alleged abduction was a hoax.

Defense lawyers Morris Lavine and George Forde for Amsler, Charles Crouch for Keenan and Gladys Towles Root for Irwin, were told by the court to outline the defense case prior to the ruling today and show why they want to recall the two Sinatras.

Today's opening session followed a three-day recess, Friday having been the day of the legal observance of George Washington's birthday and Saturday being an off-day in the courts.

TORRENCE OF BURIED TREASURES

Jan and Dean trace The Modern Sound back to 'Sh-Boom' by the Chords

Jan and Dean Explain

THE BIG BEAT

The revolution in the recording and entertainment business is called rock 'n' roll by some people. Others have named it pop music and even "The Modern Sound."

Two Californians—Jan Berry and Dean Torrence (Jan and Dean)—explain this revolution: What it means, how it affects teenagers and preteenagers, what are its economic factors and how it influences more than just young people.

In the first of a three-part series, Jan and Dean trace the overture, the beginnings of "The Modern Sound."

Jan and Dean, as a pair of football ends at University High School, cut their first record, "Baby Talk," in Jan Berry's garage. Ten weeks after it was released, it was a hit, selling 150,-000 copies a day for three months.

At present, after six years of hit records, the boys are enrolled in college—Dean an art major at USC and Jan in medical school at UCLA.

By JAN and DEAN

HAL BLAINE beats out a few rhythms on the wall and casually walks into the front door of the studio prior to a recording session.

After he makes it into the session, he sits down at his previously set up drum set, and counts off the first tune.

Hal is probably one of the many drummers in the country making close to $100,000 a year by being a contributor to what we call The Modern Sound.

Surprised? Well, so are we when we consider the changes that have transpired in the recording and music business during the past 10 years.

Our first recollections of the music business go back to about 1954. Most of our generation would date the origin of The Modern Sound back to one of two records, "Sh-Boom" by a group known as the Chords, or "Gee" by an unlikely sounding group, The Crows.

These and recordings like them were the antecedents of what was to prove as a sort of revolution in the music world.

Teenage Self Realization

Teenagers were beginning to become aware of themselves as a group, and among other symbols of identification, this new music was all their own. The early songs expressed this well.

Like Chuck Berry said in "School Days:"

**Up in the morning and off to school
The teacher is teachin' the golden rule
American history and practical math
Ya study 'em hard a-hopin' to pass
Ya workin' your fingers right down to the bone
The guy behind ya won't leave ya alone**
Copyright, Arc Music Co., 1957

Of course, we didn't confine our music to school. The weekends and summers brought parties, and parties meant a stack of records. We listened and danced; and we still remember people, places and incidents which we associated with certain particular records.

Some of the songs that were very popular at that time proclaimed the arrival and imminent durability of the new music, then termed rock 'n roll.

There was little Richard:
**All around the world
Rock 'n' roll is here to stay**

Here to Stay

It is interesting to note that the Beatles themselves have said that Little Richard's style has had a marked influence on their own recordings.

Also, Danny and the Juniors (a typically unsophisticated but yet honest name for a

Continued on Page 8, Col. 4

TORRENCE OF BURIED TREASURES

CROSSING THE BRIDGE

(Continued from Page 1)

recording group of the day warbled:

We don't care what people say
Rock 'n' roll is here to stay

Ironically, neither of these two artists stayed; but what they preached did. The young person in that day had his own music to listen to and in listening to it he found his own identity.

The adults scoffed and called the music horrible. Especially the old hat singers. Naturally the critics berated our music, saying it was a fad and wouldn't last.

We distinctly remember reading an article at that time in which Frank Sinatra blasted the new trend in music. Well, he changed his mind pretty quick when he found out that his newly formed record company, Reprise Records, could not sell enough of the old-fashioned records to keep in the black.

He hired Jimmy Bowen, an ex-rock 'n' roller himself, to take over the Artist and Repertoire chores of the firm. Jimmy took Hal Blaine and the rest of the boys with the Cadillacs, and together with a few violins and background singers stuck them behind Dean Martin and even Frank.

The rest is history. With his number one record of "Everybody Loves Somebody," Dean Martin had his first hit in some three or four years, and he has continued to sell singles and albums as well as the best in the business.

Sinatra himself has since turned to the modern sound and is now back on the charts.

What about the precursors of the modern sound. The chord structure of the songs was usually based on only three or four chords. The melodies were rarely involved. The few musicians on the record date provided simple musical backgrounds for the vocal.

The final sound was simple, not involving much harmony or use of such musical devices as counterpoint, variation, or development.

Fortunately, the most important and most universal musical device was retained—rhythm. The young listener rejected intricacies in favor of the beat and the overall sound.

Strictly Off the Record

BY WALLY GEORGE

DEPARTMENT OF IMMORTAL LYRICS—

"Hey little school girl,
Wake up sleeepy head.
Come on little darlin'
Get up out of that bed.
The school bell is ringin'
Vacation time is gone
No more watchin' the late show,
From now on."
—from "Young School Girl" by Fats Domino (Imperial).

★

TV Disc Jockey Dick Clark should be well in tune with his horde of adoring followers tomorrow night at Hollywood Bowl — for video's musical envoy to the chewing gum set will have a potent package of talent on hand as a lure.

Not the least of this talent are a couple of local teen-agers who were (as in the well-told legend of show biz) unknown a year ago, quite unaware of their forthcoming popularity.

In fact, the only entertaining Jan Berry and Arnold Ginsburg (who record under the names of Jan & Arnie) did was at private parties, where they banged out tunes on the piano and drums. At times they made up their own tunes and from this came the song "Jennie Lee."

Arwin Records waxed the rocker and it wasn't long before the boys picked up a gold disc on Clark's American Bandstand show when the platter hit the million mark.

Their second release, "Gas Money"/"Bonnie Lou," is currently showing up well on the charts and Arwin is readying a third single, "The Beat That Can't Be Beat"/"I Love Linda," for release Sept. 2.

'Dance Party' Back Again on Saturday

Teen-agers take the spotlight again this Saturday at 7:30 p.m. as the Junior Chamber of Commerce sponsors its second "Wink Martindale Dance Party" in Municipal Auditorium.

Jan and Dean, singing their latest record hit "We Go Together," headline a cast which features Dante and the Evergreens, the Untouchables, Deane Hawley, Mike Adams and the Red Jackets.

The dance party consists of a television broadcast from 8 to 9 p.m. over KCOP, Channel 13, followed by a one-and-a-half-hour stage show. About 300 Long Beach area teen-agers dance each week to music of their favorite artists and prizes are awarded.

The first of the Junior Chamber-sponsored shows was held last Saturday and Jim Selover, president of the civic group, said "if the enthusiasm of those in attendance was any indication, the 'Dance Party' is assured of being the place to go on Saturday night."

Reserved section seats are on sale at the Junior Chamber office, 121 Linden Ave., and Domenico's restaurants at 6110 Long Beach Blvd. and 5339 E. Second St. General admission tickets will be available at the auditorium box office Saturday at 6 p.m. Doors open at 7 p.m.

Anyone wishing to dance on future shows should get in touch with the Junior Chamber office, Selover said.

Selover said negotiations are under way to bring Fabian, Frankie Avalon, Rickey Nelson, Paul Anka and Bobby Rydel to future Wink Martindale parties.

TORRENCE OF BURIED TREASURES

Friday, August 6, 1965
SAN FRANCISCO CHRONICLE

Weird Film Crash

Trains Hit —Singer, 14 Others Hurt

Los Angeles County

Fifteen persons, including rock 'n' roll singer Jan Berry, were injured yesterday when a railroad engine plowed into the rear of a flatcar on a movie location scene.

Berry, 24, half of the singing team of Jan and Dean, suffered a compound fracture of the left leg. His partner and co-star in the film, Dean Torrence, 25, who figured in the 1963 Frank Sinatra Jr. kidnap trial, was unhurt.

Of the 14 others injured, 12 were film company workers on the flatcar and two were train crew members. Berry and six others suffered fractures, while the others sustained lesser injuries, police said.

The company for the film "Easy Come, Easy Go" was working near the Southern Pacific Railroad station in this San Fernando Valley community.

SIGNALS

The flatcar, carrying the film crew, was being towed by one engine and followed by another, which the crew was filming. The crew was trying to get the second engine to pull closer, officers said, but a mixup in signals brought the second locomotive up too fast.

It collided with the flatcar at between 15 and 20 miles per hour, up-ending the flatcar to a 54-degree angle and spilling Jan, Dean, the crew and their equipment along the track for 150 feet.

Also among the more seriously hurt were director Bar-

Career Nipped in the Bud

By BOB THOMAS
AP Movie-Television Writer
HOLLYWOOD (AP) — To Jan Berry, the whole affair had a feeling of unreality: the onrushing locomotive, bodies strewn about as on a battlefield, his own leg dangling at a crazy angle.

But the event was painfully real. A month later, the rock 'n' roll singer is able to gain some perspective on the catastrophe that nipped his budding film career on the day it began.

Berry is a member of the singing act, Jan and Dean, the latter being Dean Torrence. The two boys messed around with rock 'n' roll while students at University High School in West Los Angeles, scored with their first record, "Jenny Lee."

In the shaggy, semi-literate world of rock 'n' roll, Jan and Dean stand out. They are well-groomed and look like football ends, which they once were. Although they can earn as much as $5,000 per night on singing dates, they refused to let careers interrupt their schooling. Dean graduated in art at the University of Southern California. Jan got through pre-med at UCLA and is now in his second year at California College of Medicine.

Their wholesome appeal attracted the interest of Paramount Pictures, which signed them for a starring film, "Easy Come, Easy Go."

Race Before Train

Last month they began shooting the movie with a train sequence at Chatsworth in the San Fernando Valley. The first day's work was actually the tag of the film, in which the pair was to race before a train.

Jan and Dean had performed their scenes during the day, then they watched as the camera crew filmed the oncoming train. The camera was mounted on a flatcar which was pulled by another locomotive.

"This is too dangerous for me; I'm getting off," said Dean after a couple of takes.

"I'm going to watch just one more take," said Jan, remaining on the flatcar.

After the next shot began, the oncoming locomotive seemed to be gaining on the camera flatcar, which was traveling about 40 m.p.h. Said Jan: "The flagman in the other engine was waving us off but I still couldn't believe what was going on."

Within seconds it was apparent that a crash was coming. Jan joined the crew members in leaping off the flatcar.

"I saw the other guys sprawled all over the landscape, bloody and delirious," Jan recalled. "I still couldn't believe it. Then I looked down at my foot and saw that it was pointed the wrong way."

However he managed to hop to a road wher he hailed a car to take him to a hospital to set the leg. Fourteen members of the crew also suffered broken bones; director Barry Shear's injuries included four breaks in an arm, two in the pelvis and eight ribs.

Singer Tells of Train Crash on Movie Location

CHATSWORTH (Los Angeles County)—(AP)— "I could see the train wasn't going to stop," said rock 'n' roll singer Jan Berry.

"When it rammed us, I jumped off and landed on my left leg."

Berry, half of the singing team of Jan and Dean, suffered a compound leg fracture Thursday when a freight engine being filmed for a musical comedy rammed a flatcar bearing actors and film technicians.

Twelve people were injured.

Among them, was director Barry Shear, 42.

Berry's singing partner and co-star in the film, Dean Torrence, was unhurt.

The flatcar was up-ended at a 45-degree angle, spilling Berry, Torrence, Shear, the crew and their equipment.

TORRENCE OF BURIED TREASURES

Los Angeles Times 11
WED., MAR. 31, 1965—Part IV

Jan and Dean Signed

Singers Jan and Dean have been signed to make their motion picture debut in Paramount's "Jan and Dean Go-Go Wild." The film is an original screenplay by Maurice Richlin and begins shooting the last week in April at Paramount.

MOVIELAND LOCATION COMEDY STUNT SENDS SINGING STAR JAN BERRY TO HOSPITAL BED

A comedy stunt ending a new motion picture, "Easy Come, Easy Go" turned into bedlam and injury to 14 members of the cast and crew, including famed Jan Berry, as one of the railroad cars being used overturned and spilled its human contents beside the tracks. Berry, who is half of the recording team of Jan and Dean, suffered multiple fractures, and a compound fracture of his leg. His partner, Dean Torrance, had finished shooting for the day, and was not aboard the overturned train.

The sequence being shot was to end the film with Jan and Dean jumping from a flatbed car as another train zoomed up behind them. As they jumped, they were to break into little pieces, through an optical trick, and spell out "The End" as the train raced into the distance. Previous shooting of the sequence had been done at a slower speed and had been succesfully done two times. The third time, at which the mishap occurred, the speed had been upped a little to add authenticity to the filming. Railroad investigators are trying to discover why the train went out of control and crashed into the flatbed car, which held Berry and the director, Barry Shear, plus cameramen, standins, and others.

The shooting was being done in the San Fernando Valley of California, where a Southern Pacific train had been rented. Southern Pacific officials stated that SP frequently allows this area to be used for motion picture filming, at certain quiet times of the day.

Because of the mishap, filming will be delayed for an indefinite period of time, possibly making scheduled cameo appearances by leading actors, actresses and comedians difficult to obtain, because of their crowded schedule. Stars who were scheduled to appear, included Milton Berle, Terry Thomas, Jerry Lester, Gene Kelly, Joan Staley and Jack Jones.

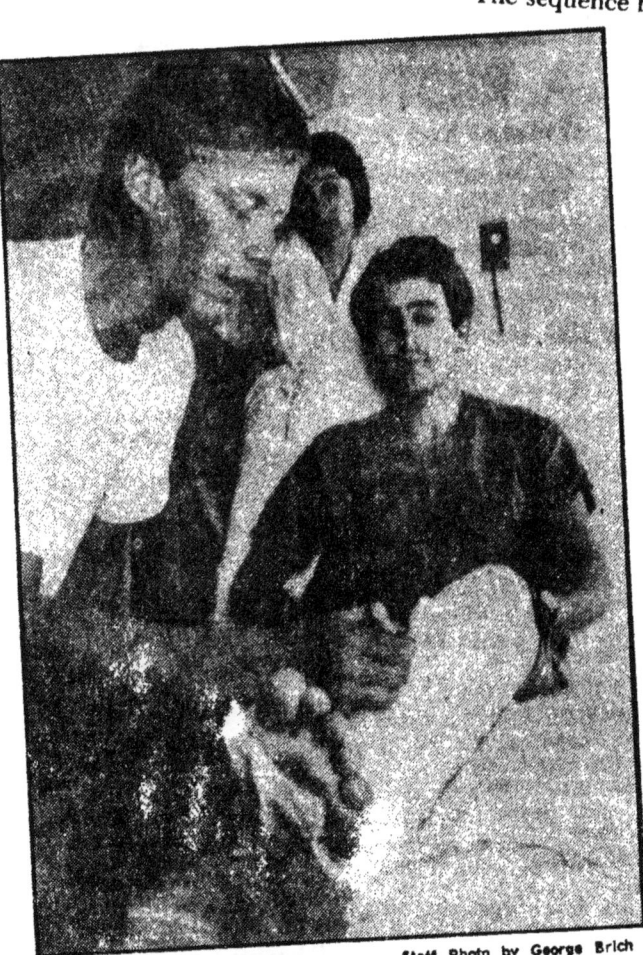

Staff Photo by George Brich

TRAIN VICTIM—Jan Barry, who broke his left leg in a train accident Aug. 5 in Chatsworth during shooting of a movie, has his cast autographed by his rock 'n' roll singing partner, Dean Torrance. Mrs. Lenore Khan, nurses aide at Northridge Hospital, adjusts Jan's bed.

ry Shear and assistant director David Salven, who both suffered fractures.

"I just went along for the ride," Berry told newsmen later. He said he and Torrence, who were not being filmed at the moment, had hoped on the flatcar to watch when: "All of a sudden the train behind us speeded up. I saw it was going to hit us, and so I jumped."

Torrence jumped, too, but landed safely, a studio spokesman said.

Torrence is an art student at the University of California and Berrry attends California Medical College.

Their Surfer recordings have sold millions of records.

Torrence's name came into the news in 1963, in the trial of three men accused of kidnaping Frank Sinatra Jr., son of the famed crooner.

Torrence was a friend of one defendant, Barry W. Keenan. Torrence denied knowledge of the case at first, but later testified Keenan had discussed the kidnaping two months before it occurred and later left $25,000 ransom money with him. The defendants were all convicted.

Associated Press

TORRENCE OF BURIED TREASURES

The Beat of the 'Modern Sound'
WILL IT LAST?

The "Modern Sound" has influenced television, the recording industry, the band business, radio, dance styles and even fashions. But how is it made, who are its successful utilizers, and how long will it last? The answers in the last of a series, follow:

By JAN and DEAN

One reason for the new awareness of the Modern Sound is that the young person is an increasingly important economic consumer.

By 1970, one-half of our population will be under 25. More important, a good number of them have money to spend on records.

We've seen how these records affect the public, but now let's look into how they're actually made.

The Modern Sound would not be possible without some of the electronic advances that have been made in recent years.

Transmitted to Wax

Until the advent of the tape recorder, records were made with the vocalist and the whole orchestra present. The sound was transmitted through the microphones, through a mixing board, right on to a wax which was the mold for the records to be pressed.

Nowadays, the tape recorder provides the record producer with up to four separate tracks on which he can record. Different sections or instruments of the orchestra can be recorded on different tracts and at different times if desired.

He then can overdub from a tape already recorded to another tape, more instruments or more vocal. In other words, the vocalist does not have to be present at the time that the background track is recorded.

Also, this means that few instruments and vocalists can give the effect of many. With splicing and editing, the producer can reach near perfection in his chores.

He does not have to put the sound on the acetate mold until he is completely satisfied with his final product. This acetate mold is to become the mold for the records.

The Money Makers

With these advances, one record session can last up to two or three months.

One of the most successful utilizers of these recording tricks is Phil Spector, young genius who has parlayed his production talent and ear for the Modern Sound into a multi-million dollar recording firm.

Another producer with full control of these facilities, is Brian Wilson, the leader of the Beach Boys.

In Detroit, producer Berry Gordy is making his contribution to the Modern Sound (termed the Motown Sound by fans) — a combination of intense percussion, thumping bass, high-pitched horns with a soulful vocal and a lyric that hits home.

A story about the everyday ups and downs of life. This has led to the success of his Tamla-Motown record company.

In New York, Lieber and Stoller have been contributing to the Modern Sound since they first began 10 years ago with the Coasters. In London, another young man, Andrew Long Oldham, has been turning out a good number of England's hits.

And still another extremely talented young man here in Los Angeles, with whom we work closely, is making his contribution.

Lou Adler has been able to capture that live, happy sound of Johnny Rivers at the Whisky A-Go-Go and put it on record. This live trend has since been followed by many other top recording stars.

There are those who thought that these sounds would not last. But new renditions of records of a few years back keep popping up again and becoming hits: "Memphis" by Johnny Rivers, "Rock 'n' Roll Music" by the Beatles, "Surfin' USA" by the Beachboys.

Of course, there will always be disbelievers who insist that our new Modern Sound is doomed. But it seems like we've been hearing that for the past 10 years; so we both say thanks for the Stingrays in the meantime.

Sunday, June 27, 1965   Los Angeles Herald-Examiner D-5

Jan and Dean Movie

"Easy Come, Easy-Go," a feature length motion picture starring Jan and Dean, will start July 26, according to Producer Bobby Roberts.

This will be the boys' first movie, Roberts said. The film is a Paramount Production in conjunction with Dunhill Productions.

TORRENCE OF BURIED TREASURES

KEEPING THE JAN AND DEAN FAN CLUB UP-TO-DATE

1962 FEBRUARY 1962

from **JAN AND DEAN FAN CLUB**
NATIONAL HEADQUARTERS
1307 BRINKLEY AVENUE
LOS ANGELES 49, CALIFORNIA

TRIFLES MAKE PERFECTION....

.... BUT PERFECTION IS NO TRIFLE. WHO SAID THAT ? WHY, JAN AND DEAN , OF COURSE ! YOU SEE, THEY WERE TO HAVE HAD A NEW RECORD OUT ON FEBRUARY 16th. REMEMBER LAST MONTH I SORTA TEASED YOU ABOUT WHAT THE TITLE WAS GOING TO BE . WELL, AFTER THE SONGS THEY HAD RECORDED WERE COMPLETED, THEY PLAYED THEM BACK AND JUST WEREN'T SATISFIED WITH THE RESULTS. (NOTHIN' BUT THE BEST FOR JAN AND DEAN'S FANS) SO THEY HAVE RESCHEDULED ANOTHER RECORDING SESSION THIS WEEK-END AND WILL DO THEM ALL OVER UNTIL THEY ARE JUST SO ! THAT LEAVES US AGAIN UNABLE TO TELL YOU JUST WHICH WILL BE THE FEATURED SIDE - - - BECAUSE THEY USUALLY DON'T DECIDE THAT UNTIL THEY COMPARE THEM ALL.

ANYWAY, THEY HAVE BOTH BEEN VERY BUSY WITH THE NEW SCHOOL SEMESTER. DEAN IS DEVOTING EVERY POSSIBLE MINUTE TO THIS STUDIES WHICH WILL MAKE HIM AN ARCHITECT. SAW HIM THE OTHER DAY WITH A FELLOW STUDENT FROM SANTA MONICA CITY COLLEGE , NAMED ARNIE , WHO IS ALSO STUDYING TO BE ONE OF THEM THAR ARCHITECTS. DEAN LOVES ART STUDIES - ALWAYS HAS SOME KIND OF PEN IN HAND - SORT OF A " SKETCH-AS-SKETCH CAN " BASIS !

JAN IS BACK AT HIS PRE-MED BOOKS AT U.C.L.A. BUT IS DEVOTING MUCH OF SPARE (?) MOMENTS TO MUSIC ARRANGING AND SONG WRITING. I THOUGHT THAT AS MEMBERS OF THIS CLUB YOU'D BE INTERESTED IN THIS STORY: SEVERAL DAYS AGO I WAS WATCHING THE LOCAL LOS ANGELES NEWS ON T.V. AND I SAW THE CUTEST TEEN-AGE GIRL SHOWN APPEARING BEFORE A LOCAL JUDGE HAVING HER RECORDING CONTRACT SIGNED. THE PAPERS THE NEXT DAY ALL CARRIED HER PICTURE, TOO. THE BIG SURPRISE CAME LATER WHEN JAN AND DEAN'S MANAGER, LOU ADLER , TOLD ME THAT JAN HAD DONE ALL THE ARRANGEMENTS FOR HER FIRST RECORD, AND THAT ONE SIDE OF IT WAS TO BE A REAL GOODIE THAT JAN AND MY SON , DON , WROTE. IT'S CALLED "Im Dying To Give You My Love" and the other side is " A Boy ". THIS ONE'S COMING OUT ON THE EPIC LABEL AND FROM ALL EARLY PREVIEW REPORTS THIS GIRL IS GOING TO GO PLACES. OH YES , HER NAME ..... SHE'S GOING BE KNOWN JUST AS " P I X I E " . WE HERE KINDA HOPE THAT JAN AND DEAN FANS WILL LIKE HER , AND HER RECORD. APPRECIATE HEARING FROM YOU WHEN YOU START HEARING IT IN YOUR CITY.

Current Comment

JOE KRYNICKY OF PHILADELPHIA WRITES: "SUNDAY KIND OF LOVE" WAS JUST PICKED AS A PICK HIT BY WXPN, THE UNIV. OF PENNA. RADIO STATION. THE REASON IT TOOK SO LONG IS WE DON'T PICK 'EM UNTIL IT GETS ON THE BILLBOARD CHART, WHICH IT DID LAST WEEK .... AND PRES. LARSON, (KRISTINE, THAT IS OF CLUB 649, MILWAUKEE) FINALLY GOT HER CLUB LISTED IN TEEN WORLD * * BUT AFTER ALL THAT WAITING THEY MISPRINTED IT AS JEAN AND DEAN -- COULD'VE BEEN WORSE, THEY MIGHT'VE GONE ALL THE WAY WRONG AND CALLED 'EM JEAN AND DAN .... AFTER I COMPLAINED LAST MONTH ABOUT THE DIRTY DIG WHICH APPEARED IN PLAIN OLD DIG (Magazine) OUR GOOD PREXY GLENDA SEALY, #650, OF BURBANK HAPPENED TO RUN INTO WAYNE SCRIVNER WHO WROTE IT, OR PERHAPS I SHOULD SAY SHE PRACTICALLY RAN O-V-E-R HIM. SHE JUST LET HIM HAVE BOTH BARRELS .... BUT HE WOUND UP CONVINCING HER THAT SOMETIMES A REMARK LIKE THAT REACTS FAVORABLY, AND THE BOYS GOT LOTS OF GOOD PUBLICITY OUT OF IT. HOPE SO.

SPEAKING OF DIGGING, I THINK YOU WILL DIG THE FULL-PAGE OF JAN AND DEAN WITH CONNIE FRANCIS IN THE APRIL MOVIE TEEN ILLUST.

CAR FANCIERS ARISE! JAN HAD HIS FIRE-SINGED CORVAIR PAINTED ALL BLACK BUT NOW THREATENS TO TRADE IT OR SELL IT. GUESS IT HAS NOT THE SAME FEEL AS WHEN IT WAS WHITE. WHAT SHOULD HE GET NOW?

FROM MARGARET MONIER, #665, UP PORT CHESTER, N.Y. WAY WE GOT A CLIPPING FROM THE JOURNAL AMERICAN WHICH READS AS FOLLOWS: JAN AND DEAN : Ancients who can recall 78 RPM discs and the Claude Thornhill orchestra and Fran Warren's version of "Sunday Kind of Love" with that great band are in for a surprise. Jan and Dean - not recording for ancients, naturally - take the standard up tempo, dress it in Marcel-style bah-bah-bah-di-di-dip breaks. And "Poor Little Puppet" on the flip, is a ballad with lyric in the teen groove ....

Our forefathers thought NOTHING of working 12 to 16 hours a day.
(I don't think much of it , either)

Greetings?

COMING UP MARCH 10th - DEAN TORRENCE'S BIRTHDAY - A "BEEG" ONE - HIS 21st. I'LL BE HAPPY TO HAND HIM A BIG STACK OF CARDS IF YOU AND YOUR MEMBERS WILL SEND THEM TO HIM CARE OF MY ADDRESS.
LET'S SHOW HIM WE WANT TO HELP HIM CELBRATE! !

Clipped and sent by Bev Skotnicki
#597 - Canton, Massachusetts

TORRENCE OF BURIED TREASURES

JAN AND DEAN FAN CLUB NEWS

MAY 1962

NOW!
WIN A CONTEST
...designed with YOU in mind

JAN and DEAN are preparing their new album for release on July 15th. All they want you to do is NAME IT !! Simple, isn't it?

Their first album was called JAN and DEAN SOUNDS. We're all certain that you can get a better title than that for this new swinger. It will, of course, have "Tennessee" on it, plus other JAN and DEAN favorites - like "Jennie Lee", "Heart & Soul", "We Go Together" and "Baby Talk", plus many new "favorites-to-be".

Here's all you and your members have to do: Write the name of the title you suggest, your name, address and club number on a piece of paper and mail to address shown below. You can enter more than once, but each entry must be on a separate piece of paper and have all the above information. JAN and DEAN FANS who are not members of your club can enter, too. We want a barrel full of responses!

HERE ARE THE PRIZES: First Prize is really a triple reward: (a) A personally dedicated copy of the new album inscribed to YOU from JAN and DEAN (b) A personally autographed really b-i-g photo of JAN and DEAN -- it's 16 x 20 -- that's four times as big as an 8 x 10, and it's a brand new never-before-used picture. plus (c) A subscription for a year to your best reading magazine from this list - DIG, TEEN, "16", TEEN SCREEN or INGENUE.

Second, third, fourth, and fifth prizes are YOUR OWN PERSONAL COPY of the new JAN and DEAN album inscribed to you by each of them.

BONUS: For the club sending in the most entries, we will send a new picture of JAN and DEAN to each entrant. That's why you should have even non-members who enter list your club number on the entry blank.

CLOSING DATE OF CONTEST - JUNE 20th. Don't know how you are going to do it, but entries must reach here by then. DO use airmail if you live "way out".

GOOD LUCK TO YOU ALL. Show JAN and DEAN you care - enter their big contest NOW.

MAIL ENTRIES TO: Jan and Dean Fan Club
1307 Brinkley Avenue
Los Angeles 49, Calif.

How's Tennessee Doing?

CLIMBING everywhere! This is going to press right before the new surveys come out, but last week it was No. 26 on both L.A. stations (you mean those things are getting honest? They never agreed before!)

Hear one d.j. say: "This new JAN and DEAN song is a WOW -- in fact it's the WOWsiest record on the air". And another, after hearing all the "pomp-pomp-pomps" questioned: "Wonder what that means in Morse Code?" When they talk about your record, it means it's going places.

Quotes Joan Phelps down Youngstown, O. way:" It's being played more and more on stations that never have played JAN and DEAN records before". From same area I got a Chart from Nancy Vaughn showing it No. 31 in its first week "on" and she calls it the fastest-riser on the list.

"I could listen to it for hours" Judi Fox writes.

It's hitting BILLBOARD and CASH BOX charts too!

Here Is All I Hear

The nicest thing I heard was an offer from JAN and DEAN to go with them to the Fair in Seattle this week-end, but I just couldn't get away. (sigh).

Caught the name of one of our prexies on KRLA - Kathy Minnick - who acts as a special reporter for her school.

Paramount High will see JAN and DEAN on Tuesday, May 29.

June 1 finds "our boys" in Dallas, and at Appreciation Night on the 16th in good ol' Denver.

Good old Soupy Sales had his Pookie and Hippy "mouth" JAN and DEAN's "Tennessee" at the request of Club #677 and did a good job of it. Say, there's a guy that is now going places!

"Tennessee is everything you said it would be, and more!" confesses Marilyn Dugekos from her point of vantage up in Pleasant Ridge, Michigan.

TORRENCE OF BURIED TREASURES

THIS IS
JAN

JAN BERRY, 21, was born in Los Angeles on April 3, 1942 and lives with his folks in the Bel-Air Section, along with sisters Luana 24, Aleta 10 and brand-new Melissa, and brothers Ken 20, Bryan 14, Bruce 11, Steve 3½ and Billy 1½. JAN is 6' 1½" in height, tips the scales at 173 and has real blonde hair, light blue eyes, and slips his tired feet into size 12's.

He attended University High School where he and DEAN belonged to the same Club and began singing together "for fun." JAN completed U.C.L.A. as a pre-med student, doing well in such tough subjects as Physics and Chemistry. He added some music courses which will be valuable to him in his song-writing and arranging activities. He will attend Med School next semester.

Jan got his letter in football in High School, and only the traveling connected with his personal appearances kept him from going all-out for the U.C.L.A. team. He's an all-around athlete -- and especially crazy about surfing, volleyball, and is a table-tennis player to be reckoned with! He's a member of Phi Gamma Delta Fraternity.

He has a real sweet-tooth -- candy bars, popsicles and orange juice are his very special weaknesses. He loves to chew on wheat kernels (don't laugh -- they're good for you) and he divinely digs Chinese foods. His favorite color combination is Silver & Black, so naturally his Fuel-Injection '63 Corvette Sting Ray is an all-silver hardtop, with a black interior.

JAN's pet peeve is people who put on airs -- he likes 'em natural.

JAN'S greatest thrill was captaining his sailboat to safety after a hectic few hours in the Pacific Ocean when a real storm came up and all small craft had been ordered out of the sea lanes. He was on his way to Catalina, but he and Dean and two friends made it anyway.

JAN has been quoted in movie magazines as saying he likes only "way out" girls. Not so! He does like those who have real life, pep, and energy, and he likes to see them dressed in high style clothes. He's still quite unattached and "looking." And, for those of you who have asked, and wondered -- she <u>need</u> <u>not</u> be in show biz.

His favorite actor is Paul Newman, actress Liz Taylor, vocalist Chuck Berry, and T.V. show Route 66.

AND DEAN

DEAN TORRENCE, 22, first saw the light of day in Los Angeles, March 10, 1941 and resides now in West Los Angeles with Mom, Pop, and sister Kathy, 17. DEAN is 6' 3/4" tall, weighs in at 170, has hair the identical blonde shade as JAN's, blue eyes, and fits into Thom McAn's size 11½.

He, too, graduated from University High School, and after a year at Los Angeles Art Center, a fine art school here, is now going full-speed ahead in his specialty of Industrial Design at U.S.C. which has a fine department. And he's quite an artist! Recently had a painting on exhibit in one of the better shows in town.

DEAN is an exceptionally fine swimmer, and was a football letterman, too. He's great on the surfboard, and in fact at anything that smacks of athletic skill. You can imagine how the feminine hearts flutter when "our boys" appear at the local beaches.

DEAN's preference is for vanilla milk shakes and club sandwiches. You can offer him these at any hour - day or night. His favorite color is red, and natch his '60 Corvette is red, trimmed in black on the fender inserts. If he has a bad habit, it's driving too fast. He just loves cars! Once (when time permitted) he was a bug on customizing cars and entering them in shows. One of his cars was once pictured in a Hot Rod magazine.

DEAN's pet peeve is people who criticize other people.

DEAN's greatest thrill was appearing on the Dick Clark Show in the Hollywood Bowl. (Since that time he has re-appeared there). Second thrill would have to be winning a trophy for his pick-up truck at an Auto Show.

DEAN, by comparison is the "shy one," but get him started and he can really talk. Both boys have a weird, dry sense of humor, and if they get a "victim" -- he'd better watch out!

DEAN, too, is the "unsteady" type. I mean he is still playing the field. His undoing will be a blonde, natural or unnatural. He likes girls who are the outdoor type but who can retain their femininity. In their clothes he's for frilly, party ones -- especially cocktail dresses.

His favorite movies are the old-timers -- Laurel & Hardy and like that. Singers, Connie Francis and Johnny Mathis get the nod from him. Like JAN, he agrees that on T.V. Route 66 was the most.

They both see their old friends and are devoted to them, but it's a little difficult these days when they travel so much. But reunions are more fun than ever. This, then, is a picture of JAN and DEAN, based on questions most asked of their Fan Clubs.

Jan and Dean Fan Club
National Headquarters
1307 Brinkley Avenue
Los Angeles 49, California

May 1963

TORRENCE OF BURIED TREASURES

ACTION SPEAKS LOUDER THAN WORDS

Action Speaks Louder Than Words They Say
And That's Why I Won't Listen To You Today
You've Promised The World And Din't Deliver A Thing
You Know Your Talk Is Cheap

You'd Better Start Showin Me Real Fast
The Things You Can Do And They'd Better Last
Your Broken Promises Are Breaking My Heart
I Shoulda Learned And Set You Straight From The Start
(If You Don't Do It Now When Will You Start)

Actions Speak Louder Than Words I Know
Cause You've Put Me On And Really Hurt Me So
But I Wont't Be Your Fool Never No More
Not Unless You Come On With What I'm Waiting For

Action Speak Louder Than Words Its True
You Tell Me One Thing But Its Not What You Do
I Guess You Just Like To Hear Yourself Talk
For All I Care Baby You Can Take a Walk

Another happy day

When I go to sleep
at nite out the stars
I look at the stars
Can't wait to wake for more

The sun is coming up
by the rain light up the skies
The train hits again
Can't wait to ride somemore

All I want to do is play
I'll ride the waves alone
And catch the ocean spray
today's gonna be
anotter happy day

No one to bother me
no kids to get n scream
She found my life at last
my life a surfur dream

I sleep beneath the stars
along the sandy beach
and night that's my ride
my beach nuthin bleak

No one to bother me
no one to say tell me what to do

until I drownd — my life a surfur dream

TORRENCE OF BURIED TREASURES

Anaheim, Azusa, and Cucamonga

THEY WEAR ORGANDY DRESSES AND HIGH BUTTON SHOES
THEY READ PLAYBOY MAGAZINE AND HOT ROD NEWS
THERE'S PATIENCE PROPER AND PRUDENCE PRIM
YOU OUGHTTA SEE EM DO THE SWIM

THEY COME FROM ANAHEIM, AZUSA AND CUCAMONGA TOO
FOR A SEWING CIRCLE AND A BOOK REVIEW
THE LITTLE OLD LADIES WAITIN WILD ANTICIPATION
FOR THE MEETING OF THE A.A.C., BR, SC&T ASSOCIATION

THEY TOOL AROUND TOWN IN THEIR BIG GRAND PRIX
SITTING IN THEIR BUCKET SEATS, SHOOTING THE BREEZE
ALL WEEK LONG THEY PUT UP JAM N' PRESERVES
WHILE THEY'RE SLOWLY BUILDIN UP THEIR NERVES

THE MEETING BREAKS UP WITH A THUNDROUS ROAR
AND THERES A MAD RUSH FOR THE BIG OAK DOOR
THEY RUN TO THEIR CARS, LIKE THE START AT LEMANS
THEN THEY GO SPINNIN DONUTS ON THE LAWNS

BETTER SURE THAN SORRY

WE WERE YOUNG AND IN LOVE AND WE KNEW ITS FOREVER
AND ALL OUR HOPES AND DREAMS WE HAD WORKED FOR TOGETHER
WE WERE SO CLOSE TO EACH OTHER
YOU'RE SO COMMITTED TO EACH OTHER ~Lean
TO TELL YOU THAT IT HURT ME SO SWEETHEART
THAT IT WAS BEST FOR US TO BREAK APART

IT IS BEST TO HAVE JOYS THAN TO HAVE SORROWS
ALL THROUGH THE YEARS WE LOOKED FORWARD TO ALL OUR TOMORROWS
AND SO THAT MOMENT THAT WE PARTED, DIDN'T HURT SO BAD
CAUSE WE KNEW IF WE PARTED OUR LOVE WE'D SEE WHAT WE REALLY HAD

IF WE'D HAVE STAYED TIED TO EACH OTHER
BY STAYING TIED TO EACH OTHER
COULD ONLY LEAD TO
TROUBLE AND PAIN
HEARTACHE IN VAIN

← BETTER SURE THAN SORRY
ALL THROUGH TH YEARS
NO REAL TEARS

WE CAN SEE NOW AND KNOW WE DID THE RIGHT THING
WHILE AT THE TIME ONLY SADNESS WE THOUGHT IT WOULD BRING
THEY SAY THAT PATIENCE IS A VIRTUE THAT ONLY VERY FEW POSSESS
AND WE FOUND FOR US ITLL ONLY BRING HAPPINESS
                                                              CLARINET

TORRENCE OF BURIED TREASURES

"THE BATTLE OF STRAWBERRY FIELD"

MAMAS AND PAPAS ARE NOWHERE AROUND
KIDS WITH REVOLVERS ARE ALL OVER TOWN
WITH LOVE IN THEIR HEARTS AND CLOVERS FOR SHIELDS
THEY'LL FIGHT THE BATTLE OF STRAWBERRY FIELD

BIRDS AND THE AIRPLANE ARE READY TO FLY
LUCY IS WAITING, SHE'S UP IN THE SKY
WHOSE SOUL IS RUBBER? WHOSE SOUL WILL YIELD?
DURING THE BATTLE OF STRAWBERRY FIELD

THE FIRST EDITION - HEADLINES THE NEWS
MESSENGER SERVICE - IGNITED A FUSE
EGGMAN'S ERUPTED, OMELETTES SUPREME
BLOOD, SWEAT AND TEARS ~~IS MIXING~~ WITH CREAM
ARMIES CONSISTING OF SPIRITS WELL HEALED
PREPARE TO DO BATTLE ON STRAWBERRY FIELD

TURTLES IN SHELLS, HERMITS IN CAVES
THE FOOL ON THE HILL IS DIGGING THEIR GRAVES
DEAD ARE NOT GRATEFUL, SURVIVORS APPEASE
THE SERGEANT COMMANDS, "ATTENTION!" "AT EASE."
GET ALL THE KINKS OUT, PULL IN THEM GUTS
THE SERGEANT'S NOT KIDDING, HE'S GOT THE CUTS
"HEY JUDE!" DRILLS THE SERGEANT, KILL OR BE KILLED
HERE COMES THE BATTLE OF STRAWBERRY FIELD

  BOMBS ARE EXPLODING, STONES ARE BEING THROWN
  THE FIFTH DIMENSION'S THE BATTLE ZONE
  SPRINGFIELDS ARE LOADED, SHOOT AT POINT BLANK
  DAWN FINDS CARPENTERS, TOP 'O THE TANK

  SOUND THE ALARM CLOCK, STONE PONIES CAN'T RUN
  COMPANY SUNSHINE GETS HIT IN THE SUN
  RHINOCEROCES CHARGE, ELEPHANTS MOVE
  COMPANY HOLDING GETS HIT IN THE GROOVE

  DEFEND THE BEACH BOYS, TEMPTATION'S TO FIGHT
  RAIDERS ARE GUARDED BY THREE DOGS A NIGHT
  BUTTERFLIES FREED FROM IRON COCOONS
  STEP ON THE WOLVES WHO HOWL AT THE MOON

  ANIMAL INSTINCTS REPLACING REFRAIN
  HOOK YOUR OPPONENT, CAPTURE HIS BRAIN
  SURRENDER'S UNKNOWN, CLEAR WATER TURNS RED
  RASCALS GO AWOL, OUR GANG'S LEFT FOR DEAD

FOR SEASONS THE BATTLE'S CONTINUES TO RAGE
POETS WRITE CLASSICS FOR PAGE UPON PAGE
IMPRESSIONS IMPLANTED YOU'LL NEVER REGRET
A DAY IN THE LIFE IS SO HARD TO FORGET

(Gvds, where's Jan & Dean)
MONKEYS SWING SLOWLY, LEAVES FALL TO THE GRASS
~~REVOLUTIONS GIVE WAY~~ (ALL THINGS MUST PASS)
THE KING IS THE VICTOR, HE'LL LEAD THE PARADE
UP ABBEY ROAD, DOWN WITH ~~ORANGE AID~~ MARMALADE

MOTHERS SHOULD KNOW WHAT MIRACLES REVEALED
BUGS WIN THE BATTLE OF STRAWBERRY FIELD

BIG MAN ON CAMPUS

YOU WERE MY HONEY
EVERYBODY KNEW IT
AT EVERY PARTY
THEY KNEW I'D BE WITH YOU
UNTIL YOU WERE DISCOVERED
BY A BIG MAN ON CAMPUS

YOU WERE TAKEN IN BY HIS NAME
THE LETTER ON HIS SWEATER
FLATTERED BY HIS ATTENTION
YOU SHOULDA KNOWN BETTER

YOU WERE MY HONEY
TILL THE OTHER DAY
WHEREVER YOU WENT
I WAS GOING YOUR WAY
NOW I GUESS I'VE LOST YOU
TO A BIG MAN ON CAMPUS

SAY THAT BIG MAN YESTERDAY
SAID ILET THE BEST MAN WIN
HE TURNED TO ME AND SAID
THAT HE'S THE BEST MAN

I WANT YOU TO KNOW
THAT I WON'T WAIT
I'll BE LOOKING ROUND
FOR A BRAND NEW DATE
AND TO HER I'll BE
A BIG MAN ON CAMPUS

"BLOW OUT"

Say ya got money
And a brand new bike
I seen you out a-ridin'
Down the old turn pike
And who's right behind you
Holdin' you tight
Man ya got my woman
Ya got her in the night

Say you look flashy
~~And you shift runs away~~
And. ~~You~~ tank is flamin'
With a crimson red

Like your good time lovin'
Comes on that way

TORRENCE OF BURIED TREASURES

BETTER SURE THAN SORRY   (A)

#1
YOU KNOW YOU LIVE TO LOVE AND WORK TO-GETH-ER
AND YOU'RE SO YOUNG AND YOU HOPE AND DREAM OF FOR-EV-ER
YOU KNOW DECISIONS MADE TOO QUICKLY, TWO LIFETIMES CAN DESTROY
BUT BY WAITING WE CAN CHANGE WHAT MIGHT BE SORROW INTO JOY

BETTER SURE THAN SORRY
BETTER LAUGHS THAN TEARS   (B)
ALL THROUGH THE YEARS
NO REGRETS

#3
or #2
WE CAN SEE NOW AND KNOW WE DID THE RIGHT THING
WHILE AT THE TIME WE THOUGHT ONLY SADNESS IT WOULD BRING
THEY SAY THAT PATIENCE IS A VIRTUE, THAT ONLY VERY FEW POSSESS
AND WE FOUND FOR US IT HAS ONLY BROUGHT US HAPPINESS   (C)

(" C
YOU KNOW THAT LOVE NEEDN'T BE BLIND   (D)
IT'S TO EASY TO MAKE IT THAT WAY
BUT IF YOU LOVE WITH HEART, AND YOU LOVE WITH MIND
IT'LL LAST ALWAYS AND A DAY

#2
or omit
WE BUILD UP DREAMS AND SCHEMES FROM YOUNG IMAGINATIONS   (E)
                                              IMAGI-NA-TIONS
FILLED AND WE KNEW IT WASN'T JUST ONE OF THOSE OLD FLIRT-FA-TIONS
                                                    FASCINATIONS
SOME SAY EXPERIENCE'S THE BEST TEACHER, SO WE PROFIT BY OTHERS MISTAKES
AND YOU KNOW THAT WE HAVE AVOIDED SOME BAD HEARTBREAKS

A B D C B ∅

LET EXPERIENCE BE THE BEST TEACHER
BUT PROFIT BY OTHERS MISTAKES
AND IF YOU DO, YOU SURELY WILL
AVOID SOME BAD HEARTBREAKS

THE BARONS of WEST L.A.

Jan Berry
Don Altfeld

WE'RE IN TROUBLE NOW, REAL BAD
SOME PEOPLE THINK WE'RE GONNA GET HAD
WE'VE GOT THE PTA AT OUR NECKS
OUR TEACHERS ALL ARE NERVOUS WRECKS

WE'RE THE BARONS OF WEST L.A.
WE CUT SCHOOL EVERY OTHER DAY
TO CRUISE AROUND IN OUR HOPPED UP CARS
AND THROW SPEED SHIFTS BY THE SCHOOL YARD

OUR SISTER CLUB HAS ALL THE GROOVY CHICKS
THEY COME WITH US WHILE WE GET OUR KICKS
TO BEACH, DRAG CITY, OR PARTY TIME
THEY STICK WITH US, CAUSE THEY'RE REALLY FINE

BRING IN FAKE NOTES THAT SAY WE're SICK
WE PULL CAPERS THAT ARE REALLY SLICK
WE'VE GOT TOP GUYS ON XXXXXXXXXX ALL THE TEAMS
WE"RE THE FAVORITES OF THE SCHOOL GIRLS DREAMS

WE"RE THE BARONS OF WEST L.A.
WE KNOW WE"LL GRADUATE SOME DAY
AND LEAVE THESE HALLOWED HIGH SCHOOL HALLS
TO HIT THE WORLD AND HAVE A BALL

TORRENCE OF BURIED TREASURES

I FOUND HER IN A BARN IN TENNESSEE
PAID FIVE BUCKS FOR MY BUCKET TEE
IT TOOK THREE YEARS OF SWEAT AND BLOOD
TO CLEAN OFF ALL OF THAT TENNESSEE MUD

CRUISIN' DOWN THE STREET IN FRONT OF SCHOOL
I WANNA REV UP BUT I GOTTA BE COOL
→ CAUSE WHEN I HIT THE ROAD I'LL GET MY KICKS
POPPIN' THE CLUTCH AND SPINNIN' MY SLICKS

OUT AT DRAG CITY SHE'S FIRST IN HER CLASS
THERE'S NOTHIN' ON THE FREEWAY SHE WON'T PASS
ALL THE GIRLS WANNA TAKE A RIDE WITH ME
CAUSE THERE'S ONLY ONE SEAT IN MY BUCKET TEE

BUCKET "TEE"

ROGER CHRISTIAN 32½
DEAN TORRENCE 15
JAN BERRY 32½
DON ALTFELD 20

FROM THE DISCOTHEQUES ON BROADWAY
TO THE GO GO'S ON THE STRIP
COKE IS IN WITH THE CROWD THAT'S HIP

IF YOU'RE GOIN' TO SCHOOL OR HEADED FOR WORK
DOIN' THE FRUG OR DOIN' THE JERK
WHEN IT'S TIME TO BE COOL, UNCAP A COKE

IF YOU'RE WAXING YOUR BOARD AT WAIMEA BAY
OR DIGGIN' THE BIG CARS DOWN INDY WAY
WHEN YOU'RE AT A PARTY AND SOMEONE YELLS, "CHUG-A-LUG"
REACH FOR A BOTTLE, A CAN, A GLASS, OR A MUG
WHEN IT'S TIME TO BE COOL UNCAP A COKE

THE LITTLE OLD GRANNYS FROM PASADENA
THE SWINGING CHICKS FROM IPANEMA
~~THE LEADER OF THE PACK FROM A BRITISH SCHOOL~~
AND THE MODS AND THE ROCKERS ~~WHEN THEY WANNA~~ BE COOL From Liverpool
~~UNCAP A COKE~~ Reach for a Coke when they wanna keep their cool

reach for coke ~~when~~ cause they wanna be cool

TORRENCE OF BURIED TREASURES

COME ON BABY

Come on, come on baby --- Come on, come on sugar ----
Come on and see me anytime, anytime you want is fine,
Won't you let me know you're mine, Oh well now come on, Oh yeah---
Come on baby.

Come on, Come on Honey --- No more, no more maybe ----
Come on now baby be my man, won't you take my little hand,
Let me know you understand. Oh well now come on, Oh yeah---
Come on baby.

    You know that I love you so, and if you love me,
    Why don't you let me know.
    Your love would be everything, Oh for you baby
    I'de do anything,   So won't you

Come on, come on baby,---- Come on, come on daddy ----
Come on and say you love me so, tell me what I want to know,
Don't you ever let me go. Oh well now come on, Oh yeah----
Come on baby.

    INSTRUMENTAL

1-2-3-4--1-2-3- I said come on,   I said come on baby -----

CALLING ALL GIRLS
CASON-RUSSELL

MARY ... JUDY ... LINDA ...
MARY LOU, PEGGY SUE, SUSIE Q, CALLING YOU

CALLIN' ALL GIRLS ALL OVER THE WORLD
SURELY ONE OF YOU TO ME CAN BE TRUE
AND BRING ME LOVE, LOVE, LOVE
DREAMS, DREAMS, DREAMS
AND ALL OF THESE THINGS
LET ME TELL YOU
GIRL, IF YOU'RE OUT THERE AND YOU'RE LONELY,
WELL HONIES, I'M TALKING TO YOU.
LET ME TELL YOU NOW I -- I NEED SOMEONE
SOMEONE TO CALL MY OWN
I'M SO ALONE

MARY LOU, PEGGY SUE, SUSIE Q, CALLING YOU
CALLIN' ALL GIRLS ALL OVER THE WORLD
PLEASE HEAR MY PLEA
AND HURRY ON TO ME
AND YOU'LL HEAR
BELLS, DING, DONG
RINGING WEDDING BELLS
AND HEARTS -- TWO HEARTS WILL BE SINGING
I PROMISE YOU
CALLING ALL GIRLS
CALLING ALL GIRLS
(FADE)

THE CLASS OF '64

There have been lots of classes, there'll be many more
But they never can surpass THE CLASS OF '64.
We'll always be true to our school
Our class is the one that it made it cool.

With classes like our she'll always soar
There's no group like old '64.
We've got the boys who make the team
And the senior chicks are only supreme.

I must admit the senior treasurer
Is the one who really gives me pleasure
She's my first love - will be my last
Everyone knows she's the class of the class*

School days are ending, It's getting late
Won't be long till we graduate
Tell you something you never knew before
It'll be a century till there"s another CLASS OF '64.

RECEIVED
NOV 4 - 1963

    * This could be an alternate title ....

TORRENCE OF BURIED TREASURES

CHILDHOOD MEMORIES

Intro:
It seems like only yesterday
When you and I were kids
Remember all the things we did
Made our folks flip wheelies

Chased the Good Humor man
About a block or more
Snuck looks at comic books
At the corner drug store

When we played kick the can
[Hide and Seek]
We'd always hide together
Had a tree house in the empty lot
Where we'd go in rainy weather

Bridge:
Childhood memories
Even tho' the times are gone
Childhood memories
Will always linger on

Threw away the bubble gum
To save ballplayer's pictures
I traded a Duke Snider and a Peewee Reese
For a "nobody" named Duane Gritchers

You once built a snowman
With a big carrot nose
An' when your ma came to see it
I'd watered it with a hose

— Bridge —

We played Monopoly
At a long and crazy pace
And when the game was over
You owned Boardwalk and Park Place

We also played post office
Spin the bottle too
My favorite part of all the games
Was when I was kissin' you

— Bridge —

People still talks about Cajun Joe
Cajun Joe was the bully of the bayou
He'd fight anything — a beast or a man
In bayou waters or on dry land
   "   "   "   "   "   "
   "   "   "   "   "   "

At sixteen years he won a victory
The longest battle fought in history
When Cajun Joe whipped Tipple Doe
He became the bully of the bayou
   "   "   "   "   "   "
   "   "   "   "   "   "

He was the bully of the bayou — bully of the bayou
Everybody knew he was the bully of the bayou
Many mans tried and many man's died
But he could whip 'em with one hand tied
   "   "   "   "   "   "
   "   "   "   "   "   "

Undefeated at twenty-one
He was was a fightin' son-of-a-gun
He had his pick of the free ole girls but
They all thought he whip the world
   "   "   "   "   "   "
   "   "   "   "   "   "

People still talks about Big Mandu
Where Cajun Joe met his Waterloo
He picked on a little one to his regret
A hundred and twenty pounds soakin' wet
   "   "   "   "   "   "
   "   "   "   "   "   "

Cajun Joe swung a mighty blow
He aimed for the head but he swung too low
Joe got set for the second blow
When the little guy tore into Cajun Joe
You couldn't even recognize the bully of the bayou

TORRENCE OF BURIED TREASURES

DRAGGING USA

THE SMELL OF BURNING RUBBER
AND THE SOUND OF GRINDING GEARS

FROM BORDER TO BORDER NOW AND FROM COAST TO COAST
THE HIPPOS AND THEIR BOYFRIENDS KNOW THAT DRAGGING'S THE MOST
AND EVERY TOWN HAS A QUARTER-MILE OF BLACKTOP SPEAKAWAY
AND THE TEENAGE POPULATION IS DRAGGING USA
— SPEED-SHIFT, SPEEDSHIFT USA

You'll thrill to:

Competition Dragsters Screaming Out of the Pit
Sling Shots, Six Pots, Injection Power Kits.

THE CANDYAPPLE STING-RAY, THIS JAG WITH WHEEL-SPANS
BOTH GUYS DRIVING HARD TIL THE BEST MAN WINS
THE STANDS ARE FILLED WITH HONEYS, WHO CAME TO SPEND THE DAY
AND ALL ACROSS THE COUNTRY, THEY'RE DRAGGING USA
SPEEDSHIFT — SPEEDSHIFT USA

You'll thrill to:

SUPERCHARGED MONSTERS LEAPING OFF OF THE LINE
BLISTERED MAGS, CHROMED MAGS, SHINY 409'S.

IT'S CATCHING ON MUCH FASTER THAN THE SUMMER SURFIN'
AND ON SUNDAY, MONDAY to SUNDAY, FRIDAY ALL ARE DRAGGIN' CRAZY DAYS
IN GAS STATION GARAGES NOW, THERE'S NO TIME TO PLAY
THE TEENS ARE GETTIN' READY TO GO DRAGGIN' USA
WIPEOUT — WIPEOUT USA

Cheyenne (Flight number nine)
slight surface-wind, bright number nine
5/1 — (?)
Cheyenne Country movin' fast
Past my eyes that never rest (?)
Cheyenne baby sings the sweet wind
Through my vacant mind
Lord its hard to leave Cheyenne this time.
(scissor)

Cheyenne pattern over below
Need no place to go
Quiet honey wildflowers?
Peaceful lands and happiness
smilin flowers good place taught my soul to rest
Cheyenne winds that love to fly
cuttin clouds across the sky
Blown airplanes on their way flying for home
Lord its hard to leave Cheyenne behind.

TORRENCE OF BURIED TREASURES

"DIANE"

Somehow it seems I manage to
Get through another day
With just the image of her face
To lift me on my way

    An' by myself -- I close my eyes
    And dream about her by my side

    That's when I find
    That DIANE'S on my mind
    And I can see
    Just where I want to be
    That's when I find
    That DIANE'S on my mind

I see her in the distant crowd
She seems to smile at me
Her golden hair and tender lips
My heart is melting softly

    I know somehow -- that she'll be mine
    I'll love her till -- the end of time
    WE'LL TAKE THE NIGHT AND MAKE IT SHINE

    And so I fins
    That DIANE'S on my mind
    And I can see
    Just where I want to be
    That's when I find
    That DIANE'S on my mind

DANCE TOGETHER

I'VE SOME ADVICE
FOR THE YOUNG GENERATION
AND IF THEY'LL ~~ONLY~~ HEED IT
IT'LL BE A SENSATION!
DANCE TOGETHER — DANCE TOGETHER

DO THE SLAUSON
AND YOU'RE MILES APART
WITH MY ~~NEW~~ "INVENTION"
SHE'S CLOSE TO YOUR HEART!
DANCE TOGETHER — DANCE TOGETHER

"WHAT FOOLS WE MORTALS BE"
A PLAYWRIGHT ONE TIME SAID
WE LOOK FOR A CHANCE TO HOLD HER TIGHT
IN ~~HER~~ WHEN IT ARRIVES
~~THEN WE DANCE~~ — WE'D DANCE SOLO INSTEAD

THE BIRD — THE ~~TWIST~~ SHUFFLE — WALK THE DOG
ALL OF THEM LACK
THE PRICELESS INGREDIENT
THAT CAN BRING ALL THE FUN BACK
DANCE TOGETHER — DANCE TOGETHER

2/9/64

TORRENCE OF BURIED TREASURES

DRAG CITY

① JUST TUNED, MY CAR NOW SHE REALLY PEELS
A LOOKIN REAL TOUGH WITH THE CHROM-REVERSE WHEELS
A BLUE CORAL WAX JOB SURE LOOKS PRETTY
GET MY CHICK AND MAKE IT
GONNA OUT TO DRAG CITY

               ① ② ③

WELL I'M GONNA DRAG CITY
RUN HER THROUGH NOW   YEAH   YEAH   YEY
YEAH GONNA DRAG CITY   HEY   HEY   WELL
WHAT'LL SHE DO NOW   WELL   YEAH   YEAH
HEY GONNA DRAG CITY   YEAH   YEAH   YEAH
RUN HER THROUGH NOW
GONNA DRAG CITY
WHAT'LL SHE DO NOW
I'M GONNA BURN UP THAT QUARTER MILE

② THE DEE-JAY IS SAYIN ON MY FAVORITE STATION
DRAG CITY RACES ARE THE FASTEST IN THE NATION
RAILS ARE THE WILDEST, AND THE STOCKERS ARE PRETTY
I'LL GET MY HONEY, GRAB SOME MONEY NOW
SPLIT TO DRAG CITY

CHORUS

③ BURNING RUBBER, THICK EXHAUST FILLS THE AIR
FINAL TUNES, TACKIN-UP AND ACTION EVERYWHERE
CHECKERED FLAGS AND WHEEL STANDS, IT SURE
     SOUNDS PRETTY
{ TO HEAR THE CHEERS RING YOUR EARS
   OUT AT DRAG CITY
{ SO BRING YOUR DOLL & HAVE-A-BALL
   OUT AT DRAG CITY

"DRAGON WAGON"

I can't help but Jenny my coupe is really class
And She sure knows how can squeel when I give her the gas
I'm always talken bout her and I can't stop Brappen
Cause I really feel cool in my Draggin wagon

She can take a trophy just any time
Her Et's somethin near close to a 9-09
She leaves the other coupes behind because their laggin
No no-one gets close to my draggin wagon

She my honey she's really fine
All of the guys are jealous she is mine

When I'm not draggin I can't around relaxin'
The engine might need tunin or the body an axin
I'm with her so much the drivers seat is sappin
I really am in love with my draggin wagon

TORRENCE OF BURIED TREASURES

DEADLY DUDLYSDRAGGIN

oooh! oh
Gonna Get that cup

BURNING RUBBER SCREAMING DOWN THE ASPHALT TRACK
EVERYBODY'S HIDING, DEADLY DUDLY'S BACK
GOT A STINGRAY ENGINE NOW FOUR ON THE FLOOR
NOW DEADLY DUDLY'S DRIVING WHO COULD ASK FOR MORE

OHHHH LOOK OUT: DEADLY DUDLY'S DRAGGIN (2)
© OHHHH LOOK OUT: DEADLY DUDLY'S DRAGGIN (2)
OHHHHHHHH: OH;
GONNA GET THAT CUP

TWO GEAR BOXES CLASHING DOWN THE AISLE
DEADLY DUDLY'S SURE TO WIN THE QUARTER MILE
HE'S A MEAN ALIGATOR WITH A WHEEL IN HIS HAND
NOW HIS SIILVER THREE WINDOW'S STREAMING XXXXXXXX OVER THE LAND

(CHOR)

NECK AND NECK AS THEY PASS THROUGH THE TRAPS
LISTENING TO THE P.A. THROUGH THE MUFFLER RAPS
THEY WERE SCREAMING MACHINES BUT WHICH X IS THE
LOOK IT'S DEADLY DUDLY THAT'S TAKEN THE RUN ONE

(CHOR & fade)

Cool Blue eyes and a face with the stub
Now a heavy foots a trampingothell Holie
    yank

"DOWN AT MALIBU BEACH"

① GET OUTTA THE SACK AT THE CRACK OF DAWN
GAS UP THE TRUCK, WE'LL SOON BE GONE
GRAB YOUR BOARD AND WAX IT DOWN
THEY'LL ALL BE COMIN FROM MILES AROUND
TELL YOUR MOM IN SCHOOL DAY TEACH
THE SURFIN'S BEST AT MALIBU BEACH

② DOWN TO SURF ROUTE ONE – OH-ONE
YOU'RE ALL IN STRIDE FOR LOTSA FUN
ALL THE LADIES WILL BE THERE TOO
THREE FOR ME AND TWO FOR YOU
YOU'RE GONNA HEAR THE TREE'S SCREECH
WHEN THE LADIES MAKE OUT FOR MALIBU BEACH

       YOUR
(CHORUS) JUMP OUTA THE WAVE YOU PADDLE OUT
INTO THE SURF YOU'RE READY TO RIDE
KNEEL ON YOUR BOARD GET READY TO RIDE
THE SETS ARE FORMIN' RIGHT OUTSIDE
A LITTLE GAS YOU MIGHT TAKE
UNTIL YOU FINALLY FIGURE THE BREAK

③ WHEN YOU THINK YOU'VE HAD ENOUGH
YOU GRAB A CHICK THAT'S REALLY TOUGH
- YOU BUILD A FIRE AS THE SAND
- TWO DANCE AND OH THAT RICHER CAMP
- FROM ANY WHERE IT'S EASY TO REACH
- SUN AND FUN AND OWN AT MALIBU BEACH

TORRENCE OF BURIED TREASURES

EVERY BODYS GO, GO WILD

GR 21211
BILL 162
ARNIE 253

WELL, THE GO-GO CROWD HAVE THEIR FOUR SPEED STICKS NOW
(TO GO BETTER, GO BETTER, GO, GO, GO)
THEY RIDE 40 FOOT WAVES JUST TO GET THEIR KICKS NOW
(TO GO BETTER, GO BETTER, GO, GO, GO)
BUT WHEN THEY REALLY WANNA GO
YOU KNOW THEY
THEY REALLY WANNA STOP FOR
A REAL COOL COKE, IT'S THE ONE THEY'RE HOT FOR

THINGS GO BETTER WITH COCA-COLA
THINGS GO BETTER WITH COKE (COKA-COLA)
LIFE'S MORE FUN WHEN YOU'RE REFRESHED
AND COKE REFRESHES YOU THE BEST
THINGS GO BETTER WITH COCA-COLA

THE GIRLS ARE TWO TO ONE WHERE THE GO-GO CROWD GOES
(GO BETTER, GO BETTER, GO BETTER, GO)
AND IT'S THE JERK AND SIDEWALK SURFIN' THAT THE GO-GO CROWD KNOWS
(GO BETTER, GO BETTER, GO BETTER, GO)
YOU'LL NEVER SHUT 'EM DOWN, YOU'LL NEVER PASS 'EM OVER
THEY ARE SUPER STOCKED WITH COOL COCA-COLA

THINGS GO BETTER WITH COCA-COLA
THINGS GO BETTER WITH COKE (COCA-COLA)
FOOD GOES BETTER WITH, FUN GOES BETTER WITH
YOU GO BETTER WITH, LIFE GOES BETTER WITH
THINGS GO BETTER WITH COCA-COLA

FAN TAN

Girl + Boy
married long time
Girl gets a package[?] Fan Tan
neither has tasted it before — thing
Take off in their sting Ray
Get to beach
Sit down on sand
(crowded beach — summer)
Radio Playing — ~~Beach Adventure~~
(Disc Jockey)
Em for the 1st time tastes fa
"Excuse me, going to store."
She goes and buys whole
carton. and start chewing
til she mad.
Goes back sits down. Boy
was asleep — wakes up. Boy:
"What you doin." Girl: "you'd
better try it." — Boy: "Aw you
dunda[?] (?)" Goes back to sleep.

TORRENCE OF BURIED TREASURES

Here's one I've really worked on. I've tried several melodies; however, I am not satisfied as of yet. See what you and Jan can come up with.

"THE FOOL OF THE SCHOOL"

I want to walk you home
Got no other place to roam
For I feel just like a fool
The fool of the school.

Tried to play your foolish game
Knew you'd put me to shame
Hurt me bad when you were so cruel
Made me fool of the school

(Chor:) Yesterday in English class
My you were a sassy lass
You-ou never answered my note
never even read what I wrote
Six days since you put me down
After that I wandered all over town
Why'd you break the golden rule
Made me fool of the school

chick chick

INST. BRIDGE

(Chor:) This mornin' in history
Tried to make you listen to me
Wouldn't give me the time of day
Just turned your head away

Breakin' up, it's a dirty shame
Rumor's got it it's me they blame
Better learn how to play it cool
Or play the fool of the school.

(I want to walk you home(Repeat to fade out))

FREEWAY FLYER

① FREEWAY FLYER'S GOTTA GET HIS QUOTA TODAY

THE FASTEST CARS AROUND THERE AIN'T NO DOUBT
ARE THOSE BIG BLACK AND WHITE JOBS ~~THESE~~ THAT REALLY MOVE OUT
YOU'LL SEE EM ON THE FREEWAY FLYIN PAST
FLATTIN UP HOT SHOES DRIVIN TOO FAST
       (HEAVY FOOTS)
OR

CHORUS)
FREEWAY FLYER - GONNA SHUT YOU DOWN NOW
FREEWAY FLYER - GONNA WRITE YOU UP NOW
FREEWAY FLYER - DON'T EVEN TRY NOW
                                    (IN)
FREEWAY FLYER OR THEY'LL TAKE YOU BYE BYE NOW
                                   - FOR A RIDE -

② THEY HIDE BEHIND THE BUSHES ON THE SIDE OF THE ROAD
JUST WAITING FOR THEIR NEXT WRITING EPISODE
THEY SHARPEN UP THEIR PENCILS AND STRAIGHTEN UP THEIR PAD
THEY CAN'T WAIT TO PUNCH OUT, THEY THINK THEY'RE REALLY BAD

③ YOU DON'T STAND A CHANCE
YOU CAN'T OUTRUN NO MATTER WHAT YA DRIVE
WHEN HE PULLS YA OVER DON'T YA GIVE EM ANY JIVE
CAUSE BIG JOHN LAW DON'T TAKE NO LIP
~~UNLESS YOUR A CHERRY LOOKIN CHICK~~
                      MIGHTY
UNLESS YOUR A CHICK WHOSE PRETTY HIP

TORRENCE OF BURIED TREASURES

① HIS NAME IS MR. FERN BUT ~~THEY~~ WE CALL HIM FRED
HE'S THE MAN DOWN AT SCHOOL WHO TEACHES DRIVER'S ED
HE WEARS VELOUR SHIRTS AND CONTINENTAL CLOTHES
AND HE'S ALWAYS REAL POPULAR WHEREVER HE GOES

(CHORUS) THE PARENTS & THE TEACHERS ALL ARE DOWN ON FRED
BUT THE STUDENT DRIVERS TELL ME HE'S A REAL COOL HEAD
~~THEY~~ HE DON'T SAY TOO MUCH BUT HIS LECTURES ARE A GAS
CAUSE ALL HE GIVES IS "A's", ~~THEREFORE~~ THATS WHY NO ONE CUTS HIS CLASS

② YA BETTER WATCH OUT WHEN FREDDY'S ON THE LOOSE
THE (THEY) COPS DON'T EVEN WRITE HIM UP ~~NO MORE~~ CAUSE WHAT'S THE USE
HE GETS A LOTTA HEAT FROM THE BOARD OF EDUCATION
EVERY TIME THEY HAVE TO FIX ANOTHER SPEEDING VIOLATION

(CHORUS) or instrumental

③ HE USED TO RACE EVERY WEEKEND OUT AT THE STRIP
TILL THE HIGH SCHOOL PRINCIPAL FINALLY GOT HIP
MISTER FERN SET EXAMPLES THAT THEY SAID WERE BAD
AND USING THE DRIVERS ED CAR REALLY MADE 'EM MAD

~~THERE~~ IT'S GOES FRED ERICK FERN THE DRIVERS ED TEACHER

TORRENCE OF BURIED TREASURES

THOSE BAD LOOKIN' GUYS WITH THE MOPPY-LONG HAIR
THE ROLLIN' STONES
GERRY & THE PACEMAKERS, BILLY J. TOO
~~THEY'RE ALL GONNA MAKE IT~~ NOW; SO WHY DON'T YOU
→ HEY EVERYBODY'S MAKIN-IT, SO WHY DON'T YOU

live   18   LA LA —
       15th
       8-12

can't you just hear everybody singin
the biggest sound you've ever heard
clappin & stompin while guitars are screamin
better go spread the word

LOTTA SWINGIN HONEYS FOR EVERY GUY
~~THE GROOVEST IN THIS WHOLE WORLD~~
(THE MUSIC GOES ON ALL NIGHT LONG)
WE'RE EXPECTIN A REAL BIG CROWD
JERKIN AND STOMPIN WHILE GUITARS ARE SCREAMIN
AND THERE'S NO ADULTS ALLOWED

"GINNY ON MY MIND"

Somehow it seems I manage to
Pull through another day
With just the image of her
To lift me on my way
When I'm alone, I close my eyes
And dream of her by my side
That's when I find
That Ginny's on my mind
   And I can see
   Just where I wanta be
   That's where I find
   That Ginny's on my mind

I saw her in a distant crowd
And I thought she smiled back at me   pleasant smile
Her golden hair and ~~tender lips~~
My melted heart could see
I don't know if she can be mine   My eyes cannot fool
~~And now~~ I know I've gotta try   my heart is poundin all the
That's when I find   while
That Ginny's on my mind

And I can see
Just where I wanta be
That's where I find
That Ginny's on my mind

TORRENCE OF BURIED TREASURES

```
from the desk of                            Date_____
    HORACE ALTFELT

                    G I R L S '   C U R L S


        Girls Curls
        Where do they get them?
        I know -- they spin and they set them
        Oceans and oceans of
        All kinds of lotions
        Make Girls Curls


        Girls Curls
        Mustn't upset them
        They"ll shriek if you ~~only~~ just touch them
        Hours and hours
         After their baths and showers
        Make Girls' Curls.


        ~~Praxymax~~
        Every one's a slave
        To some kinda permanent wave
        They rat 'em and tease 'em
        Nothin' seems to please 'em
        And the process goes on, on and on .....

        Girls' Curls
        We're all mad about 'em
        What-in-the-world would we do without 'em
        There's no place like home
        With that old brush and comb
        For Girls' Curls !

2/10/64
```

```
                THE GREATEST SHOW ON EARTH




        LOVE IS JUST A THREE RING CIRCUS

        ALL THE GLITTER AND THE GOLD

        I FEEL LIKE THE HIGH FLYER

        FLYING HIGHER GETTING BOLD


        IT'S A WORLD OF MAKE BELIEVE

        I NEVER KNEW BEFORE

        A WORLD FULL OF PRIZES

        NO ONE KNOWS WHATS IN STORE


        AND LIKE EVERY THREE RING CIRCUS

        IT'S GONNA BE A SURE BET

        YOU'LL ENJOY EVERY MINUTE

        IT'S A SHOW YOU WON'T FORGET


        SO GET ON THE BAND WAGON

        YOU'LL GET YOUR MONEYS WORTH

        CAUSE LOVES JUST GOTTA BE

        THE GREATEST SHOW ON EARTH.
```

PUBLISHER (DICK GLASSER)
CORNERSTONE (LIBERTY RECORDS)
6920 SUNSET BLVD.
LOS ANGELES, CALIF.
HO 4-8101

WRITERS
JACK GREENBACH
MEL LARSON
JERRY MARCELLINO
420 POPE ST
SAN FRANCISCO, CALIF

TORRENCE OF BURIED TREASURES

GIRL, YOU'RE BLOWIN' MY MIND

FLUSTRATIONS HANG UP THE DAY
TROUBLES COME MY WAY
HIDDEN FEELINGS DARKNESS FINDS
NIGHTTIMES ONE BIG GRIND
I'M BLOWIN' MY MIND

I'M SACKED OUT MOST OF THE DAY
I JUST CAN'T MAKE IT NO WAY
I'M NOWHERE 'TILL WE MAKE LOVE BABY
THAT'S WHEN I UNWIND, GIRL YOU'RE BLOWIN'
MY MIND

I SEE BLAZIN' COLORS FLASHIN' 'CROSS MY CEILING
I CAN'T LET GO, THIS UNIVERSE IS REELIN'
NOW DON'T YOU DIG THE SAME THING THAT I'M FEELIN'
NOW DON'T YOU KNOW THE KIND OF GLOW I'M REVEALIN'

I'M WALKIN' 'ROUND IN A DAZE
I SEE THE WORLD THROUGH A HAZE
BUT WHEN YOUR RIGHT HERE BY MY SIDE
A DIFFERENT GUY YOU'LL FIND, GIRL YOU'RE
BLOWIN' MY MIND - 5X ON LAST ONE

INSTRUMENTAL

AGAIN

(I'LL NEVER FORGET)
THE GIRL FROM WAIMEA BAY

I KNOW I'LL NEVER FORGET
THE LITTLE SURFER GIRL THAT I MET.
LAST SUMMER AT WAIMEA BAY
WHO PICKED UP AND WENT AWAY

SHE LEFT ME THERE WITH AN UNRAVELLED HEART
SHE STOPPED OUR LOVE BEFORE IT COULD START
I CAN NEVER FORGET HER HANGING TEN
SO I TRAVEL ON, HOPING WE'LL CROSS PATHS AGAIN

LITTLE GIRL
CURL
SO I GO TRAVEL AROUND

ONE DAY THOUGHT SAW IHBR
SOMEBODY ELSE

DON —
DONNA CALLED —
CALL YOUR DAD —

Lynn
Tori Becker

113 Hallmark House
In H'lwd.
464-8344
Lynn Carson

554-1210

TORRENCE OF BURIED TREASURES

HE DON"T LOVE ME

HE'S NUMBER 1 ON THE FOOTBALL TEAM
YOU KNOW I HAD A DATE WITH HIM
HE PUT ME DOWN, THERE GOES MY DREAM
HE DON"T LOVE ME, HE DON"T LOVE ME

I MEMORIZED WHERE HE'D BE ROUND SCHOOL
I"D BE WAITING THERE FOR HIM
HE"D SORTA LOOK AND THEN ACT SO COOL
HE"DON"T LOVE ME, HE DON"T LOVE ME

I THINK ABOUT HIM ALL THROUGH EVRY CLASS
MY HEART WOULD BREAK JUST WONDERING WHO HE"D ASK
FOR A DATE, AND FOR A KISS
FOR A SMILE AND TENDERNESS

IF I KEEP IT UP I KNOW ILL NEVER PASS
I BEEN AROUND FOR A YEAR OR MORE
AND ALL THAT TIME I"VE LOVED HIM
I DON"T KNOW WHAT I KEEP CHASING HIM FOR
HE DON"T LOVE ME, HE DON"T LOVE ME.

HONOLULU LULU (QUEEN OF THE SURFER GIRLS)

SHE'S GOT STARS IN HER EYES
AND KNOTS ON HER KNEES NOW
HER CRAZY GRASS SKIRT SHIFT....
REALLY SWAYS IN THE BREEZE NOW

RIDING DOWN A HEAVY
OR RELAXIN' IN THE SAND
SHE'S THE HIPPEST SURFER GIRL IN THE LAND SHE'S MY

CHORUS   HEY SHE'S MY   BIG ONES

WELL SHE HANDLES ALL THE BREAKERS
EVERY YEAR AT MACAHA
ALL THE SURFERS KNOW HER
AND EVERYBODY KNOWS HER
FROM RINCON TO BAJA

WHEN THE BEACH IS QUIET
AND I KNOW WERE OUT A LUCK   OUT IN
WHILE MARY OUT IS SIT INSIDE OF OUR TRUCK
WE PRAY FOR SURE AND SIT INSIDE OF OUR TRUCK
WITH MY   LITTLE
JUST ME AND   YEAH MY

CHORUS

I TELLYA ONCE UPON A TIME
YOU KNOW SHE GOT A LITTLE BOLD
WHAT SHE TRIED A HULA SPINNER
BUT HER WAY WOULDN'T HOLD

→ WOOPS OVER THE FALLS
STEAD OF HANGIN TEN
BUT THEN SHE D PADDLE OUT AND TRY IT AGAIN
CAUSE SHE'S MY

CHORUS

TORRENCE OF BURIED TREASURES

Hawaii

Hawaii's got 2 or 3 of my good years
Hawaii is where I'm going from K.H.
Hawaii is the place I'd rather stay
The summer's vacation to the sea
I'll hop a plane that will fly just for me.

Hawaii is where I met my girlfriend
Hawaii I'll find her at South Bend
Together the islands we will see
Riding round on her new motorcycle

I'll grab my surfboard and make it to the sand
Take the waves no matter how I can
Following where ever they may lead me
Radio blaring —
K Poi's always playin music now

HIGH SCHOOL FLIRT
Rewrite 1/2/64

I CAN STILL HEAR THE SCHOOL BELL RING
FUNNY HOW IT DON't MEAN A THING
YOU DON'T KNOW HOW I BEEN HURT
CAUSE I GOT PUT DOWN, BY THE HIGH SCHOOL FLIRT

NOW I GUESS IT'S OVER SHE WON'T COME BACK TO ME
MY TEARS HAVE FALLEN SINCE SHE SET ME FREE
BUT MY LOVE GOES ON, THO I &BEEN HURT
CAUSE I GOT PUT DOWN, BY THE HIGH SCHOOL FLIRT

CHORUS:

SHE SURE IS A ~~HIPPIE~~ WILD, AND AS FICKLE AS CAN BE
NOW SHE,S MAKIN PASSES AT EVERYONE BUT ME
HER NEW STRING OF BOYFRIENDS LONGER THAN A MILE
BEATING PATHS TO HER DOOR, LINED UP SINGLE FILE

SO WHEN I WALK DOWN THESE HIGH SCHOOL HALLS
I"M KINDA FILLED WITH SADNESS WHEN MY MIND RECALLS
AND WHEN I SIT IN ENGLISH CLASS IT REALLY STARTS TO HURT
CAUSE THESE ANOTHER GUY WITH THE HIGH SCHOOL FLIRT
YEAH, THERES ANOTHER GUY WITH THE HIGH SCHOOL FLIRT

TORRENCE OF BURIED TREASURES

HEY LITTLE FRESHMAN YOU LOOK SO PRETTY
YOU'RE THE CUTEST COED IN THIS WHOLE WIDE CITY
THE LETTERMEN LOVE YA AND THE CLASS BRAINS TOO
BUT SOON I'LL BE THE GUY WHO'S GOIN' STEADY WITH YOU

YEAH SHE'S REALLY TURNIN' ON ALL THE GUYS
WITH HER CUTE LITTLE WALK AND HER BIG BLUE EYES
IN EVERY SINGLE CLASSROOM SHE'S GETTIN' THE LOOKS
AND ALL THE GUYS ARE FIGHTIN' JUSTA CARRY HER BOOKS

CHORUS
I REALLY FLIPPED NOW WHEN I FIRST MET HER
SHE SURE LOOKED GREAT IN THAT REAL TIGHT SWEATER
HEY LITTLE FRESHMAN YOU TURN ME ON SHE'S

SHE'S GOTTA GREAT PERSONALITY AND LOTTSA CURVES
GONNA ASK HER OUT WHEN I GET THE NERVE
BUT SHE'S GETTIN TOO POPULAR MUCH TOO QUICK
SO I GOTTA TRY AND GET HER FOR MY STEADY CHICK

He'll never change   W B 12235

He'll never change, he'll never change
he asks me to forget, & he asks me to forgive
the the things he does to hurt me inside

when your in love you're bound to wonder why

you want him to look into your eyes

He cheats on me

I know I'm not to blame, he'll always be the same
even when I love to leave him behind
He cheats on me   He treats so terribly
he breaks my heart into, and sees that I am blue
then he holds my face and says I love you

TORRENCE OF BURIED TREASURES

Horace - The Swingin' School Bus Driver

(1) Hey! He Picks Up The Kids And He Takes Em To School Now
And Everybody Digs Him Cause He Acts So Cool Now
Well You Can Catch See Him Every Day At Three On The Dot
In His Big Yellow Hotty Tackin Up In The Lot

CHORUS Horace - Horace The Swingin' School Bus Driver
Knows Every Cop In Town - He's Always Shutin Em Down
Horace - Horace The Swingin' School Bus Driver
We Never Have To Hitch - We'd Rather Fight Than Switch
From Hot Roddin' Horace

(2) You Know Well
And He Flips All The Girls - They Say He's Too Much Now
And You Gotta See The Way He Can Double The Clutch Now
With His Lettermens Sweater And A Ivy League Hat
He's Got A Quarter Mile E.T. Of One Minute Flat

(3) The Kids Are Always Jumpin' Up And Down On Their Seats
Cause His Radio's Blastin' Out That Rock N Roll Beat
Top 40 Beats

He Digs All The Chicks Up And Down The Street
And He Gives Good Head - You Should See Him Eat!!

Horney - Horace, The Swingin' School Bus Driver
Sells Dirty Pictures, And The Wildest Pills.
He's Got Eardrums, If Your Too Young
And He's Got Extensions If Your Underhung!!

"HIGH ON A RED CARPET FLIGHT"

I decided one day to fly the earth
Not enough bread for a first class berth
A decision I had to make to keep sane
Should I fly now or wait for the plane
I climbed in sat in front and overheard
The two guys flyin' this big silver bird

Said listen here captain
There's one thing I found
Before you fly you've got
To get off the ground
Sittin' here like this is a real bummer
Hold the wheel captain while I check the number

CHORUS
There we were off into the sky
Sure felt great to fly
Pull it up captain, ten feet aint so high
Go up five more or were sure to die

Stewardess came up to me in third class coach
Said you don't get a whole number
All you get is a roach
Turn me on with some bread and fly first class
You get good food and real good grass

TORRENCE OF BURIED TREASURES

IT CAN'T LAST FOREVER

WHEN IT SEEMS LIKE HEAVEN IS ONLY
A HALF-STEP AWAY
AND YOU LIVE FOR TOMORROW INSTEAD
OF TODAY
AND YOU HOPE INSIDE YOUR HEART
THAT YOU'LL NEVER BE TURN APART
BUT YOU BETTER YOU KNOW YOU WILL
IT CAN'T LAST FOREVER

WHEN YOUR HAPPINESS GOES BEYOND
YOUR WILDEST DREAMS
AN EVERYTHINGS JUST AS GREAT
AS IT REALLY SEEM
YOU REALLY TRY TO HOLD ON
YOU REALLY GOTTA GO ON
BUT YOU KNOW
IT CAN'T LAST FOREVER

YOU'VE BEEN LOOKING THROUGH ALL
THE YEARS
ALL YOUR YEARS ON BEYOND ALL YOUR
AN YOU'VE KEPT ON
52 YEARS

HOLDING ON TO HAPPINESS IS
YOU KNOW YOU CAN'T HOLD ON TO
HAPPINESS
YOU KNOW IT ALWAYS SEEMS TO
HAPPINESS
YOU KNOW IT ALWAYS SEEMS TO
SLIP AWAY
YOU CAN'T HOLD ON TO HAPPINESS
SO JUST TAKE IT DAY BY DAY

```
                Lyrics              F Wieder

                XXXXXXXXXXXXXXX
                    It's So Easy(to be in love with you)

         It's so easy just to walk by your side
         Squeeze your hand, smile, a love I can't hide
         Doesn't matter where you go or what you do
         It's s easy, oh-h-h- it's so easy
         It's so easy to be in love with you

         It's so easy while we talk on the phone
         Makes it better when I must sit home alone
         Doesn't matter what you say when I'm blue
         It's so easy, oh-h-h-h it's so easy,
         It's so easy to be in love with you

         It's so easy when we kiss goodnight,
         Kiss me again while I hold you tight
         Doesn't matter if the eveningsnever xxxx through
         It's so easy, oh-h-h-h it's so easy,
         It's so easy to be in love with you

BRIDGE   I can look into your eyes - feel my pulse rise - I grt a certain special
             type of feeling,
         I run my hands through your hair - we have love so rare - It's my heart
             that your stealing.

HHHHHHHHHHHHHHHHHHHHHHHHHHHHHHHHHHHHHHHHHHHHHHHHHHHHHHHHHHHHHHHHHHHH

Ideas

"When I'm With You"
"Supermarket Shutdown" - about the little old ladies racing their pushcarts
                          around the supermarket. As they burn out aisle one
                          little old lady tachs up to 26 CPM (cans per
                          minute) , the second sideswiped tomatoes and potatoes
                          they cornertheir screamin machines by the Boston
                          Baked Beans  and the ring of the register signals
                          they're done with the trophy run. (Work on this
                          idea if you like it.

"Kisses, Kisses, Kisses"

"Number One"

"You Don't Have Me(Where YOU Want Me)"
```

TORRENCE OF BURIED TREASURES

I'LL NEVER RACE AGAIN

I KNOW I'LL NEVER RACE AGAIN
I'LL NEVER SCREAM AROUND THE BEND
PUT MY DEUCE UP FOR SALE
CLUB COAT HANGS ON A NAIL
I'M THROUGH --- I'll NEVER RACE AGAIN

I WON'T BE THERE AT SAUGUS TRACK
TO TURN 13 SECONDS FLAT
GAVE MY CARBS TO MY BEST FRIEND
BRINGS MY RACIN' DAYS TO END
I'M THROUGH --- I'LL NEVER RACE AGAIN

Bridge

I KNOW I'LL NEVER RACE AGAIN
MY HEARTS UNRAVELLED SINCE THEN
TURNED MY BACK ON THE TRACK
ITS SOMETHING I CAN'T HACK
I'M THROUGH --- I'LL NEVER RACE AGAIN

I'LL NEVER DRIVE AGAIN
RACE(?) / DRIVE(?)

I KNOW I'LL NEVER DRIVE AGAIN
I WON'T BE SCREAMIN ROUND THE BEND
PUT MY DEUCE UP FOR SALE
CLUB COAT HANGS ON A NAIL
I'M THROUGH --- I'LL NEVER DRIVE AGAIN

I WON'T BE THERE AT SAUGUS TRACK
TO TRY TO BUST 'TEN SECONDS FLAT
GAVE MY CARBS TO MY BEST FRIEND
BRINGS MY DRAGGIN' DAYS TO END
I'M THROUGH --- I'LL NEVER DRIVE/RACE AGAIN

~ Instrumental ~

I KNOW I'LL NEVER DRIVE AGAIN
MY HEARTS UNRAVELLED SINCE THEN
NO MORE CHECKERED FLAGS FOR ME
NO MORE KEEPIN' FAST COMPANY
I'M THROUGH --- I'LL NEVER DRIVE AGAIN

IT'S GREAT TO HAVE YOU BACK AGAIN

IT WAS NO FUN TO BE THE ONE PUT DOWN
I SURE MISSED YOU HANGIN' 'ROUND
LINDA MADE A MISTAKE PARTY
NOW SHE'S LOST TWO FRIENDS - YOU AND ME
IT'S GREAT TO HAVE YOU BACK AGAIN
IT'S GREAT TO HAVE YOU BACK AGAIN

IT'S BEEN A LONG TIME SINCE WE KISSED
YOU CAN'T KNOW HOW MUCH I MISSED
THE WAY YOU

                                I'M
MY GIRLFRIENDS THINK A CRAZY FOOL
TO START GOING BACK WITH YOU
BUT THEY CAN'T KNOW, HOW GREAT IT IS

TORRENCE OF BURIED TREASURES

IT'S A SHAME

It's a shame to say goodbye
'Cause we hardly said hello
I can see no reason why
~~You'd desert a heart you hardly know~~

It's a shame you choose to part
'Cause it seems we ~~barely~~ only met
Our love ~~had~~ barely had a start
And my head is reeling yet

Was at the dance I found you
Locked in another's arms
One look & you overwhelmed me
~~With~~ your simple beauty and charm
I was smitten and I knew it
'Cause inside I felt so warm

It's a shame you have to leave me
A future I dread to face
Just when I've given myself completely
You're drifting back to his embrace

Oh well you can't win 'em all!

"I'm Coming Back"

I'm comin' back, I've been, away too long
I'm comin' back, this is, where I belong
There was a time, so very, long ago
I wasn't sure, at all oh, but now I know
I just don't count, those times I fell down
Cause I always, got up, and came around
To find the right, that's here, inside of me
Cause I was born, in truth, so my mind is free

TORRENCE OF BURIED TREASURES

It's A Shame

(It's a shame to say goodbye, when we barely said hello
It's a shame to say goodbye, when I could have loved you so

It's funny how simple it started
You were standing above on the sand
You walked slowly up to me
And casually reached for my hand

You took my hand in yours
Even before you knew my name
It was such a beautiful beginning
That's why parting's such a shame

It's a shame to say goodbye, when we barely said hello
It's a shame to say goodbye, when I could have loved you so

We stood there looking at each other
As time seemed to stand still
Your dark eyes shined with amazement
And seemed to say "I will"
      → Then quite suddenly you kissed me
You tiptoed up to kiss me
As the surf came crashing down. A kiss like yours I've never known
Nothing like this ever happened
And I've travelled the world around

Refrain

As summer winds tossed jet black hair
Across your golden face
You said your name ____ (Lajanh).
As I pictured you in white lace
Visioned
But ~~today came~~ the ultimos are just a vacation
And today is my last day ____ (native)
You could beg my little Hawaiian girl
But I won't be able to stay

Refrain

Toots
Jean A Thielman

Tomorrow's the last day and our school
is through
Tomorrow's the last day that I'll be
with you — cause we're through
Forget me
It's as easy as one, two, three.

It's time that we parted now
It's summer time
I want someone new and I will
make him mine —
Forget me —
It's as easy as one, two, three

Please won't you go away,
I want to play
Summer is here & I want to
be free ___ La, la, la la la la la

When summer is over and I've
had my fun —
You'll come back to me and we
will be as one
You wait & see
It's as easy as one two three

TORRENCE OF BURIED TREASURES

MUSIC: JAN BERRY
WORDS: ROGER CHRIS
TAN
2-28-68

I KNOW MY MIND

TODAY I KNOW MY MIND
I HAVE'NT ANY FEAR
AND I CAN SEE FOR MILES AND MILES
MY DESTINATION'S CLEAR
NOW I CAN SEE MY LIFE
UNFOLDING BEFORE ME
WITH A FIGURE THAT IS REAL
IN SEARCH OF REALITY

TODAY I KNOW MY MIND
AND YESTERDAY IS PAST
GONE WITH TOMORROW'S DREAMS
AND PLANS THAT COULD NOT LAST
I HAVE THE RIGHT TO STAY HERE OR LEAVE
TO LIVE MY LIFE AGAIN

TODAY I KNOW MY MIND
I HAVEN'T ANY FEAR
AND I CAN SEE FOR MILES AND MILES
MY DESTINATION'S CLEAR
NOW I CAN SEE MY LIFE
UNFOLDING BEFORE ME
THIS HOUR OF MY LIFE
SEEMS LIKE AN ETERNITY
TODAY I KNOW MY MIND

I BEEN A BAD GIRL

You caught me now
I've been a Bad Girl
Please Johnny, Don't be mad
There's still a chance
to save our Romance
So C'mon, please take me back

I'm sorry that
I been A Bad Girl
I did some I shoulda done-oo
when I'm your girl
I'm ontop of the world
So lets try to start it again
C'mon I wanna start nothin' new

I never woulda been bad in the 1st place
If you'd show our plans and gave love
But I'm through running around now love
take me, and hold me, and gimme some

Never Again will
I Be A Bad Girl
I learned my lesson real good
Now I've got you back
I'll stay on a new
I'll stay on the right track
I'll do everything that I should

TORRENCE OF BURIED TREASURES

IN MY MIND — Don Bendy

This is the new generation
Starting now and going into the future
Thinking of a girl while you were asleep
Then the next day you forget
Time changes really fast

The playground is a street
~~prostitute~~ ~~street~~ San Francisco
Everybody's working a lot faster
To keep up you've got to work too
Sat. Sunday, it's easy to work then

- ~~Saturday~~
- Call Danny
- Call Vincent's
- Pick up tire at Speedway
- ~~Go to french class~~
- ~~Go bodysurfing with Rich~~
- Bake Cake (for Elaine at Midnight)
- deposit $15 – $20 Before Monday

I'm IN A STATE OF SHOCK

I'm in a state of shock
Everything around seems to be a haze
Since I first caught sight of you
I'm in a perpetual daze.

I'm in a state of shock
You alone occupy every thought
I try and try to concentrate
But all my efforts are for naught.

Without even hearing my professor
I mutter a muffled "Yes Sir"
And I seem to float from place to place
All I see, in front of me, is your face.

I'm in a state of shock
I just can't face up to life.
And I guess I'll stay in this condition
Until the day when you're my wife.

2/10/64

TORRENCE OF BURIED TREASURES

I BEEN A SAD GIRL

YOU CAUGHT ME NOW
I BEEN A SAD GIRL
PLEASE JOHNNY, DON'T BE MAD
THERES STILL A CHANCE
TO SAVE OUR ROMANCE
SO C'MON, PLEASE TAKE ME BACK

I'M SORRY THAT
I BEEN A SAD GIRL
(For DON) ~~I DID SOME THINGS~~ I SHOULDN'T DO
WHEN I'M YOUR GIRL
I ALMOST OWN THE WORLD
SO C'MON, LET'S START IT ANEW

I NEVER WOULDA BEEN SAD IN THE FIRST PLACE
IF YOU'DA SHOWN ME SOME LOVE
I'M THROUGH PLAYING AND RUNNING AROUND NOW
SO TAKE ME, AND HOLD ME, AND GIVE ME SOME LOVE

NEVER AGAIN WILL
I BE A SAD GIRL
I LEARNED MY LESSON REAL GOOD
I'VE GOT YOU BACK
I'LL START ON A NEW TRACK
AND DO EVERYTHING I SHOULD

THE JOKER

"Extra, extra, read all about it
the Joker's on the loose again

Emerging from the shadows of downtown Gotham city
It's that green-haired crime-clown, clever and witty
With his sardonic smile, he schemes in the night
Plotting an evil and treacherous plight
HE TRIES TO GET THE CAPED CRUSADERS INTO A FIX
~~Hoping to get Batman and Robin in a fix~~
The cunning Joker ponders his bage full of tricks
Soon at the scene of the crime a calling card appears
It's the sigh of the Joker's diabolical jeers

This harlequin of hate has struck again
and taken the loot to his demon's den
But don't start to count the jewels you stole
Cause the Batman is holding the Ace in the hole

Instr.
Sock, Zap, Pow -- Siren

Anncr: "And so Batman once again foils that crime jester,
the Joker, and has him safely behind bars, but

Joker: Drat, My nemesis, Batman, has won again. But they can't
hold the Joker for long .. I'll have the last laugh.
Ho ho ho, ha ha ha

JUST FOR TONIGHT

I wish I may --- I wish I might, Have your arms --- around me tight

If you're not sure love --- then give me your love, just for tonight.

I've tried and tried, to catch youre eye, but cried and cried - each time you've

passed me by.

Oh hear my plea love, let it be me love, just for tonight.

So let me borrow, your love for just awhile

And no more sorrow will there be.

And come tomorrow, I will own the world

because my darlin' you're the world to me

I'm you'rs to hold, the whole nite through, you couldn't by, A heart so true,

And mine is free love, why not try me love, Just for tonight ------------------

TORRENCE OF BURIED TREASURES

Jill _____ (how's this?)

LONG TIME NO SEE

MEETING YOU HERE IS SUCH A SURPRISE
YOU KNOW BABY YOU'RE A SIGHT FOR SORE EYES
I THOUGHT OF YOU I'D SEEN THE LAST
AND OUR HAPPY MEMORIES ALL HAD PAST.

LONG TIME, NO SEE
THAT'S NOT THE WAY IT OUGHTTA BE
I WANT TO HUG YOU REAL TIGHT
HOLD YOU CLOSE AND KISS YOU RIGHT

(1) I'LL NEVER FORGET WHEN I FIRST MET YOU
(2) YOU TRIED TO KISS ME BUT I WOULDN'T LET YOU
or (3) I'LL NEVER FORGET OUR VERY FIRST DATE
    I WAS SO SCARED AND YOU CAME LATE
(4) SEEING YOU NOW MAKES ME TINGLE INSIDE
(5) I GOTTA HAVE YOU BY MY SIDE

LONG TIME, NO SEE
I KNOW INSIDE YOU BEEN MISSIN' ME
I WANT TO HUG YOU REAL TIGHT
HOLD YOU CLOSE AND KISS YOU RIGHT

LETS PICK UP THE PIECES AND PUT'EM TOGETHER
AND VOW FOR US NO MORE STORMY WEATHER
I KNOW YOUR THE ONLY ONE FOR ME
THAT'S JUST THE WAY IT'S GOTTA BE

—— Don

"SAN, THE FAN TAN MAN"

SAN, SAN, THE FAN TAN MAN —
LOOK WHAT HE'S GOT IN HIS HAND —

THE FLAVORS RIGHT — HE CHEWS
IT WITH ALL HIS MIGHT —

DON'T TAKE FROM HIS HAND THE
ORIGINAL FAN TAN — CAUSE
SANS MY FAN TAN MAN —

OH SAN, OH SAN - HOW YOU LOOK JUST
FAN TAN — WHAT A MAN —
WHAT A MAN —

OVER THIS ENTIRE LAND — THERE'S
NOTHING LIKE THAT
FAN TAN

TORRENCE OF BURIED TREASURES

MUSIC - JAN BERRY
WORDS - GENE WEED
BOB APPLEGATE
2-27-68

LOVE HOLLOW

LIFE CAN BE WHAT WE WANT IT TO BE
I SEE A REFLECTION OF SOCIETY
THERE'S A PLACE FOR YOU AND ME
I OFTEN SEE THIS PLACE OF OURS
FOLLOW THE SUNLIT PATHWAY THERE
YOU'LL NEVER KNOW THE FEELING I GET
FOLLOW ME TO LOVE HOLLOW

I'LL TELL YOU WHAT I REALLY SEE
FLOWERS TURN TO BUTTERFLIES
NATURE MAKES IT HAPPEN FOR ME
IN OUR GROTTO WHERE NO ONE LIES
FOLLOW ME I'LL TAKE YOU THERE
IN LOVE HOLLOW WE CAN SHARE
All The Love that we DARE
HAPPINESS WITHOUT A CARE
FOLLOW ME TO LOVE HOLLOW

WE TOUCH THE GRASS, WE HOLD THE TREE
THIS MY LOVE IS REALITY (THIS MY LOVE IS REALITY)
WE KISS THE FLOWERS, FEEL THE WIND
CAN SOCIETY COMPREHEND
KISS THE FLOWERS, FEEL THE WIND
THIS IS OUR LOVE HOLLOW, LOVE HOLLOW, L H
LOVE HOLLOW, LH, LH, LH
LH, LH, LH, LH, LH, LH, LH

You told me you were tired of the hangin' Round
"You said you little wanted to be set free
But listen girl, you'd better think twice
Cause I'll

Now OH LITTLE GIRL

YOU TOLD ME YOU WERE TIRED OF ME HANGIN' ROUND
YOU SAID YOU WANTED ME TO SET YOU FREE
BUT LISTEN LITTLE GIRL, YOU'D BETTER THINK TWICE
BUT LISTEN LITTLE GIRL, YOU'LL REALLY MISS ME
CAUSE I'LL LEFT ME FOR ANOTHER GUY
JUST CAUSE YOU'VE GONE AND FOUND ANOTHER GUY
DON'T THINK HIS LOVE WILL LAST
THEN YOU WILL REMEMBER
AND WANT THINGS JUST LIKE IN THE PAST
BUT THEN LITTLE GIRL I'LL BE FAR AWAY
WITH ANOTHER GIRL WHOSE REALLY NICE
AND IT'S ALL YOUR FAULT
CAUSE YOU DIDN'T THINK TWICE.

BAR BAR A
HOW I WANT TO TAKE YOU TO THE PROM
HOW I WANT TO HAPPENED HOW I WANT HOW LONG
SPEND THE SUMMER LONG
JUST LOVING YOU

TORRENCE OF BURIED TREASURES

```
" LITTLE GIRL -- LITTLE BOY "

LITTLE GIRL, LITTLE GIRL BLUE
TELL ME WHAT HAVE I DONE TO YOU
DID I MAKE YOU SAD
DID I MAKE YOU CRY
DID A TEAR ROLL FROM YOUR EYE?

LITTLE BOY, LITTLE BOY SAD
WHAT DID I DO TO GET YOU MAD
DIDN'T CHEAT ON YOU
DIDN'T RUN AROUND
BEEN THE BEST GIRL YOU'VE EVER FOUND

WHY DO WE ALWAYS HAVE DISAGREEMENTS
WHEN WE ONLY SAY " I LOVE YOU"
WE GO ROUND SUSPECTING EACH OTHER
WHEN EACH ONE IS REALLY TRUE BLUE

LITTLE GIRL, LITTLE GIRL BLUE
HAVE I EVER BEEN FALSE TO YOU
YOU'RE THE ONLY ONE
I'VE EVER REALLY LOVED
C'MON AND BE MY LITTLE TURTLE DOVE

LITTLE BOY, LITTLE BOY SAD
ALL I WANNA DO IS MAKE YOU GLAD
THAT YOU PICKED ME OUT
FROM ALL THE REST
AND THAT YOU 'LL ALWAYS LOVE ME BEST

GUESS WE' VE LEARNED TO TRUST EACH OTHER
WITH A LOVE THAT'S SO REAL
IT'LL GROW AND WEE WILL MARRY
```

```
LAUREL & HARDY

IN A WORLD GROWN COMPLICATED
IT COMES AS QUITE A SURPRISE
THAT A COUPLE OF SIMPLE PEOPLE
ARE STILL MASTERS IN OUR EYES

MANY TIMES YOU'VE SEEN THEM LAUGHING
SPREADING JOY FOR ALL TO SEE
MISTER LAUREL AND MISTER HARDY
I'LL TELL YOU WHAT THEY MEAN TO ME

ROLLER COASTER'S ON THE RAINBOW
RUNNING ON LIKE ENDLESS TIME
STAN AND OLLIE IN THE FRONT
AND MAHARISHI BACK BEHIND

YEARS HAVE PASSED AND THEY'RE STILL HERE
WITH A SMILE THAT TIME CAN'T VOID
AND LAUGHTER RINGS THROUGHOUT THE WORLD
THEIR ART PRESERVED ON CELLULOID

IN A WORLD FILLED WITH CONFUSION
I JUST WANT TO GO BACK WHEN
LIFE WAS FILLED WITH SIMPLE PLEASURES
WILL THEY EVER COME AGAIN?

THEY WERE BORN TO PUT THE WORLD ON
SLAPSTICK CLOWNING FANCY FREE
MISTER LAUREL AND MISTER HARDY
I'LL TELL YOU WHAT THEY MEAN TO ME

ROLLER COASTER'S ON THE RAINBOW
REACHING FAR ACROSS THE SKY
MISTER LAUREL AND MISTER HARDY
NEVER REALLY SAID GOODBYE

MANY TIMES I'VE SEEN THEM LAUGHING
MANY TIMES THEY'VE MADE ME CRY
AND I KNOW THEY KEEP FOLKS HAPPY
IN THAT BIG "LAUGH-IN" IN THE SKY
```

D — WHEN I GO TO SLEEP
    I NEVER COUNT SHEEP
    I COUNT ALL THE CHARMS

J — ABOUT ~~LINDA~~ LA LA

D — AND LATELY IT SEEMS
    IN ALL OF MY DREAMS
    I WALK WITH MY ARMS —— ABOUT LINDA

J — BUT WHAT GOOD DOES IT DO ME
    CAUSE LINDA DOESN'T KNOW I EXIST
    CAN'T HELP FEELING GLOOMY
    THINK OF ALL THE LOVIN' I'VE MISSED

D — WE PASS ON THE STREET
    MY HEART SKIPS A BEAT
    I SAY TO MYSELF ~~~

J — HELLO ~~LINDA~~ LA LA

IF ONLY SHE'D SMILE
I'D STOP HER A WHILE
AND THEN I WOULD GET —— TO KNOW LINDA

BUT MIRACLES STILL HAPPEN
AND WHEN MY LUCKY STAR BEGINS TO SHINE
WITH ONE LUCKY BREAK I'LL MAKE
LIN-DA   MINE

TORRENCE OF BURIED TREASURES

"LOVE FOREVER" — "LOVE FOREVER"
You are kind & you are sweet
Just to be near you is such a lucky treat,
When you frown it makes me feel blue
& when you smile my heart smiles too
When you have to stay my heart is happy all the day!
But when I feel you by my side my heart will brust with pride—
In the joy of your sweet kiss I'm filled throughout with bliss,
Shine — Shine — Shine
By Jan Berry
Jill

Little Mustang

```
LATE ONE NIGHT I WAS CRUISIN' ALONG
MINDIN' MY BUSINESS DOIN' NOTHIN' WRONG
When ALL OF A SUDDEN I HEARD THE ROAR
OF A FIFTY-SEVEN "T"-BIRD RUNNIN' FULL BOAR bore

WELL I'LL TELL YOU NOW FRIEND THAT GIRL LOOKED SWEET
BUT SHE ALMOST RAN ME OFF THE STREET
GETTIN' BEAT BY A GUY WOULDN'T MAKE ME MAD
BUT WHEN A CHICK SHUTS YOU DOWN IT MAKE YOU LOOK BAD

MOVE OUT, MOVE OUT, GO LITTLE MUSTANG
MOVE OUT, MOVE OUT, GO LITTLE MUSTANG
COME ON NOW YOU BETTER HUSTLE QUICK
CAUSE A GOTTA TRY AND CATCH THAT CHICK

I HAD TO CATCH UP AND SET HER STRAIGHT
BESIDES FROM WHAT I COULD SEE, MAN, SHE SURE LOOKED GREAT
I LEFT IT IN THIRD NOW UNTIL IT RED-LINED
THEN I THREW IT IN HIGH AND LET IT UNWIND

WHEN I FINALLY CAUGHT UP TO HER, I HEARD HER SAY,
"I DIG YOUR MUSTANG, HONEY, YOU GOIN' MY WAY?"
WELL SHE'LL RACE NO MORE NOW I GUARANTEE
CAUSE FROM HERE ON IN SHE REDES WITH ME.

CHORUS
```

Little Ferrari

When I park her on the strip the crowds congregate
To see my low slung Ferrari they just can't wait
She sits low down real close to the street.
If ya choose her on the drag (ya know) she can't be beat

I saved n' scraped for nearly ten years
To get my loaded Ferrari with the racing gears

There's only one like her in my whole town
She takes on the sting rays an' shuts em all down

Little Ferrari you're real low slung
Little Ferrari you're number one

"Let Yourself Go"

4 Bars

Everybody gather round yea
Everybody let your hair down uh
Everybody sing and play yea
Com' on throw your books away, yea
It's a shame to feel so low go
Com' on and dance, yea, let yourself go.

4 times

Good times here for a little while yea
Com' on, yea, and start to smile uh
Everybody start to move yea
Grab your chic, get in the groove yea
It's a shame to feel so low go
Com' on and dance, yea, let yourself go.

Tomorrow is another day
Who cares what the people say
Have yourself a real good time
You can dance with that girl of mine
It's a shame to feel so low
Com' on and dance, let yourself go.

TORRENCE OF BURIED TREASURES

Little Roadster

① I got a little roadster and I cleaned it up
With a 427 that runs like a pup
Its fuel injected and its hard to beat
With racing mag. and a big four speed

wind little roadster wind ya know you can't beat
wind   wind your the fast on the street

② I took my roadster down to the drags
To see if it could get the checked flag
It sure looked good when it got on the line
The crowd went wild as it started to wind

wind little roadster wind get up off that line
wind   wind get the fast time

③ At the drop of the flag I shoved her down
You could hear my slicks bite the ground
I was flyin high and flyin low
Theirs the flag I knew she'd go

wind little   wind you got your checked flag
wind roadster wind you got your checked flag

Jam
write music for this
Smash (Please).

TORRENCE OF BURIED TREASURES

My Street Rod

Little roadster, yellow paint
Chopped top, lowered frame

Dig out at every light
As the slicks take a bite

Down main street, around the square
Turn the corner on a prayer

It's oh, oh --- my street rod

All the kids in Centerville
Know when my rod hits the hill

By my pipes with throaty roar
And pedal jammed to the floor

Draggin' with an XK-E
While a girl holds on to me

It's oh, oh --- my street rod

My street rod is really great
Envy of the guys of every state
When I punch out it'll really go
Faster than a herd of wild buffalo

Spinnin' wheels, gettin' torque
Six grand, maybe more

Hittin all the side streets now
Head for Pop's and all the crowd

To sip cokes, put cars to test
Where one stands out above the rest

It's oh, oh --- my street rod

Manhattan

Summer journeys to Niagra
And to other places aggravate all our cares
We'll save our fares

I've a cozy little flat in
What is known as old Manhattan
We'll settle down
Right here in town

We'll have Manhattan,
The Bronx and Staten Island too
It's lovely going through the zoo
We'll go to Coney

And eat boloony on a roll
In Central Park we'll stroll
Where our first kiss we stole
Heart to soul

And tell me what street
Compares with Mott Street in July
Sweet push carts gently gliding by
The great big city's a wondrous toy
Just made for a girl and boy
We'll turn Manhattan into an isle of joy

You'll be so perty
At "Bye Bye Birdie" Friday nite
I just can't wait to hold you tight
The city's clamor can never spoil
The dreams of a boy and goil
We'll turn Manhattan into an isle of joy

TORRENCE OF BURIED TREASURES

---

words, J. Jacobs

THE MAGIC OF MAKING LOVE

I know your goin round the town
And I know its great to get around
And feel the things you want to be
because you think it makes you free

I know how many times you lied
and how your old love made you cry
But baby now its time we touch
Because I'm feeling you so much

{ and I'll show you, the Magic of MakingLove

You say that your too young to stop
and you say your gonna be on top
but whos the one to teach you how
Come...on home with me right now

and I'll show you, The Magic of MakingLove

ZAX-ALTFELD & ASSOCIATES, INC.
NOW MUSIC (ASCAP)
ARIANNA MUSIC (BMI)

3308 MANDEVILLE CANYON ROAD
LOS ANGELES, CALIFORNIA 90049
(213) 476-5883

MEDITATE
(whisper: this is-to you..from me..)
LIFE

Things keep changing in my mind
And what's the mystery of time
What is really going on
And where have all the answers gone

If you really seek some more
And need to open up your door
To find a way that's really true
And understand the whole you   (whisper)
Meditate -- Meditate

Can you teach me how to see
The Deeper truer part of me
What's the secret of my life
Free from pain & free from strife

Really feel & not just touch
Find that life can be so much
The universe is in your hand
If your mind you'll let expand
meditate...meditate

Be alive & free of strife
Loving all that's real in life
Go the way I say is true
To really live inside of you
Go the way I say is true
To really live inside of you

It's not to late-
To Meditate, Meditate ... Meditate - Meditate.

TORRENCE OF BURIED TREASURES

MYSTERIOUS THINGS ARE HAPPENING

WE ARE FREE, YOU AND ME
WE'LL FLY THRU THE SKY
TO THE STARS, SEE THE UNIVERSE GO BY
MYSTERIOUS THINGS ARE HAPPENING TO ME
AND TO KNOW, YOU MUST GO FLY WITH ME
AND NOW THAT YOU'VE GROWN DEEP IN MY HEART
I FEEL YOU'RE AN ANGEL HERE ON EARTH
COME TO SAVE MY LIFE
MYSTERIOUS THINGS ARE HAPPENING
A BOY AND A GIRL MUCH IN LOVE
NOW WE'RE FREE YOU AND ME

WE ARE FREE YOU AND ME
WE'LL FLY THRU THE SKY
TO THE STARS SEE THE UNIVERSE GO BY
MYSTERIOUS THINGS ARE HAPPENING TO ME
AND TO KNOW YOU MUST GO FLY WITH ME
WE'RE FREE
MYSTERIOUS THINGS ARE HAPPENING
MYSTERIOUS

WORDS AND MUSIC
BY JAN BERRY

MOTHER EARTH

MOTHER EARTH YOUR SONS HAVE COME
TO PLOW YOU UP AGAIN
WITH-IN YOU RESTS THE MEMORY OF ALL   RGOTTEN MEN
AND WHEN THE SEED I PLANT IN YOU
HELPS ME TO SURVIVE
MOTHER EARTH I THANK YOU FOR THE CHANCE TO KEEP ALIVE

CHORUS   AND YOU'VE STOOD ALONE NEATH THE WIND AND RAIN
AND THE SUNS BURNIN HEAT
YOU'VE STOOD THE TIME OF ALL MENS GUNS
AND ALL MENS WANDERING FEET

WHEN I WAS YOUNG I MOVED TO TOWN
IN THE CITY'S NEON GLARE
HOPING TO BECOME SOMEONE GOIN ' SOMEWHERE
I WASN'T BORN A DEALIN MAN
FORGETTING WHO I AM
SO MOTHER EARTH I LONG FOR YOU, I'M COMIN HOME AGAIN

MOTHER EARTH I KNOW YOU FEEL
THE CHANGING OF YOUR SOIL
LYING UNDER WARS OF WASTE AND NATURES ENDLESS TOIL
AND NOW I SEE YOUR GENTLE LAND
QUIETLY AT REST
I SHALL BECOME A PART OF YOU WHEN I AM GONE AT LAST

CHORUS   AND YOU'VE STOOD ALONE NEATH THE WIND AND RAIN
AND THE SUNS BURNIN HEAT
YOU'VE STOOD THE TIME OF ALL MENS GUNS
AND ALL MENS WANDERING FEET

TORRENCE OF BURIED TREASURES

Music City

There's a place on the coast
Where the kids all go to
To have themselfs a ball
It's a paridise they call Music City
The home of Rock n' Roll
Guys wear their hair as long as they please
And dirty old jeans worn out at the knees
Everybody there is in with the crowd
And there's a sign on the gate
No adults allowed

There's always some kinda party crowin'
Where a guy and girl can meet
Everybody's singin' every place you go and
Dancin' in the street
You can hear your favorite sounds of the day
Just let your transistor radio blast away
No grown ups there to tell you keep it down
And everybody gets a Honda to drive around

The latest dance craze is the headline news
And you oughta see em jerk to that rythm & blues
You don't need bread - everythings for free
Just bring some old 45's and some new L.P.s

When your engine is hot and foot hollers drag
Get your wheels on the line cause you won't run stag
Hold your clutch down tight and rev it up to go
You're bout to do business with my mighty G.T.O.

On the way to the strip *you know* she shows lottsa style
~~And you know~~ *And nobody* in takes her ~~standin~~ *with* quarter mile
~~She's got~~ 3 pots on the manifold and louvers on the hood
~~With~~ a competition steering wheel that's made
                                          out of wood

HOT4088   729 2700
       929 2700

If you're lookin' for speed you can get your kicks
~~Cause~~ *yeah* you can wind her up to sixty in four pt. six
The stingrays and the cobra's never even show
~~Yeah~~ *cause* none ~~one~~ *of em* can catch me in my mighty G.T.O

TORRENCE OF BURIED TREASURES

①

MY QUEEN MY QUEEN LET ME TELL YOU ABOUT MY QUEEN

WHERE EVER WE GO SHE ALWAYS MAKES THE SCENE

THE FIRST TIME I SAW HER SHE WAS STANDING BY A COKE MACHINE

I SAID TO MY SELF SHE LOOKS LIKE A MODEL FROM A MAGAZINE

SO CUTE SHES GOT TO BE SWEET 16 ~~AGAIN~~

SHE'S TO CUTE TO BE A MINUTE OVER ~~SIXTEEN~~

MY QUEEN MY QUEEN LET ME TELL YOU ABOUT MY QUEEN

WHEN SHE DANCES SHE SURE CAN SHAKE IT

(I) TOLD HER TO COOL IT NO NEED TO BREAK IT

MY FRIENDS ASK ME WHO'S THE QUEEN

I (TELL) THEM SHE'S A MODEL FROM A MAGAZINE ~~FOR~~

SHE'S SO CUTE SHE'S ONLY ~~FOURTEEN~~

MY QUEEN MY QUEEN LET ME TELL YOU ABOUT MY QUEEN

SHE'S LEARNING TO DRIVE A CAR

SHE LIKES TO ROAM NEAR AND FAR

IF SHE HITS SOMETHING THAT WON'T GET IT

IF SHE'S GOOD THEN (I'LL) ADMIT IT

SO COME ON MY QUEEN LETS GET WITH IT

GO GO GO MY QUEEN

GO GO GO MY QUEEN

SLOAN

② 5/24/65

MY QUEEN MY QUEEN LET ME TELL YOU ABOUT MY QUEEN

WHERE EVER WE GO SHE ALWAYS MAKES THE SCENE

THE FIRST TIME I SAW HER SHE WAS STANDING BY A COKE MACHINE

I SAID TO MY SELF SHE LOOKS LIKE A MODEL FROM A MAGAZINE

SHE'S TO CUTE TO BE A DAY OVER SIXTEEN

MY QUEEN MY QUEEN LET ME TELL YOU ABOUT MY QUEEN

WHEN SHE DANCES SHE SURE CAN SHAKE IT

I TOLD HER TO COOL IT NO NEED TO BREAK IT

MY FRIENDS ASK ME WHO'S THE QUEEN

I TELL THEM SHE'S A MODEL FROM A MAGAZINE

SHE'S SO CUTE SHE'S ONLY SIXTEEN

MY QUEEN MY QUEEN LET ME TELL YOU ABOUT MY QUEEN

SHE'S LEARNING HOW TO DRIVE A CAR

SHE LIKES TO ROAM NEAR AND FAR

I TOLD HER IF SHE HITS SOMETHING THAT WONT GET IT

BUT IF SHE'S GOOD THEN I'LL ADMIT IT

SO COME ON MY QUEEN LETS GET WITH IT

GO GO MY QUEEN GO GO

GO GO MY QUEEN GO GO

TORRENCE OF BURIED TREASURES

MY BOBBY WON'T BE HOME AGAIN

WE HAD A FIGHT FOR THE FIRST TIME IN A YEAR
HE HEARD THINGS HE WASN'T SUPPOSED TO HEAR
THEN HE LEFT BY THE VERY FRONT DOOR
SAID HE WASN'T COMING BACK NO MORE
GUESS MY BOBBY WON'T BE HOME AGAIN

MY FAVORITE DREAM

EACH TIME I CALL YOU UP YOU'RE ALWAYS FREE
YOU BREAK THE DATES YOU'VE GOT JUST TO
BE WITH ME
GEE WHIZ, THAT'S NOT THE WAY IT IS
(BUT THAT'S MY FAVORITE DREAM)

YOU TELL ME I'M THE TYPE YOU CAN'T RESIST
YOUR LIPS ARE ALWAYS THERE READY TO BE KISSED
GEE WHIZ, THAT'S NOT THE WAY IT IS
(BUT THAT'S MY FAVORITE DREAM)

(R)
⎧ WE SPEND EACH NIGHT TOGETHER
⎨ BUT YOU DON'T EVEN KNOW
⎩ (CAUSE INSPITE OF ALL MY DREAMS
   SOMEHOW IT SEEMS
   I'VE NEVER EVEN DARED TO SAY HELLO, BUT ✱ *REPEAT*

I BELIEVE MY DREAMS MAY STILL COME TRUE
SOMEDAY YOU'RE GONNA SHOW THAT YOU WANT ME TOO
GEE WHIZ, THAT'S NOT THE WAY IT IS
(BUT THAT'S MY FAVORITE DREAM)   (B)
↑
FAVORITE DREAM   ← ENDING

MARY-ANN

THERE ONCE WAS A LITTLE GIRL
AND HER NAME WAS MARY-ANN
SHE LIVED IN A BEE-LITTLE BEACH SHACK,
BY THE SEA, BY THE SHORE, BY THE SAND

SHE HAD A '40 WOODY, IT WAS REALLY LOADED FOR BEAR
AND EVERY TIME LITTLE MARY-TEARED ON IT.
IT WOULD GET ON ITS HAUNCHES AND TEAR
IT WAS PAINTED CANARY YELLOW WITH A 348 CORVETTE
AND THERE HASN'T BEEN A CAR MADE
THAT COULD MAKE LITTLE MARY'S YET

WELL SHE WHAM WHEELIN' DOWN THE HIWAY
DOIN' A 100 HUNDRED OR MORE
WHEN ON HER PORT PASSED A SUPER SPORT
AND HE HUSTA HAD HI/FOOT ON THE FLOOR
WELL LITTLE MARY'S-VETTE STRAINED AND THOSE CARBURETORS
DRAINED AS SHE CAUGHT HIM GOIN INTO THE TURN
YOU COULD HEAR HIM SIGH AS THE WAVED BYE-BYE
AND THE SOUND OF RUBBER BURNED

CHORUS

WELL LITTLE MARY'S-VETTE STRAINED AND THOSE
CARBURETORS DRAINED AS SHE CAUGHT HIM
GOING INTO THE TURN
YOU COULD HEAR HIM SIGH AS SHE WAVED
BYE-BYE OH BYE-BYE MARY-ANN, BYE-BYE,
I SAID BYE-BYE MARY-ANN, BYE-BYE

TORRENCE OF BURIED TREASURES

MULHOLLAND

WHERE THE MOUNTAINS REACH UP TO THE SKY
   MULHOLLAND
HIGH ABOVE ALL THE LIGHTS WAITING THERE
   FOR ME
   up up up
2 I'M COMING UP TONIGHT THATS FOR SURE
   MULHOLLAND
I DON'T KNOW WHAT'S HAPPENING ALL DAY
   LONG I'M DOWN I AM
3 BUT EVERY TIME ~~~~ TURNED ON
   MULHOLLAND

THE AIR IS CLEAR THE PAST IS NEAR
AND NOW ITS TIME TO LEAVE
4 I FEEL WASTED ALL DAY LONG
   MULHOLLAND
NOTHING HOURS HOW THEY DRAG
TIL NIGHT TIME COMES AROUND

Mulholland

The scene allright but a lyttle bit right *null*

Mulholland a place for me where I
will be spending all my time

" THE MAGIC OF MAKING LOVE "

I know you're goin' round the town
And I know it's great to get around
And feel the things you ~~wanna~~ ~~won't~~ be
Because you think it makes you free
I know how many times you lied
And how your old love made you cry
But baby now it's time we touch
Because I'm feeling you so much
And I'll show you, the Magic of Making Love

You say that you're too young to stop
And you say you're gonna be on top
But who's the one to teach ~~you~~ how
Come on home with me and stay with me right now
And I'll show you, the Magic of Making Love

Littel girls get hurt so bad
By so many guys ~~that~~ that ~~they couldn't keep~~ make them glad
With promises that ~~they~~ they don't keep
Just to get one sweet nights sleep
But thats ~~to good~~ don't last when morning comes
And you're so too fine to live on crumbs
So kick this life and live with me
I'm the guy ~~that'll~~ will set you free
With the Magic of Making Love
The Magic of Making Love
The Magic of Making Love

TORRENCE OF BURIED TREASURES

> Now that Bobby wants Me
>
> My life changed
> Never felt greater
> had to happen later
> sooner or later
> Now that Bobby Wants Me
>
> I feel good
> flyin on a cloud now

MUSIC CITY

① HEY EVERYBODY SEE EM ARRIVIN'
THE GREATEST STARS YOU'LL EVER SEE
SOME ARE FLYIN AND SOME ARE DRIVIN'
FROM LIVERPOOL TO TENNESSEE
CHUCK BERRY'S CHECKIN' IN FOR ST. LOO
THOSE SWINGIN' 4 SEASONS
YOU KNOW LESLIE GORE IS GONNA BE HERE TOO
RINGO, JOHN, PAUL & GEORGE ARE ALWAYS AROUND-
THEY'RE DRIVIN IN THE STREETS, YEAH THEY'RR
     LAYIN EM DOWN---

HERE THEY COME — COME, COME, TO MUSIC CITY
  "   "   "   "   "   "   "   "   "
  "   "   "   "   "   "   "   "   "
YOU KNOW THE GUITARS ARE GROOVIN'
EVERYBODY'S MOOVIN'
SO COME ON, COME ON, COME ON
THEY'RE COMIN' FROM ALL OVER THE WORLD

② LOTTSA SWINGIN' HONEY'S FOR EVERY GUY, NOW
THERE'S GONNA BE A REAL BIG CROWD
JERKIN' AND STOMPIN' WHILE THE GUITARS ARE SCREAMIN'
AND THERE'S NO ADULTS ALLOWED
YOU'RE GONNA HEAR THE MUSIC CITY SOUNDS OF THE DAY
THE BABY-LOVIN' SUPREMES & MARVIN GAYE
THE KING OF THE BLUES, MISTER JAMES BROWN
THE BEACH BOYS SINGIN', NOW, I GET AROUND

(CHORUS)

TORRENCE OF BURIED TREASURES

I GOT IT BAD FOR THE NEW GIRL IN SCHOOL
THE GUYS ARE FLIPPIN' BUT I'M PLAYING IT COOL
EVERYBODY'S PASSIN' NOTES IN CLASS
THEY REALLY DIG HER NOW SHE'S SUCH A GAS

THE CHICKS ARE JEALOUS OF THE NEW GIRL IN SCHOOL
THEY PUT HER DOWN AND THEY TREAT HER SO CRUEL
BUT THE GUYS ARE GOIN' OUT OF THEIR MINDS
CAUSE SHE'S THE FINEST GIRL YOU'LL EVER FIND

WON'T BE LONG UNTIL WE'RE HAVIN' A BALL ~~TILL SHE'S MY STEADY DOLL~~
WE'LL WALK AND TALK AND WE'LL HOLD HANDS IN THE HALL
NEVER THOUGHT I'D MAKE IT THRU THIS YEAR
SURE WAS A DRAG TILL SHE TRANSFERRED HERE

I GOT IT BAD
I GOT A LOT

~~NEW IN TOWN~~ — NO MESSIN' AROUND

2nd THE GUYS ARE SAYIN MY CARS NO DARN GOOD
     BUT THEY DIDN'T LOOK TO SEE WHAT'S PACKED UNDER THE HOOD
     I DON'T CARE WHAT THOSE BIG MOUTHS SAY
     (GUESS) I'M GONNA STAY
     — I'M NEW IN TOWN
     — AND I DON'T WANT NO MESSIN AROUND

3rd THOSE BRAGGARTS BETTER QUIT THEIR GOOFIN' AROUND
     CAUSE THEY'LL HURT MY PRIDE AND START A BIG SHOWDOWN
     I'M A PRETTY GOOD-NATURED GUY
     BUT THEY'LL PUSH ME BY AND BY
     ~~I'M NEW IN TOWN~~
     — I'M NEW IN TOWN

FLY
BY
PUSHE

FROWN
BROWN
CROWN
CLOWN
SHOWN
POUND

I JUST MOVED OUT HERE FROM A CITY ON EAST COAST
THE FOLKS BACK THERE SAID THE WEST'S WOULD BE THE MOST
BUT I'M FINDIN IT PRETTY TOUGH
THE GUYS SEEM KINDA ROUGH
I'M NEW IN TOWN
AND I DON'T WANT NO MESSIN AROUND

THE GUYS THEY FINALLY PUSHED ME TO FAR
I HAD TA BEAT 'EM FIRST IN MY CAR
THEN I PUNCH'D UPSIDE THEIR HEADS
SENT 'EM HOME TO BED
I'M NEW IN TOWN
AND I WON'T STAND NO MESSIN AROUND

54

TORRENCE OF BURIED TREASURES

NO MESSIN' AROUND   GIBSON / ALTFELD

I JUST MOVED HERE FROM A CITY ON THE FAR EAST COAST
MY FOLKS BACK THERE SAID THE WEST WOULD BE THE MOST
BUT I'M FINDING IT PRETTY ROUGH
THE GUYS SEEM KINDA TOUGH
I'M NEW IN TOWN
BUT I WON'T STAND NO MESSIN AROUND

THE GUYS ARE SAYIN' MY CAR IS NO DARN GOOD
BUT THEY NEVER SAW WHATS PACKED UNDERNEATH THE HOOD
I DON'T CARE WHAT THOSE BIG MOUTHS SAY
WHEN THEY PASS MY WAY
I'M NEW IN TOWN
AND I DON'T WANT NO MESSIN' AROUND

THOSE BRAGGARTS BETTER QUIT THEIR GOOFIN AROUND
CAUSE THEY'LL HURT MY PRIDE AND START OUR BIG SHOWDOWN
I BEEN A DARN GOOD NATURED GUY
BUT THEY'LL PUSH ME BY AND BY
I'M NEW IN TOWN
BUT I WON'T STAND NO MESSIN' AROUND

THE GUYS THEY FINALLY PUSHED ME ONCE TOO FAR
I HADTA BEAT 'EM FIRST IN MY CAR
THEN I PUNCHED 'EM UPSIDE THEIR HEADS
SENT 'EM HOME TO BED
I'M NEW IN TOWN
BUT I DIDN'T STAND NO MESSIN' AROUND

(((((((((DON'T SAY WORDS IN)))))))))

~~I AIN'T GONNA STOP MY STING RAY~~
          or
    MY LITTLE RED STINGRAY

(CAPITAL LETTERED)
(WORDS ARE FOR   )
(↓LOW VOICE   )

WELL I GOT MY LITTLE STING RAY GOING REAL FAST   tank filled Up with the Highest Test gas
I've got my Little Sting ray going real Fast

Flying down the road at a hundred and ten   Passing fast cars like they never been

Flying Down the road just a gettin the Rubber, got a 4th gear and a looking for trouble...

Flying down the road just a ~~howling~~ sucking up trouble   JUST A GETTIN PEELING OFF RUBBER

Flying down the road just a (BLOWER SUCKING IN wind)

(Sound---(½ REV OFF)   30 seconds (Drag Slicks And Blower)

(LOW) ---(GET-IT) ONE WORD LITTLE RED STING RAY

(Sound(LAST REV Off) 30 seconds
    (LAST ½)
                     (Possibly Low)
                     (Really burning up that quarter mile)
(High)----Really burning up that quarter mile ,
(LOW)-- GET SOME RUBBER
        It really cleans everything at the Drag Strip, I mean nothing can stay ahead

I've Got a bad Little Sting Ray and it's about to shut everything down
it's about to shut everything down, it's about to shut everything down...(/UP)
SOund------ Rev off or Squealing (until out of site) (matter of speaking)

TORRENCE OF BURIED TREASURES

POM-POM PRISCILLA
(PATTY)
(PAULA)

SWINGINEST CHICK IN ALL THE SCHOOL...
(CHAMP OF THE CHEERLEADER GIRLS)

SHE WEARS A REAL SHORT SKIRT, AND A NICE TIGHT SWEATER
ALL THE BOYS IN SCHOOL WISH THEY KNEW HER BETTER
HAIR IN A FLIP - A WALK THAT'S TOUGH
I JUST CAN'T SEE HER ENOUGH

SHE'S MY POM-POM PRISCILLA
SHE'S MY POM-POM PRISCILLA
CHAMP OF THE CHEERLEADER GIRLS

LEADS IN THE AIR - PUTS ON A REAL SHOW
PUSH 'EM BACK, PUSH 'EM BACK - GO TEAM GO
FULL OF SPIRIT - EYES THAT SHINE
ALL THE GUYS KNOW SHE'S MINE

SHE'S MY POM-POM PRISCILLA
SHE'S MY POM-POM PRISCILLA
CHAMP OF THE CHEERLEADER GIRLS

(ON THE ~~STATE~~ BEACH)

ONE GIRL FOR YOU AND TWO FOR ME

WE'RE GOIN TO THE BEACH
WE'RE GOIN HAVE A GOOD TIME
WE'RE GOIN TO THE BEACH
WHERE THERE'S LOTS OF GIRLS
SO WILL BE MAKIN SOME TIME
WE'RE GOIN TO THE BEACH

WELL ~~THERE~~ THERE BE LOTS OF HONEYS WRITHIN AND
SEE, ONE FOR YOU AND TWO FOR ME
SO WE'RE GOIN TO THE BEACH TO MAKE SOME SCENE
" " " " " ...TO FIGHT THE GIRLS
" " " " " ...TO MAKE SOME OR —

ONE GIRL FOR YOU AND TWO FOR ME

WELL LOOK THIER'S JENNY + PEGGY SUE
WE'RE GOIN TO THE ~~BEACH~~ BEACH ITS HAPPIN ON THE BEACH

THEY LOOK SO GOOD GONNA DO
LET'S SEE WHAT HAPPEN ~~THIER~~ THE BEACH
BEFORE I'LL TAKE JENNY AND BETSY SUE
WELL I'LL TAKE JENNY NOW HOW ABOUT YOU.
I'VE GOT MINE

WELL SIT AT AROUND ~~THE~~ A FIRE O
AND ROAST SOME WINNIES
IT'S HAPPIN ON THE BEACH
WITH JENNY + PEGGY IN THIER BAKINIS
IT'S HOPIN AT THE BEACH
WELL ITS THE GREATEST IT'S THE MOST

WELL ITS GONNA GOIN ON ALL OVER THE COAST

TORRENCE OF BURIED TREASURES

POPSICLE

THAT OLD SCHOOL TEACHER'S GOT ME
MY CLASSES GOT ME DOWN CAUSE I'M WORKIN' TOO HARD
RELAX AFTERSCHOOL SITTIN OUT IN THE YARD
JUST ME AND MY BABY - I'M HOLDIN' HER HAND
THEN POP — TING A LING HERE COMES THE POPSICLE MAN

ORANGE, LEMON, CHERRY AND LIME
FUDGE, TUTTI-FRUTTI, AND GRAPE THAT'S FINE
BOY ONE FOR ME AND ONE FOR MY CHICK
A LOT A GOOD EATIN' ON A POPSICLE STICK

POPSICLE,
POPSICLE
IF YOU WANNA KEEP COOL — IT DOES THE TRICK
AND IT COMES ON A STICK

SOME PEOPLE EAT POPSICLE'S JUST FOR KICKS
BUT ME AND MY BABY - WE SAVE THE STICKS
TO KEEP BROTHER AND SISTER AS QUIET AS A MOUSE
WE GIVE 'EM POPSICLE STICKS TO BUILD A POPSICLE
—HOUSE

CHORUS

WHEN YOU HEAR THE BELL GO DING A LING
IT THE POPSICLE MAN AND HE'S THE GOODIE KING
SAVE POPSICLE STICKS WRAPPERS AND BEFORE LONG
YOU WILL WIN A PHONOGRAPH TO PLAY THIS
RECORD ON

POT OF TEA

Come and see my Pot of Tea
Let us drink my Pot of Tea

One day as I walked thru fields of green
I met a maiden not so clean
She took my hand and I was glad
We arrived at Lil' Red Riding Hoods pad

She said if you will stay with me
I will make a Pot of Tea
Like the little lady on the shore she
Gathered herself up once more

And then like good ole' mother Hubbard
She cut a trail for her cupboard
But no goodies did I see just a/
Just a little Pot of Tea

Well, they pot ran out, and all the same the dish was hot
But who's to blame, I could have found her real cool,
But then she played like a darn old fool.

Laurel & Hardy

Laurel & Hardy knocked at the door
But know one answered.
They slowly sneaked around the back
And saw two bikini;s on the fake rack.

The girls were swimming in the pool
When they caught a glimpse of the two ole' mules.

Laurel & Hardy were quite amazed
And ran for the gate but fell over a skate

They got themselves up and started once more,
When all of a sudden the girls locked the door

Well the moral of the story is don't explore
If you don;t get an answer when you knock on a door.

TORRENCE OF BURIED TREASURES

"SWINGIN' BUS DRIVER"

HE PICKS UP THE KIDS AND HE TAKES 'EM TO SCHOOL
AND EVERYBODY DIGS 'EM CAUSE HE ACTS SO COOL
HE FLIPS ALL THE GIRLS THEY SAY HE'S TOO MUCH
AND YOU SHOULD SEE THE WAY HE CAN DOUBLE CLUTCH

YOU'LL SEE HIM EVERYDAY AT THREE ON THE DOT
IN HIS BIG YELLOW "HOTIE" TACHIN' UP IN THE LOT
HE WEARS A LETTER SWEATER WITH AN IVY LEAGUE HAT
AND HIS QUARTER MILE ET IS ONE MINUTE FLAT

HIS BUS HAS A RADIO THAT PLAYS ROCK AND ROLL
AND IT'S REALLY BLASTIN' NOW WHEREVER WE GO

HIS BUS IS NOSED AND DECKED WITH DUAL EXHAUST
IT HAD A CARBURETOR GOVERNOR BUT IT GOT LOST

YOU SEE THE KIDS CROWDIN' ROUND AND MAKIN' A FUSS
CAUSE DON'T YOU KNOW EVERYBODY WANTS TO RIDE ON HIS BUS
CAUSE HE'S THE SWINGIN SCHOOL BUS DRIVER

I WANNA BE A SURFER AND LIVE BY THE SEA
CAUSE IT'S A WAY OF LIFE AND THE LIFE FOR ME
I KNOW WHAT I WANT, I'VE GOT IT ALL PLANNED
I WANNA SURF ALL DAY AND SLEEP ON THE SAND

I'VE SURFED ON THE COAST FROM MONTEREY TO BAHIA
AND RODE THE BIGGEST HEAVIES IN HAWAII AT MAKAHA
WHERE THE SURF IS BREAKIN BIG I WANNA BE FOUND
HOTDOGGIN ON MY BOARD TIL THE SUN GOES DOWN

WHEN THE SUN COMES UP, I WAX DOWN AND MOVE
DOWN TO THE BEACH WHERE THE SURFER'S ALL GROOVE
CAUSE I WANNA BE A SURFER AND LIVE BY THE SEA
IT'S A WAY OF LIFE AND THE ONLY ONE FOR ME.

TORRENCE OF BURIED TREASURES

SURF HEARSE

(1) I'VE GOT A 1937 CADILLAC HEARSE
IT'S NOT TOO CHERRY BUT IT COULD BE WORSE
THE SURFERS ALL DIG IT, THEY SAY IT'S COOKIE
BUT THE HONEY'S ~~WON'T GET IN IT~~ PUT IT DOWN YA KNOW, THEY SAY IT'S SPOOKY

(2) IT MAKES ALL THE OTHER WOODIES LOOK INFERIOR
AND EVERYBODY DIGS THAT PURPLE VELVET INTERIOR
IT'S GOT A LOT A FANCY INGRAVIN' ON THE SIDE
BUT NONE OF THE SURF-BUNNIES'LL GO FOR A RIDE

(3) WHEN I DRIVE IT BY THE CEMETERY LATE AT NITE
I GUESS I JUST IMAGINE THAT IT PULLS TO THE RIGHT
THE ENGINE SURE IS QUIET, CAUSE LIKE MAN ALIVE
THIS WEIRD WOODIE AIN'T ~~BEEN~~ GONE OVER THIRTY-FIVE

SURF HERSE
I'VE GOT A 1937 ~~CADILLAC~~ CADILLAC HERSE
IT'S NOT TOO CHERRY BUT IT COULD BE WORSE
THE SURFER'S ALL DIG IT, THEY SAY IT'S COOKIE
BUT THE ~~GIRLS~~ HONEY'S WON'T ~~GET IN IT~~ DEY SAY IT'S SPOOKY
    CHORUS   SURF HERSE

IT MAKES ALL THE OTHER WOODIES LOOK INFERIOR
~~BUT I REALLY GO FOR~~ AND EVERYBODY DIGS THAT PURPLE VELVET INTERIOR
IT'S GOT A LOT OF FANCY INGRAVING ON THE SIDE
BUT NONE OF THE SURFBUNNIES ~~WILL~~ GO FOR A RIDE
    CHORUS

WHEN I DRIVE IT BY THE CEMETARY LATE AT NITE
I GUESS I JUST IMAGINE THAT IT PULLS TO THE RIGHT
THE ENGINE SURE IS QUIET, CAUSE LIKE MAN ALIVE
THIS WEIRD WOODIE'S ~~NEVER~~ AIN'T GONE OVER THIRTY-FIVE
    CHORUS

TORRENCE OF BURIED TREASURES

Surf "Route 101"

Gonna gas up my woodie, and head for Route 101
My board's waxed and racked gonna have some fun
Gonna hit all the beachs and catch some breakers
Then back on the road I'm lookin for some takers

From the Tijuana sloughs up to Wind and Sea
My wax, board, and woodie were my only company
Then I met a surfer girl up at Huntington Pier
Who said "I dig your woodie lover, lets disappear"

So we hit the surf shack for chow and some jivin'
Then back to 101 for an hours worth of drivin'
Gonna turn on the speed, don't wanna be late
Cause the afternoon breakers up at Rincon are great

We tandemed on my board, and got wiped out twice
But takin' gas with this bunny was really pretty nice
Didn't mind waxin her board but I did get mad
When I caught her makin eyes at a big hoedad

The Spirit that Pulled me Through

If I'd never known myself
As I was before,
Then my eyes would be closed
To my lifes loud roar.

To think that I was called
and almost went.
Now happy to I'm living what
you have lent

If we borrow, what isn't due
, Then thank the Spirit
that pulled me through, Or
Through to see, and love again
that someone up there gives a
hand

TORRENCE OF BURIED TREASURES

"Slock Rod"

I buy all my parts from a mail order house
And everybody says my car is mickey mouse
Guy's put me down all over the block
They say my rod is nothin but slock

I've got a brush paint job and port a'walls
I burn cheap gas, and she always stalls
With 4 bald tires full of nails
Got twin antennas with racoon tails

There's big chrome stars on the side of the hood
And these purple tail lites sure look good
Headlite hoods in front and mudflaps in back
With a monkey on the mirror there's nothin zlack

Got a big chrome knob on the steering wheel
For drivin' and huggin' it's really ideal
The rod's are knockin and the lifters scatter
But my rod's paid for so it dosen't matter

Simple Sailor

In the early early morning
On the day I was born
There were people making plans
Making plans of their own
And you know just there I was
No help, did'nt want to be
                No part of

In the later later part of the century

He was a simple sailor
Sailing cross the sea
Now he's seen the ocean
He's come to set me free
    Come to set me free

TORRENCE OF BURIED TREASURES

"SING SANG A SONG"

Are ya comin' to the party with me?
To the marshmallow jamboree
You give out candy kisses
And that's all right -- by me

That campfire leads me to the dance
And moonshadows made you take a chance
You move me with your song
And that's all right -- by me

The pow-wow pounding in the air
The pom-pom pow-wow girl's so fine
She sing, sang a song

The party people on the run
Cookin' marshmallows just for fun
You rock me with your lovin'
And that's all right -- by me

The pow-wow pounding in the pines
The pom-pom pow-wow girl's all mine
She sing, sang a song

STREET MACHINE

Got a honey of a street machine now
Looks real cherry, and she's really clean
With a stick transmission and a big truck clutch
My speeding tickets keep me in dutch
Lay off on my street machine

She don't do the trick on the local dragtrack
But on the city streets she keeps comin' back
To eat up chevies, sting rays, and corvettes
I tune her up, and run her through
-- my oh my -- street machine

She's got six pots stickin through the hood
With her Mallory coil she runs mighty good
I'm always lookin out for the local police force
But I'm clean down to the street
As I scream down the local drag course
And she screams down the po police force
But we gotta look out for the po police force

TAR
SA MYECT -
RICH Sr

All the farmers in the Midwest LAND
are surfin in their dell THE
And the hippies from the east
Really think that surfin's swell
Yea you don't need an ocean
For you to understand
That the surfin craze BOOM is here
And its taken over the land.

Over Doctors Lawyer and Indian Chiefs
All the are shooting the curl and dodging the reefs
All the rebels in South Arc Bay THE
Androchee High Society Chicks @ Hump Seaside
In the Chauder driven woodies
Are spittin to the shore and pickin on
Surfin Goodies
Yea surfin really rates in
All the fifty states

Welcome to the surf scene
Makes no difference you are
Your welcome to the surf scene

TORRENCE OF BURIED TREASURES

SOMEDAY
Jan Berry
Don Altfeld

SOMEDAY- YOU'LL GO WALKIN' BY
YOU'LL WINK YOUR EYE
AND MAYBE SAY HI

YOU'LL BE ALL DRESSED UP IN FANCY CLOTHES
THEY'LL SEE ME BUT NO ONE KNOWS
YOU ONCE LOVED ME SO

WE WERE SO HAPPY TOGETHER
BUT YOU WENT AND GOT TIRED OF ME
I KNOW I'LL LOVE YOU FOREVER
BUT THAT'S HOW ITS GOTTA BE

SOMEDAY YOU'LL GIVE ME A SMILE
I'LL CRY ALL THE WHILE
AS YOU WALK DOWN THE AISLE

© 1963 Aldon Music

She's the Queen of the Surfer Girls

She shimmies on her surfboard as she shoots the girl
With style that's special for a girl
A Hawaiin tall palm trees bristle in the breeze (tanned brown)
To the bristle of the palm trees
king Shimmering in the breeze

With Polynesian Beauty Lulu catches every wave
that makes even surfer guys rave
And all the people in wahini baby
Dig Lulu in a special way

She's my Honolulu lulu, she's my honolululu
She's the Queen of the surfer girls

HONOLULU

To the bristle of the palm trees
Shimmering in the breeze
She shakes her body every way
She's a real delight to the people of Wahini bay
She's my Honolulu
lulu is the Queen of the Surfer Girls
pla

sailors
playground for tourists
Oahu
Polynesian playground
- Waikiki
Pineapple
hippy
hipswaying
"paradise
of the Pacific"
Pacific
paradise

STREET MACHINE

GOT A HONEY OF A STREET MACHINE
LOOKS REAL CHERRY AND SHE'S REALLY CLEAN
GOT HER FROM AN OLD LADY DOWN PASADENA WAY
AN I WORKED AN WORKED TO FIX HER UP THE WAY SHE IS TODAY

FIRST I CUT DOWN HER TOP SO I COULD BARELY SEE
THEN I SANDED DOWN THE BODY AND PAINTED OLIVE GREEN
I THREW IN A CHEVY MILL OF 353 CUBES
THEN I REALLY STARTED FLYING WHEN I TAPE EM DOWN THE TUBES

GOT A BIG TRUCK CLUTCH, HEAVY DUTY TRANSMISSION

TORRENCE OF BURIED TREASURES

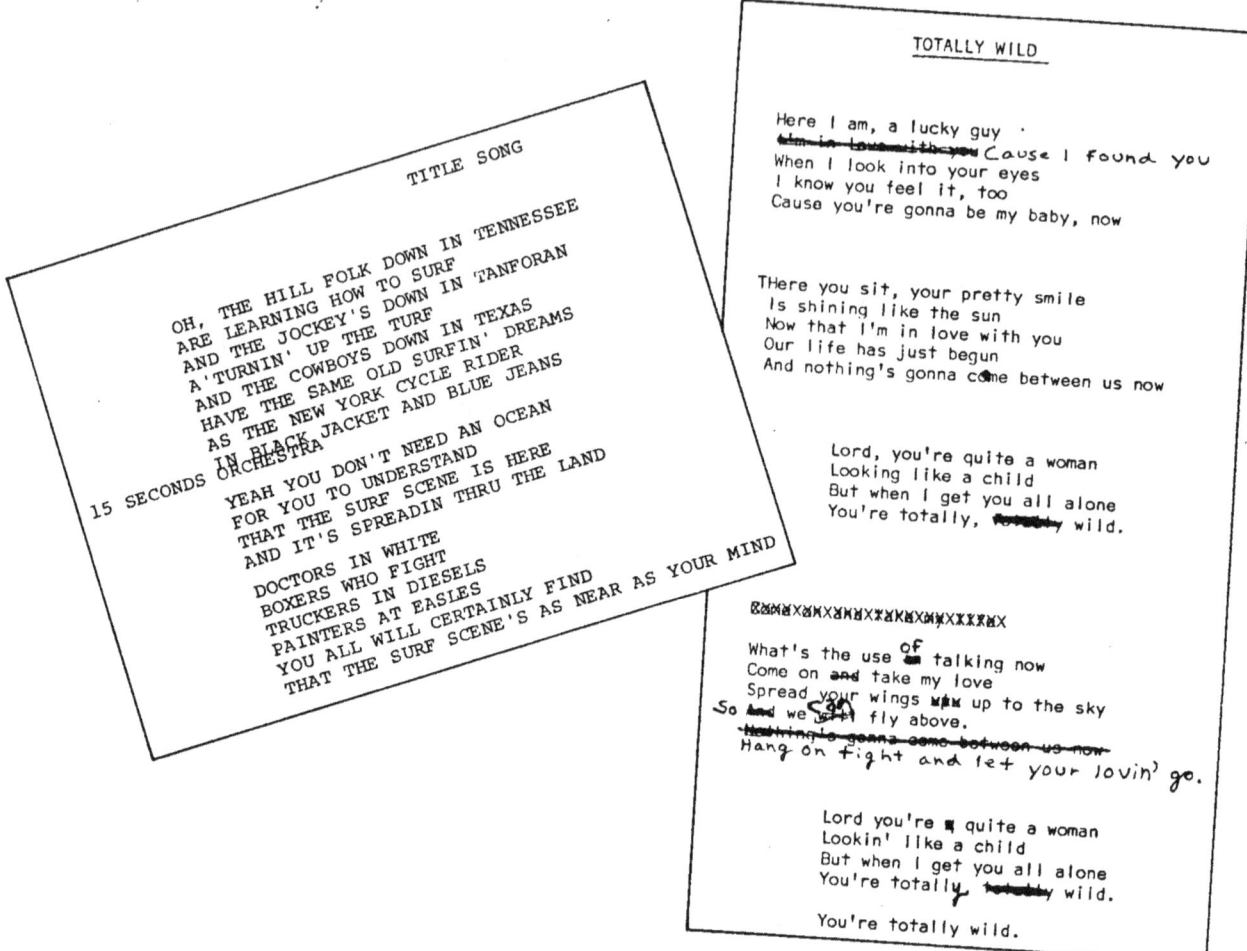

TORRENCE OF BURIED TREASURES

```
                THEY DO NOT KNOW              4/10/59

     Lonesome and blue -- an ache in my heart
     To whom can I turn , since we are apart?
     They do not know -- they do not know
             -- And little they care

     Life goes along -- and leave me behind
     I'm lost in a fog - no comfort I find
     They do not know -- they do not know
             -- And little they care

     "To each his Own" was just an expression to me
             -- I hardly knew what it meant
     Return, my own , and lift this depression from me
             -- Be my angel, heaven-sent
     I can't face the crowds -- dread being alone
     Friends pas me by - I'm all on my own
     They do not know -- they do not know
             -- And little they care
```

Totally Wild

Continuous

2ND Verse
There you sit your pretty eyes
Are shining Like the Sun
Here I am in love with you Our life
has Just begun
Nothing's gonna come between us now

3rd Verse
Everyday I listen close [to something
new you say
Night's of lying by your side
I NEED you all the WAY
Don't believe we're Gonna lose it
Now

4th Verse
What's the use of talking now,
Come on and take my love
What's the use of thinking more,
Come on and feel my love.

(Hang on Tight and let your lov'in
Go)

TORRENCE OF BURIED TREASURES

Tinsel Town

Hitch a ride to Hollywood
Hitch a ride to Hollywood
You're comin' out my way
And now I know you'll be beside me in Tinsel Town
Deep LOVE beside me in tinsel town

Hitch a ride to Hollywood
Hitch a ride to Hollywood
Can't stand to be alone
So hurry up come home to LOVE me Tinsel Town
Rain fallin' over me in Tinsel Town in
Since you been gone
When ever the action changes
We'll ride on the city ranges
And we will be together together

Hitch a hike to Hollywood
Sell your bike for Hollywood
This city's moving fast
won't give me rest with out
my head you in Tinsel town
Keep thinking all about you in tinsel town
Don't want to be with out you in tinsel town
Hurry come to me in Tinsel Town
We're gonna be High in Tinsel Town

Jon Hirsch
117 Sloane Street
S.W. 3 London, England
Bd 4718

"Trophy Run"

Worked so hard on this machine
And draggin isn't always fun
But I'm as proud as I can be
When I take my trophy run

The heats were fast but not like me
I'm proud of what we's done
Cars that machines m part of me
When I take my trophy run

Waited so long to prove to my
to show I could take a trophy
that my buggy could really rock

My Homies standin by the line
She's so proud that I have won
She'll give me a kiss and I'll be so happy
When I take my trophy run

Tinsel Town

Hitch a ride to Hollywood
Hitch a ride to Hollywood
You're comin' out my way
And now I know you'll be beside me in Tinsel Town
Deep love beside me in Tinsel Town

Hitch a ride to Hollywood
Hitch a ride to Hollywood
Can't stand to be alone.
So hurry up come home to love me in Tinsel Town

Rain fallin' over me since you've been gone
When ever the action changes
We'll ride on the city ranges
And we will be together gether

Hitch a HIKE to Hollywood
Sell your bike for Hollywood
This city's moving fast
My head won't let me rest without you in Tinsel Town
Been thinking all about you since you've been gone
Don't want to be with out you in Tinsel Town
So hurry come to me in Tinsel Town
'cause we're gonna be HIGH in Tinsel Town

Those California Drivers

*Those California Drivers
Are the terrors of the street*

I just hit the coast and was diggin the scene
While at Sunset and Vine I was cruisin a green
When some guy in a little red MG
Comes hangin' a left smack in front of me
I hit my brakes in the nick of time
And my '50 Chevy stopped on a dime

I kept on movin down the big boulevard
Along came a vette and jag drivin' hard
They forced me off the road by the Truesdale Estates
And as they went by I saw those black N yellow plates
I hustled and swung down Beverly Drive
My only hope now was to escape alive

I thought I was safe in sedate Beverly Hills
But that's where I got some really thrills
First a big blue chauffer driven Lincoln Capri
Signalled right, turned left --- almost into me
Then a litte T-Bird, filled with groovy chicks
Cut me off three times just to get some kicks

*Those California Drivers
Are the terror of the streets*

I'm not going back to that no-mans land
Where a tourists only chance is like Custer's last stand
Those California natives are out for a kill
If the youngsters don't getya, then the oldsters will
If I gotta go back, I won't wind up on a slab
Cause I'll be sure to take a yellow taxi-cab.

TORRENCE OF BURIED TREASURES

UNIVERSAL COWARD

He's young he's old he's
in between and he's so
very much confused
He's scrambling around protesting
all day long he joins the
pickets at Berkely and he
burns up his draft card.
And he's twisted into
thinking fighting is all
wrong he's a pessimist
extremist a communist
just a yank a demonstrater,
an agitator. just a nave
an conscientious objecter
a fanatic defecter and
he doesn't know that he's digging
his own grave awh he just
can't get it through his
thick skull why the mighty
U.S.A. has got to be the
watch dog of world
else pretty USSR will
bury us from afar. and
he'll never see the missiles
being hurled. He's the universal
coward and he runs from
anything from a giant
from human from elf he runs
from Uncle Sam he runs
from Viet Nam but most of
all he's running from
himself

TORRENCE OF BURIED TREASURES

WHEN IT RAINS, IT POURS

WHEN YOU THINK YOU'VE
FINALLY HAD YOUR SHARE OF SADNESS
YOU'VE HAD MORE THAN YOUR SHARE
IT'S SHEER MADNESS, DON'T YOU TRY TO HIDE
JUST LOOK OUTSIDE, THE CLOUDS
ARE CRYING ~~TOO~~
WHEN IT RAINS IT POURS

YOU'RE HEARTBROKEN

DEEP INSIDE HE HURT YOU,
LIKE ~~HA~~ YOU NEVER BEEN HURT BEFORE

WHEN IT RAINS IT POURS
NOW YOUR TEARS COME DOWN
FROM HEAVEN

~~YOU SIT BY YOUR WINDOW~~

YOU'VE HAD TROUBLE ENOUGH.

WHEN IT'S OVER

WHEN IT'S OVER
WILL WE HAVE TO PART
WHEN YOU LEAVE ME
WILL I HAVE A BROKEN HEART
WILL YOU GO YOUR WAY
AND I GO MINE
WHEN IT'S OVER — WHEN IT'S OVER

WHEN IT'S ~~DONE NOW~~ OVER
~~WILL YOU FIND NEW LOVE~~   WILL I HAVE A CHANCE
WILL YOU LEAVE ME   ~~WILL YOU FIND NEW ROMANCE~~
~~AFTER WE'VE BEEN TRUE LOVE~~ AND FIND NEW ROMANCE
                              ~~OR WILL I HAVE A CHANCE~~
WILL YOU SOON FORGET
THE HAPPY DAY WE MET
WHEN IT'S OVER — WHEN IT'S OVER

I CAN'T BEAR TO THINK AHEAD
TO WONDER WHAT WILL BE
I JUST CAN'T IMAGINE
WHAT MY LIFE WOULD BE
OH, PLEASE DON'T LEAVE

WHEN IT'S OVER
YOU DON'T HAVE TO GO
OH JUST STAY HERE
LET ME LOVE YOU MORE
~~LET'S AT LEAST PRETEND~~ ME NOW CAN'T I JUST PRETEND
WE'LL START OUR LOVE AGAIN
WHEN IT'S OVER — WHEN IT'S OVER

WHEN IT'S OVER

WHEN IT'S OVER
WILL WE HAVE TO PART
WHEN YOU LEAVE ME
WILL I HAVE A BROKEN HEART
WILL YOU GO YOUR WAY
AND I GO MINE
WHEN IT'S OVER

WHEN IT'S OVER
WILL I HAVE A CHANCE
WILL YOU LEAVE ME
AND FIND A NEW ROMANCE
WILL YOU SOON FORGET
THE HAPPY DAY WE MET
WHEN IT'S OVER – WHEN IT'S OVER

I CAN'T BEAR TO THINK AHEAD
TO WONDER WHAT WILL BE
I CAN'T IMAGINE
WHAT MY LIFE WOULD BE
PLEASE DON'T LEAVE ME

NOW THAT' IT'S OVER
YOU DON'T HAVE TO GO
PLEASE JUST STAY HERE
AND LET ME LOVE YOU MORE
CAN'T I JUST PRETEND
WE'LL START OUR LOVE AGAIN
WHEN IT'S OVER — WHEN IT'S OVER

SUMMER

TORRENCE OF BURIED TREASURES

WHY DOES EVERYTHING GO WRONG
GIBSON
ALTFELD

I'LL NEVER KNOW
WHY DOES EVERYTHING GO WRONG
I LOVE YOU SO
WHY DOES EVERYTHING GO WRONG
I GAVE YOU ALL I HAD
YOU CHEATED ME REAL BAD

I'LL NEVER, EVER TRUST ANOTHER GUY
YOU LEFT ME TORN APART
I'LL GO AWAY AND
HIDE MY BROKEN HEART

I DON'T KNOW NOW
WHY DOES EVERYTHING GO WRONG
I FEEL SO SAD
THAT WE HAD TO SAY "SO LONG"
THERE'S GOT TO BE A WAY
TO GET YOU BACK SOMEDAY

BUT UNTIL THAT TIME YOU GO AWAY WITH HER
AND LEAVE ME SAD AND BLUE
HOW WILL I EVER
GET OVER LOSING YOU

~INSTRUMENTAL~

I WAS BURNED
WHY DOES EVERYTHING GO WRONG
NOW I'VE LEARNED
I GUESS I'LL RUN ALONG
I STAYED THERE BY YOUR SIDE
WHILE YOU TOOK ME FOR A RIDE

I'LL NEVER, EVER TRUST ANOTHER GUY
YOU LEFT ME TORN APART
I'LL GO AWAY AND
HIDE MY BROKEN HEART

Who Cares?

Who Cares, I thought
When you said we're thru?
Who Cares I felt
If I'm left feeling blue
Who cares - not you - not you, not you!

Who Cares, I thought
When I slipped from #1 to 2
Who cares said I
When tossed aside like an old shoe
Who cares - not you not you not you

Ours was a wild
a whirlwind love

TORRENCE OF BURIED TREASURES

Verse version
What's He Got?

What's he got I haven't got?
True love -? No, it's not
So he's handsome - dark & tall
Listen honey - looks aren't all.

What's he got   I haven't got?
Sting Ray - or maybe a yacht.
A big white "E" on a red sweater
Honestly - other things are better

Some sweet day
When he outwears his glamor
The "big rush" will end
With its noise & its clamor

~~He~~
What've I got   he hasn't got.
His love's cold - mine's still hot
Little ol' me - waiting faithfully
Then you'll see that you <u>always</u> really loved me

10-11-78
Blow Out Music
Words by Joan Jacobs BMI

Way Too Much

See you goin' spinnin' around my mind
Its like your leavin' the world behind
Your out in front way ahead of your time
A flash of honey on a sunny hit of big time

Its O.K. downtown to be into your stuff
I know I'm gonna be good enough
An schools no place to be actin' this way
Its not my game unless were both gonna play

Wiggle an a stand up, in front a my eyes
I'm not gonna show you that I'm surprised
Your a game little mama, a hit to behold
A real heart breaker, with a heart of gold

We went up the safe way, careful and all
its not your mama or my mama's fault
Its just we're too tough to play it this way
An loves gonna help it, to come out O.K.

Chorus

Zoot suit honey, high to touch
Hawaiian tee shirts -
An (they're) showin' way to much
An (they're) showin' way to much

↑
may want
to leave out

YOU WANT TO THANK THE GUY WHO WROTE THE SONG
THAT MADE YOUR BABY FALL IN LOVE WITH YOU - WELL

WE PUT THE BOMP IN THE BOMP
THEY PUT THE RAM
THEY PUT THE ~~BOP DI-DIP-DI DIP BOP~~ IN THE - BOB
WE PUT THE DIP IN THE DIP-DI
WE WERE THOSE GUYS, I HOPE YOU REALIZE
WE MADE YOUR BABY FALL IN LOVE WITH YOU

WHEN YOUR BABY HEARD BOMP
EVERY WORD WENT STRAIGHT INTO HER HEART
AND WHEN ~~THEY~~ SHE HEARD THEM ~~STARTED~~ SINGING - RAMA LAM
SHE SAID YOU'D NEVER HAVE TO PART . WELL

EACH TIME YOU WERE ALONE - BOOGITY -BOOGITY
SET YOUR BABY'S HEART ALL A GLOW
AND ~~EVERY~~ TIME YOU DANCED TO DIP-DI-
SHE ALWAYS SAID SHE LOVED YOU SO - WELL

TORRENCE OF BURIED TREASURES

UNITED AIR LINES

WHAT NOW COBRA,
BEWARE COBRAS

Hey little cobra you're now going to pay
cause your about to be stung by a deadly
stingray
with 480 horses to make her go
my corvette grandsports not to slow

Lookin like a stingray right from the drags
with big huge goodyears on polish mags
I've done a quarter mile et. of 10.99
my corvette grandsport is nothin' but
fine

Being a thousand pds lighter she can
almost fly
and I get fourth gear rubber and I
don't even try
So hey little cobra you're at the end
of your string
and you're going to be sure to feel
my sting

JAN & DEAN
ACT

YOUR SWEET SWEET LOVE

(1). I just couldn't survive without your love__
And I just couldn't get by without your love__
And there's nothin' that I'd rather do__
than to be here mellow with you__
your love__ your love__
your sweet_sweet_sweet_sweet__

(2). Just one song in the world portrayed your love__
And just one phrase or a word explained your love__
there'd be nothin' left to say or sing
'cause that would be everything__
your love__ your love__
your sweet_sweet_sweet_sweet__

LA_LA_LA_ etc.

And there's nothin' I'd rather do__
than to be here mellow with you__
your love__ your love__
your sweet, sweet, sweet, sweet love.

TORRENCE OF BURIED TREASURES

I've been cheated
It's been repeated
that you've been going out on me
You made me blue now
You couldn't be true now
That's why I'm going to set you free
You go your way & I'll go mine
You didn't love me, but that's all right
because now
You broke my heart a mil times
So you go your way, & I'll go mine
This is it now
I'm gonna quit now
I just can't go on with you this way
You'll keep on lying
But baby I'm through trying
I just can't let it happen one more day
(refrain)

---

from the desk of
HORACE ALTFELD

Why should you hold me
And not let me go
When I tried to stop loving you *Shall I lean ---*
And still need you so   *-- -- or 'on with the show'*

Either you love me xxxxxxxxxxxxxxxxxx
And show me you do
Or you give me my freedom
Release me from you

There's a ~~time proven saying~~ *much quoted saying*
I ~~must repeat~~ to you *that's proved to be true*
You my dear, are trying
to have your cake -- and eat it too

I'm under your spell, and
I want to be free, but
I'd much rather stay
If you really want me

Why should you taunt me
And ~~give me fals hope~~
AND KEEP ME AT BAY
JUST SAY THE WORD
AND I'LL BE IN YOUR ARMS TO STAY.

WEIDER - ALTFELD

YOU TAKE MY HAND
AND YOU SAY I'M SORRY
FOR ALL OF THE THINGS
THAT YOU HAVE DONE

NO STARS IN THE SKY
NO BIRDS ARE SINGING
OUR LOVE IS GONE,
YEAH, OUR LOVE IS GONE

I WON'T SEE YOUR SMILE ANYMORE
I WON'T HEAR THE WORDS I HEARD BEFORE

I TURN TO YOU
AND SAY IT IS OVER
I CAN'T STAND HOW
YOU'VE DONE ME WRONG

THE LEAVES ARE STILL
THE BREEZE IS SIGHING
OUR LOVE IS GONE
YEAH, OUR LOVE IS GONE

I WON'T FEEL YOUR SOFTNESS ANYMORE
I WON'T TASTE YOUR LIPS LIKE BEFORE

TORRENCE OF BURIED TREASURES

6/20/65

BABY I CALLED YOU ON THE PHONE
BUT YOU SAID CALL BACK IM NOT ALONE
→ THEN I THOUGHT OF YOUR SWEET LIPS
→ THE ONES I WANT TO KISS
I THINK OF YOU ALL THE TIME YOUR UNDER MY SKIN
YOUR HEART CAPTURES THE MOOD IM IN
BUT IT HURTS MY HEART LOVE
CAUSE IM TRYING TO BE A PART OF
A WORLD I JUST DON'T BELONG IN

BABY IT MUST HAVE BEEN A DREAM
OR COULD IT HAVE BEEN A TERRIBLE SCHEME
TO YOU NOW THERE'S NOTHING I COULD BRING
MAKES ME FEEL THIS WORLD'S A MEANINGLESS THING
OH BABY I KNOW WHAT I SHOULD DO
BUT I CAN'T HELP MY SELF I'LL COME CRYING TO YOU

BABY IF YOU'D PROMISE TO BE MINE AND NEVER PART
I'D ALWAYS HOLD YOU CLOSE IN MY HEART
BUT IM NOT THE ONE YOU WANT BABY
IM NOT THE ONE TO PICK YOU UP AFTER EVERY FALL
TO COME RUNNING BACK EVERY TIME YOU CALL
OH NO BABY NO NO ITS NOT YOU I WANT BABY

All last summer when you should have been
With me at the beach enjoying a swim
What did you do but go surfing with Jim
I wonders what spring will bring!

Then came fall and the weather turned cool
Instead of joining me for a dip in the pool
You went surfin with Joe, I felt like a fool
I wonder what spring will bring!

In winter I wanted to an evening at home
Just holding hands, talking alone
but you and Johnny sleigh rides thing have gone
I wonder what spring will bring!

I guess you'd say I'm optimistic
Some day you'll want only me.
I still believe I can win
So when the grass turns green

TORRENCE OF BURIED TREASURES

HOW CAN YOU TELL WHEN LOVE IS REAL
WHAT IS THE CLUE - HOW DOES ONE FEEL.
IS IT TRUE INSTEAD OF BEATING STARTS ~~(illegible)~~ POUNDING
AND YOUR PULSE RATE DOUBLES - IN ANY SURROUNDING
HOW CAN I TELL WHEN LOVE IS REAL

HOW CAN YOU TELL WHEN LOVE IS REAL
DO YOU IMAGINE YOU HEAR THOSE WEDDING BELLS PEAL
DOES IT AFFECT YOUR EATING - WORKING - THINKING
AND DOES "TOGETHERNESS" OVERPOWER & ~~SMELLS~~ KEEP SINKING
HOW CAN YOU TELL WHEN LOVE IS REAL

I'VE OFTEN SEEN OTHERS GOING 'ROUND IN A FOG
OR PERHAPS STUPOR'S A BETTER WORD
BUT I ATTRIBUTED IT TO MY IMAGINATION
NOW I WONDER IF IT'S TRUE WHAT I HEARD

HOW CAN YOU TELL WHEN LOVE IS REAL
COULD INFATUATION ~~(illegible)~~ ~~(illegible)~~ ACT THE SAME
        AS ~~TRUE~~ LOVE TRUE, IDEAL
~~(illegible line crossed out)~~

BUTCHERS, BAKERS AND CANDLESTICK MAKERS
ARE WAXIN THEIR BOARDS. WAITIN FOR THE BREAKERS

~~(illegible)~~
CHAUFFER DRIVEN WOODIES WITH SOCIETY CHICKS
ARE HEADIN FOR THE BEACH TO GET THEIR KICKS

FROM THE EASTERN SEABOARD TO THE COAST
THE SURFIN CRAZE IS REALLY THE MOST
SURFIN ON THE GREAT LAKES AND DOWN THE MISSISSIPPI
ALL PRAYIN' FOR SURF FROM HOEDAD TO HIPPIE

THE
THE SURFIN SCENE IS REALLY GOOD NEWS
SAND SURF AND SALTAIR WILL CURE YOUR BLUES

TORRENCE OF BURIED TREASURES

D. I've spent my life just playin' games
E. To smart was I to give my heart
G. To anyone in sweet romance

D. Girls I met were meant to conquer
F. Then forget and throw away
C G" WITHOUT A THOUGHT WITHOUT A 2ND GLANCE
G. Yes that was me - that was me
C. That wild young love-maker me
G. That foolish dummy world shaker me
E. That cruel young heart-breaker me

A. I'd look so deep into their eyes
D I'd speak of love and whisper lies
I've told a hundred times befo re
~~shut~~
The sweet young things the way they cried
I'd hold their hands and laugh inside
~~It was just a kick to me and nothing more~~
I DID IT JUST FOR KICKS AND NOTHIN MORE
Chorus

But now I swear it's not the same
No-lon its not a game I'm playin' when I say
she's all that I'm dreamon of

She don't believe a word I say
She laughs and tells me to go away
I'm no one she would ever care to love

Yeah the tables turned - too late I've learned
That wild young love-maker
That foolish young world-shaker
That crueal young heart-breaker's - you

The future was so grim
as the trees they came to me
and they told me of him
that he would show no mercy
and unleash the sea &
on the city &
the same old song

When you look into your eyes
do you wonder where you have gone.
whats takin you so long
between the dawn
to revise the distance

~~Start~~
Well how long do you think
that we'll will have to wait
before this whole place goes
on the blink breaking & just
hope its not to late

Well there is one thing that we
all share and I'd just like to
show you how I felt this one
things always happening and
it's known as the eternal now
its said right now this very minute
now now now
there no escapin it

Well there one thing that
~~would be to tell the use~~

TORRENCE OF BURIED TREASURES

UNITED/WESTERN STUDIOS
6000 Sunset Blvd.
Hollywood, Ca. 90028

CLIENT: JAN & DEAN
DATE: 10/4/79

MASTER NO	CODE	TAKE	TITLE	
			Diane's on My Mind	1
		✓	She Sing Sing a Song	
		✓	Don't You Just Know It	3
	✓	✓	Totally Wild	1A
		✓	Fun City	
			I'm Coming After You	2
	✓	✓	Hide Your Love Away	2A
		✓	Tinsel Town	
			Blow Up Music	
Joan J.			Your Sweet Sweet Love	
		✓	~~How~~ How I Love Her	

FS - FALSE START LFS - LONG FALSE START M - MASTER ITC - INTERCUT PB - PLAYBACK C - COMPLETE

Paramount 461-4811

Hal "Jan & Dean Back on the Scene"

- "Tinsel Town"
- "Mother Earth"
- "The Magic of Making Love"
- "Blow Out"
- "Flight Number Nine"
- "I'm Coming Back"
- "Look out"
- "To Day I Know my Mind"
- "A Long Way to go"
- "High in the Sky"   Don Moss = Title

TORRENCE OF BURIED TREASURES

News from JAN AND DEAN FAN CLUB
NATIONAL HEADQUARTERS
1807 BRINKLEY AVENUE
LOS ANGELES 49, CALIFORNIA

/ MAY 1963 /

JAN & DEAN take LINDA SURFIN'

● LINDA ● MR. BASS MAN ● SURFIN' SAFARI ● RHYTHM OF THE RAIN ● WALK LIKE A MAN ●
● THE BEST FRIEND I EVER HAD ● MY FOOLISH HEART ● SURFIN' ● THE GYPSY CRIED ●
●● WALK RIGHT IN ●●● LET'S TURKEY TROT ●●● WHEN I LEARN HOW TO CRY ●●

I don't know how much of the U.S.A. got to see the TEEN AGE FAIR when they selected Miss Teen U.S.A. -- but if you did, you got to see JAN and DEAN and good ol' Wink Martindale (m.c.) give a plug for their new Liberty Album. So many have written in asking "what's on it" that I took this **bold** way to tell you. I like what Nancy Vaughn (Pres. No. 661) says: " Congrats to the Boys for their too-lively-for-words SURFIN' album! Played it at a recent party and the kids went wild .... the very favorite (mine too) was "My Foolish Heart". It's one of the nicest things they've ever done -- would make a knock-em-dead single. The album cover is beautiful -- I look at it hourly and get Californiaitis". Take a tip from Nancy and see the two pictures on the album jacket. Like, WOW!

Your record shop surely has it by now, because it is already the 12th best-selling album in Los Angeles. It's available in regular monaural , or stereo. So there !

LOOK WHAT'S NEW IN  *AND YOU'LL LOVE IT!*

excitement of the future   After a resounding H-I-T like "Linda" has been , you'd expect it to very difficult to find a record for JAN and DEAN to follow-up with, and be assured of another smash! But they've done it -- at least all the reports indicate that their new single - due to be on the racks about May 16 is perfectly timed, perfectly tuned, and with a better beat than a Mixmaster - is going to keep their names high on the Top Charts.

The featured side is "SURF CITY" and how did you ever guess that it is a surfin' song like they do so well? They had planned to come out with another platter they had already recorded, and I even hinted that to some of you by letter, but when they came across "SURF CITY" they knew this had to be their next single. The flip side is a li'l cutie to be known henceforth as " She's My Summer Girl".

JAN and DEAN can't tell you how gratified they were with the support they got from clubs everywhere when "Linda" was launched. DEAN says " Proves that it's the fans who MAKE the singers, and not vice-versa". He's a modest guy, but I can vouch for the fact that you all had a hand in zooming "Linda" right up there. Even now, after twelve weeks on the chart it is No. 27 in CASH BOX (record-industry's guide) and still climbing. Debra Sue Neff tells me it is No. 2 in Cincinnati; Stacie Staidle says it jumped from #27 to #12 in one week in the Cleveland area. The general reports were that JAN and DEAN have not had such favorable reaction and as many air plays for a long time, and they have become brand-new favorites to thousands. I can tell, too, because every day I get inquiries from more and more "newies".

More good news: After much grumbling by this reporter, and J & D fans all over, I am happy to announce that their new record "SURF CITY" with all the goodies inside, is gonna be just as nice on the outside -- Liberty is making a special JAN and DEAN sleeve (or jacket) for this disc, and we know (don't we?) that when the teens see that, instead of a plain ol' envelope, they'll want the record no matter what it sounds like. Thanks, LIB!

Would like to quote Angela Amoroso, faithful Prez, on her own way of "helping" LINDA. (Quote) "I've now discovered a rather sneaky way of promoting a song, and getting the girls to sing it. I might say, 'Irene, how does LINDA go again? I keep forgetting'. Irene then starts. Soon others join in, and before you know it we have a regular chorus going. ..... Another tactic is to sing a few lines while at the locker, etc. Somebody always says : 'What's that?' and one answers LINDA by Jan and Dean! and , voila a staged commercial".

So, the merry-go-round starts again, and this time our goal is SURF CITY . All aboard ....

THIS 'n THAT

One of my most enthusiastic correspondents of late has been Linda Klaus of Pittsburgh. She has more questions than a geometry teacher. But I thought you might all be interested in some of the answers I've had to come up with so here they are - random fashion. DEAN'S Taunus (German Ford) is now all back together. Did it himself. One slight problem. It doesn't run. 'Member JAN'S Corvette that was burned in the fabulous Bel Air Fire? He's having it all fixed, and is going to sell it. One Corvette in the drive is enough ...... How many years till JAN is a doctor? Four - then interning, residence, etc. .....

TO GET THE NEXT ISSUE YOU MUST SEND IN A STAMPED ENVELOPE ✓

JAN and DEAN are for

TORRENCE OF BURIED TREASURES

Aug. 63

JAN AND DEAN NEWS EXTRA

Help! HELP!! Help! Help!

JAN and DEAN Fan Club members are important to their radio stations. they will listen to you -- because <u>you</u> listen to them !

That's why we would like to all pull together and give them an earful about playin the new release "PERFIDIA" by the Matadors. It's on the Colpix label.

Why should we want to push that one?

JAN and DEAN Fans who have heard the record recognize JAN'S touch --- because he arranged and produced it , <u>and</u> they like it ! JAN would like our support because it would mean a lot to him to have it be a smash! (It was written up in current Cash Box and a pick hit of the new groups, so your d.j. will know all about it)

Fans anywhere can call, write or see their local d.j. and tell him they want to hear "Perfidia", and they can ask local record shops if they have it yet. All this will help it get on the air, but fast !

Many places have a "Voice-Your-Choice" type program where they <u>ask</u> you to select your favorites. Here in L.A. area we beseech every loyal fan to get as many friends as possible to phone Wink Martindale (KFWB) at HO 1-9344 ; HO 1-9932 or HO 1-9210 between 6 and 7 in the morning (Yipes!) and vote for "PERFIDIA" (This very morning Wink said it is getting a lot of votes, but it didn't quite make the top five) You can then roll over and go back to sleep knowing your good deed is done.   Wouldja?

The same goes for other areas where a vote "in time" can make "Perfidia" start chart-climbing. You did it with "LINDA" ; you gave "SURF CITY" a tremendous shove , now if you'll do it for "PERFIDIA" -- I wouldn't kiddya -- we'll all be grateful to you, and you'll have the pleasure of knowing you helped.

We'll soon be telling you about JAN and DEAN's new single, but let's get behind "PERFIDIA" right now. OK?   O.K.
and T-H-A-N-K-S

And if you wanna tell JAN you helped, just fill this in and send it to me and I'll see that he gets it personally.

JAN: In order to help "PERFIDIA" I _____

_____

(Signed) _____

TORRENCE OF BURIED TREASURES

JAN & DEAN NEWS JAN & DEAN
MARCH 1964

NEW GIRL RACES DEAD MAN UP THE CHARTS !!

As we threatened (or promised) you - JAN and DEAN have themselves a two-sided S-M-A-S-H . It certainly has been interesting to see how they have been struggling with each other for the lead on the charts. Nationally, using CASH BOX Magazine as our guide, it has gone something like this, so far: First week it was DEAD MAN out front at position 72, and NEW GIRL coming along at 80; second week DEAD MAN'S lead was cut - it was 62 and NEW GIRL 60. Well, NEW GIRL sneaked ahead on the far turn and led the third week 51 to 50; and in the latest report NEW GIRL has increased her lead and is out front as we go to the printers 32 to DEAD MAN'S No. 40.

National reports don't keep pace with local activity because some places it is way up top, and others, just getting o start. Like - let's see - in FRESNO, CALIF. it was off to a zooming start and is current #2 on one station and #3 on another. The Windy City of Chicago is behind, and we just blew in there at #40 -- but that was after only one week of play. (BEATLES, watch out').

Down MIAMI way we're in at #5, up BOSTON town there using the old bean and have us both in good position - DEAD MAN #15, and NEW GIRL #22.

We want you to know this is really the first two-sider J & D have had. It is _most_ unusual to have two songs going this well, and only a few artists ever do that like maybe the BEATLES (who they?) Elvis, and The Beach Boys. So "our group" is among the chosen few, and of course greatly appreciate you fans and your help in making this dream a reality. Read on ......

CONTEST REPORT

Perhaps you have guessed this from the news above, but if you haven't, I'm pleased to report that THERE IS STILL TIME TO WIN IN THE "GET-IT-IN-THE-TOP-TEN" Contest announced in the February Newsletter.

So far, we have four winners out of ten and the Grand Prize is still available. First in so fast my head is still swimming was Gary Arnold of Fresno, followed shortly by Gary McNally of the same city but reporting us doing Chart tricks on the other station in town. And just yesterday I got the third winner from Sue Collins of Detroit and #4 comes from Doug Braxton of Miami.

That means we have six prizes unaccounted for, and wish you to be among the winners. So call, write, wire and pester your d.j. (and your congressman if you think it'll help) and let's finish the job we've started so well.

Complete list of final winners in next issue out about April 15, if possible.

Will your town be there? Remember, we will count EITHER SIDE in the Top Ten - NEW GIRL IN SCHOOL , or DEAD MAN'S CURVE.

SEE JAN AND DEAN AT MELODYLAND THEATRE IN ANAHEIM APR. 14 THRU 19 ON THE CONNIE FRANCIS SHOW. MATINEES ON THE 18th & 19th.

WANT NEWS REGULARLY!

Any member can get the Newsletter, free , by merely sending in a stamped and addressed envelope. We'll hold it and mail the next edition to you. If there's no stamp or no address, we just can't send it. We do this to save time and labor in this office.

Drop Us A Line... 1907 Bradley Ave. Los Angeles, Calif. 90049

WORDS FOR DEAD MAN'S CURVE

I was cruisin' in my Sting Ray late one night
When an X.K.E. pulled up on the right
He rolled down the window of his shiny new Jag
And challenged me then and there to a drag.

I said "You're on buddy, My mill's runnin' fine
Let's come off the line now at Sunset and Vine,
But I'll go you one better if ya got the nerve,
Let's race all the way to DEAD MAN'S CURVE" .

(Chorus)

I flew past La Brea, Schwabs' and Crescent Heights
And all Jag could see were my six tail lights.
He passed me at Doheny and I started to swerve
But I pulled her out - and there I was at
DEAD MAN'S CURVE

CHORUS: It's No Place To Play
You Best Keep Away
I Can Hear Them Say
Won't Come Back From DEAD MAN'S CURVE.

I can't tell you how many fans wrote in to tell us about the gourgeous color pictures of JAN and DEAN in the March (Issue No. 3) of TEEN SCREEN MAGAZINE. Get your copy while still here, on the newstands.

SEE JAN AND DEAN IN HAWAII ONE WEEK BEGINNING APRIL 3.

Dean's Corner

" I finally got around to taking my new Sting Ray out to the strip , and came home with a trophy. I think it will prove to be one of the FASTEST stock Corvettes around. I'll have some photos taken of it for the Newsletter."

In answer to many inquiries, it looks like EVERYTHING is turning out A-OK for our DEAN, and take it from me, he's a great guy .

TORRENCE OF BURIED TREASURES

NOTES FOR HANDWRITTEN LYRICS (PAGES 12-77 INCLUSIVE)

PAGE 12: "ANOTHER HAPPY DAY" in a slightly altered form became "A SURFER'S DREAM", appearing on Jan & Dean's Liberty Records' lp RIDE THE WILD SURF (LRP 3368/LST 7368) issued in August 1964.

"ACTION SPEAKS LOUDER THAN WORDS" remains a mystery.

PAGE 13: "ANAHEIM, AZUSA AND CUCAMONGA" first appeared as the flip side to Jan & Dean's Top 20 chart success "RIDE THE WILD SURF". It also graced the duo's THE LITTLE OLD LADY FROM PASADENA lp, released on Liberty Records (LRP 3377/LST 7377) in September 1964.

"BETTER SURE THAN SORRY" with lyrics by Don Altfeld remains a mystery.

PAGE 14: "THE BATTLE OF STRAWBERRY FIELDS" and "BIG MAN ON CAMPUS" remain a mystery.

"BLOW OUT" is an alternate version of "BLOW UP MUSIC", an instrumental released by Jan Berry (under the name 1 JAN 1) on Ode Records (ODE-66050-S) in August 1974.

PAGE 15: "BETTER SURE THAN SORRY" alternate lyrics.

"THE BARONS OF WEST L.A.", an ode to Jan & Dean's school club called The Barons, is shown here in lyrical form. An instrumental titled "BARONS, WEST L.A." was featured on Jan & Dean's DEAD MAN'S CURVE/THE NEW GIRL IN SCHOOL album released on Liberty Records (LRP 3361/LST 7361) in May 1964. Were these the proposed lyrics?

PAGE 16: "BUCKET T" first appeared as recorded by Jan & Dean on their DEAD MAN'S CURVE/THE NEW GIRL IN SCHOOL album. Songwriting credits for this release were Roger Christian-Don Altfeld. The song was also re-issued by Liberty Records as the flip to the duo's early 1966 chart success "BATMAN".

"BUCKET T" was also recorded and released by:
RONNY & THE DAYTONAS - Mala Records #492 (December 1964). This peaked at #54 on the National charts. Songwriting credits on this occasion were Roger Christian-Jan Berry.
THE WHO - Included on the group's MAGIC BUS album released in October 1968. Songwriting credits were Don Altfeld-Roger Christian-Dean Torrence.

Although Jan & Dean did record a number of commercials for the "Things Go Better With Coke" campaign for the soft drink Coca Cola, these lyrics were not put to use.

PAGE 17: "COME ON BABY", written by Bodie Chandler, was recorded by Jill Gibson and Judy Lovejoy with production courtesy of Jan Berry although it remains unreleased. Also recorded by the duo during the same period were "WHAT'S IT GONNA BE" and the Jan Berry-Jerry Fuller composition "JUST FOR TONIGHT".

"CALLING ALL GIRLS" written by Buzz Cason and Bobby Russell was recorded in demo form and submitted to Jan & Dean who decided against utilising it.

"THE CLASS OF '64" remains a mystery.

TORRENCE OF BURIED TREASURES

PAGE 18: "CAJUN JOE (THE BULLY OF THE BAYOU) was recorded in instrumental form at Radio Recorders, Los Angeles.

"CHILDHOOD MEMORIES" with lyrics by Don Altfeld remains a mystery.

PAGE 19: "CHEYENNE (FLIGHT NUMBER NINE)". Lyrics by Joan Jacobs and music by Jan Berry. The song was originally titled "HIGH ON A RED CARPET FLIGHT".

"DRAGGING U.S.A." remains a mystery.

PAGE 20: "DANCE TOGETHER" remains a mystery.

"DIANE" features music and lyrics by Jan Berry, Tom Sumner and Alan Wolfson. Demoed but unreleased.

PAGE 21: "DRAG CITY" written by Jan Berry-Roger Christian-Brian Wilson first appeared in October 1963 as the 'A' side for Liberty Records single #55641. The following month it also appeared as the title song for the Jan & Dean album DRAG CITY (LRP 3339/ LST 7339). Both the single and album charted nationally, #10 and #22 respectively.

"DRAGON WAGON" as featured here bears no relationship to the song "DRAGGIN' WAGON" recorded and released by The Surfer Girls for Columbia Records (# 4-43001) in May 1964.

PAGE 22: "DOWN AT MALIBU BEACH" written by Jan Berry-Roger Christian-Don Altfeld, was featured as recorded by Jan & Dean on their Liberty Records lp RIDE THE WILD SURF (LRP 3368/LST 7368) released in August 1964. Roger Christian's handwritten lyrics are featured.

"DEADLY DUDLY'S DRAGG'N" remains a mystery.

PAGE 23: "EVERY BODY'S GO GO WILD" features the lyrics for Jan & Dean's 90 second Coca Cola commercial (released as 347/65) recorded and pressed on disc for the "Things Go Better With Coke" promotional campaign in 1965. 10, 30 and 60 second commercials were also recorded and issued. The 60 second commercial featured the first verse, chorus and final chorus of the 90 second commercial and was arranged by Ralph Burns. Jan Berry produced all four commercials.

"FAN TAN", written by Jan Berry-Jill Gibson-Don Altfeld, was eventually released under the Jan & Dean moniker in 1967 on the custom Jan & Dean Record label (designed by Dean Torrence) as #11.

PAGE 24: "THE FOOL OF THE SCHOOL" remains a mystery.

"FREEWAY FLYER", written by Don Altfeld-Roger Christian-Jan Berry, was recorded by Jan & Dean and released as the flip to their #56 chart success "FROM ALL OVER THE WORLD", issued in February 1965 on the Liberty Records label (#55766). Lyrics shown here are in Roger Christian's handwriting (#1) and Don Altfeld's (# 2 and #3).

PAGE 25: "FRED FERN" remains a mystery although music exists.

PAGE 26: " THOSE BAD LOOKIN' GUYS ..." as such, are the original ideas for

TORRENCE OF BURIED TREASURES

PAGE 26: (Continued) what eventually became the "THEME FROM THE T.A.M.I. SHOW" AKA "(HERE THEY COME) FROM ALL OVER THE WORLD" released as a single by Jan & Dean in February 1965 as Liberty #55766. Credited songwriters were Phil Sloan and Steve Barri, Jan & Dean's one-time backing vocalists dubbed The Fantastic Baggys

"GINNY ON MY MIND", written by Jan Berry-Alan Wolfson-Tom Sumner remains unreleased although rhythm tracks were recorded at A&M Studios in Los Angeles circa June 1976. Present at the session were musicians Hal Blaine (drums), Ray Pohlman (bass), Mike Lang (piano), Tommy Tedesco and Ben Benay (guitars).

PAGE 27: Both "GIRLS' CURLS" and "THE GREATEST SHOW ON EARTH" remain a mystery.

PAGE 28: "(I'LL NEVER FORGET) THE GIRL FROM WAIMEA BAY" remains a mystery although it may have been an intended possible inclusion for Jan & Dean's Liberty Records' lp RIDE THE WILD SURF (LRP 3368/LST 7368).

"GIRL YOU'RE BLOWIN' MY MIND", written by Pierre Hunt, originally bore the working title of "MY LIFE'S GOING TO POT", then "IT ALL GOES TO POT" and finally "TELL ME IT'S SO" before evolving into its recorded and released form. Various recorded versions of the song exist although only one was eventually released, appearing on the Warner Brothers' record label in September 1968 as WB #7240.

PAGE 29: "HONOLULU LULU" first appeared on Jan & Dean's Liberty lp SURF CITY & OTHER SWINGIN' CITIES (LRP 3314/LST 7314) issued in June 1963 and then headlined the duo's follow-up single to their chart topping "SURF CITY" in August 1963 (Liberty #55613), peaking at #11 nationally. The album release of "HONOLULU LULU" bore the songwriting credit of Jan Berry while the single bore the credit Jan Berry-Roger Christian-Spunky. "Spunky" was in fact Lou Adler.

"HE DON'T LOVE ME", written by Jan Berry-Don Altfeld-Jill Gibson was recorded and released by Shelley Fabares as Colpix #721 in March 1964. Record production was by Jan Berry.

PAGE 30: "HAWAII", written by Jan Berry and Jill Gibson, appeared under the Jan & Dean name in 1967 on the custom record label Jan & Dean as #10.

"HIGH SCHOOL FLIRT" remains a mystery.

PAGE 31: "HEY LITTLE FRESHMAN", written by Roger Christian and Don Altfeld was recorded and released by Jan & Dean on their Liberty lp DEAD MAN'S CURVE/THE NEW GIRL IN SCHOOL. It was one of a number of songs reputed to have been written by Jan Berry but whose name was left off to avoid contract problems.

"HIGH SCHOOL FLIRT" remains a mystery

PAGE 32: "HIGH ON A RED CARPET FLIGHT" are the original lyrics to Jan Berry's and Joan Jacob's song "CHEYENNE (FLIGHT NUMBER NINE).

"HORACE THE SWINGIN' SCHOOL BUS DRIVER", written by Phil Sloan and Steve Barri, was recorded by Jan & Dean and included on their Liberty lp THE LITTLE OLD LADY FROM PASADENA (LRP 3377/LST 7377) issued in September 1964. Lyrics as featured here include an extra last verse.

TORRENCE OF BURIED TREASURES

PAGE 33: "IT'S SO EASY (TO BE IN LOVE WITH YOU) remains a mystery.

"IT CAN'T LAST FOREVER" featuring handwritten lyrics by Don Altfeld remains a mystery.

PAGE 34: "I'LL NEVER RACE AGAIN", "I'LL NEVER DRIVE AGAIN" and "IT'S GREAT TO HAVE YOU BACK AGAIN" all feature handwritten lyrics by Don Altfeld yet still remain a mystery.

PAGE 35: "IT'S A SHAME TO SAY GOODBYE", written by Jill Gibson and Don Altfeld, was recorded by Jan & Dean and released as the flip side to their Top 30 national chart success "I FOUND A GIRL" issued as Liberty #55833 in September 1965. The song was also included on the duo's Liberty lp FOLK 'N ROLL (LRP 3431/LST 7431) released in November 1965 and the lp JAN & DEAN'S POP SYMPHONY NO.1 (LRP 3414/LST 7414) issued in late 1965 under the name of The Bel-Aire Pops Orchestra. A Screen Gems Music demo of the song exists with considerable lyrical change to the released version and to the version shown here. Although the backing/instrumental track of the demo is virtually identical to that released by Jan & Dean, the lead vocal is not by the duo.

"I'M COMING BACK", circa late seventies, remains a mystery.

PAGE 36: "IT'S A SHAME ..." features additional alternate lyrics to the released version.

"IT'S AS EASY AS 1 2 3", written by Don Altfeld and Jill Gibson, first appeared as recorded by Jan & Dean on the duo's Liberty lp THE LITTLE OLD LADY FROM PASADENA, performed jointly by Jan Berry and Jill Gibson as a duet. The song was also issued as a solo recording (utilising the same instrumental track) by Jill Gibson for Imperial Records - Imperial #66068, released in August 1964. The lyrics included here are from Jan & Dean's version.

PAGE 37: "I KNOW MY MIND" (AKA as "FREE FREE FREE"), written by Jan Berry and Roger Christian, appeared under the Jan & Dean name in June 1968 as the 'A' side of the duo's second single for Warner Brothers #7219.

"I'VE BEEN A BAD GIRL" remains a mystery.

PAGE 38: "IN MY MIND" and "I'M IN A STATE OF SHOCK" remain a mystery.

PAGE 39: "I'VE BEEN A SAD GIRL" is a rewrite of "I'VE BEEN A BAD GIRL".

"THE JOKER", written by Don Altfeld-Jan Berry-Jill Gibson-Fred Weider, under its full title "THE JOKER IS WILD" was featured on Jan & Dean's Liberty lp JAN & DEAN MEET BATMAN (LRP 3444/LST 7444) released in March 1966.

"JUST FOR TONIGHT", written by Jan Berry and Jerry Fuller, was recorded by Jill Gibson and Judy Lovejoy, but remains unreleased.

PAGE 40: "JAN THE FAN TAN MAN" is perhaps the original inspiration that produced "FAN TAN", a song which appeared as a single under the Jan & Dean name in 1967 on the custom label Jan & Dean as #11.

"LONG TIME NO SEE" remains a mystery.

TORRENCE OF BURIED TREASURES

PAGE 41: "LOVE HOLLOW" AKA "MEDITATE" remains a mystery although a music score exists.

"LISTEN LITTLE GIRL" remains a mystery.

PAGE 42: "LITTLE GIRL - LITTLE BOY" remains a mystery.

"LAUREL & HARDY" underwent various changes before finally being released under the Jan & Dean name in June 1968 as the flip side to "I KNOW MY MIND", the duo's second single for Warner Brothers. The released version bore the songwriting credit Roger Christian-Jan Berry.

"LINDA" was an old standard written by Jack Lawrence as rumour has it for the daughter of a friend - that daughter Linda Eastman was to become Mrs. Paul McCartney. In late 1962 Jan & Dean decided to record the song in their own inimitable style and subsequently achieved a Top 30 national chart success with it in early 1963 upon its release on Liberty Records as Liberty #55531.

PAGE 43: "LOVE FOREVER" remains a mystery.

"LITTLE MUSTANG" under the full title "MOVE OUT LITTLE MUSTANG" first appeared under the group name The Rally Packs as a single for Imperial Records (#66036) in May 1964 and then as a filler on the Jan & Dean lp THE LITTLE OLD LADY FROM PASADENA. Although both credit the artist as being The Rally Packs and Jan & Dean respectively, the song in fact is performed by Phil Sloan and Steve Barri.

PAGE 44: "LITTLE FERRARI" with handwritten lyrics by Don Altfeld remains a mystery.

"LET YOURSELF GO", written by Jan Berry-Artie Kornfeld, appeared as a single by The Matadors (Tony Minichiello, Vic Diaz and Manuel Sanchez) on the Colpix label (#741) in mid 1964 with Jan Berry producing. The Matadors apart from being friends of Jan & Dean also contributed background vocals to the duo's early Liberty recordings.

PAGE 45: "LITTLE ROADSTER" remains a mystery.

PAGE 46: "MANHATTAN", written by tunesmiths Richard Rogers and Lorenz Hart, was another old standard updated by Jan & Dean. It was featured on the duo's SURF CITY & OTHER SWINGIN' CITIES lp.

"MY STREET ROD" with handwritten lyrics by Don Altfeld remains a mystery.

PAGE 47: "MEDITATE" AKA "LOVE HOLLOW" remains a mystery.

"THE MAGIC OF MAKING LOVE" recorded by Jan Berry during the late seventies still remains unreleased.

PAGE 48: "MYSTERIOUS THINGS ARE HAPPENING" circa late seventies remains a mystery although music exists.

"MOTHER EARTH", written by Jan Berry-Joan Jacobs, appeared in late 1972 as Jan Berry's first single for Ode Records - #66023.

TORRENCE OF BURIED TREASURES

PAGE 49: "MUSIC CITY" remains a mystery.

"MY MIGHTY GTO", written by Gene Weed-Roger Christian-Jill Gibson, was issued as both a single and and album filler by Jan & Dean during May 1964, although both appearances were different recordings of the same song. In addition, songwriting credit also varied with Gene Weed-Don Altfeld receiving recognition on the single (Liberty #55704) and Gene Weed-Jill Gibson-Roger Christian on the album DEAD MAN'S CURVE/THE NEW GIRL IN SCHOOL. However during a court case in 1964 it was alleged that Jan had in fact contributed to the song but had not received credit in an effort to avoid contractual hassles with the publishing company Screen Gems.

PAGE 50: "MY QUEEN" remains a mystery.

PAGE 51: "MARY ANN" remains a mystery.

"MY BOBBY WON'T BE HOME AGAIN" remains a mystery.

"MY FAVORITE DREAM", written by the songwriting duo Barry Mann and Cynthia Weil, was recorded and released by Jan & Dean as the flip side to their third Liberty single (#55496) in October 1962.

PAGE 52: "MULHOLLAND" with words by Roger Christian and music by Jan Berry was earmarked for inclusion on Jan Berry's proposed solo album for Warner Brothers in 1968. Although recorded the song nor album was released.

"THE MAGIC OF MAKING LOVE" with an extra verse .

PAGE 53: "MUSIC CITY" in this case subsequently became "(HERE THE COME) FROM ALL OVER THE WORLD" which headlined Liberty single #55766 issued in February 1965. This version was written by Phil Sloan and Steve Barri and peaked in the mid-fifties nationally.

"NOW THAT BOBBY WANTS ME" remains uncompleted and still a mystery.

PAGE 54: "THE NEW GIRL IN SCHOOL", written by Jan Berry-Brian Wilson-Roger Christian-Bob Norberg (Norman), has had somewhat of a checkered career, originating as "GONNA HUSTLE YOU" (written by Wilson and Norberg), then "GET A CHANCE WITH YOU" until finally surfacing in the form of "THE NEW GIRL IN SCHOOL", first as a double-sided single for Liberty (#55672) issued in February 1964 and then as the title track to Jan & Dean's Liberty lp THE NEW GIRL IN SCHOOL./ DEAD MAN'S CURVE. The song charted in the Top 40 nationally.

"NO MESSIN' AROUND" with handwritten lyrics by Don Altfeld remains a mystery.

PAGE 55: "MY LITTLE RED STINGRAY" remains a mystery.

"NO MESSIN' AROUND" written by Jill Gibson & Don Altfeld remains unrecorded and unreleased.

PAGE 56: "ON THE BEACH" remains a mystery.

"POM POM PRISCILLA" with handwritten lyrics by Don Altfeld remains a mystery.

PAGE 57: "POT OF TEA" remains a mystery.

TORRENCE OF BURIED TREASURES

PAGE 57: (Continued)
"POPSICLE, written by Buzz Cason-Bobby Russell from Nashville, first appeared under the title "POPSICLE TRUCK" on Jan & Dean's Liberty lp DRAG CITY (LRP 3339/LST 7339) released in November 1963. In May 1966 it was re-issued under the shortened title "POPSICLE" (Liberty # 55886) and surprisingly entered the national charts, peaking at #21.

PAGE 58:
"SWINGIN' BUS DRIVER", written by Phil Sloan and Steve Barri (although the lyrics shown here are in Roger Christian's handwriting) appeared on Jan & Dean's Liberty lp THE LITTLE OLD LADY FROM PASADENA under the full title of "HORACE THE SWINGIN' SCHOOL BUS DRIVER".

"SURFIN' WILD", written by Jan Berry-Roger Christian-Brian Wilson, was featured as recorded by Jan & Dean on the duo's Liberty lp RIDE THE WILD SURF.

PAGE 59:
"SURF HEARSE" which became "SURFIN' HEARSE" was written by Jan Berry and Roger Christian (Christian's handwritten lyrics are shown on the lower half of the page) and appeared as recorded by Jan & Dean on the duo's DRAG CITY lp (LRP 3339/LST 7339) in November 1963.

PAGE 60:
"SURF ROUTE 101", written by Jan Berry-Roger Christian-Brian Wilson, was recorded by Jan & Dean for their DRAG CITY lp. It is NOT the same song that Gary Usher and The Super Stocks recorded for Capitol, although Roger Christian also shared songwriting credit on it. Christian's handwritten lyrics are featured here.

"THE SPIRIT THAT PULLED ME THROUGH" remains a mystery.

PAGE 61:
"SLOCK ROD" which surfaced as "SCHLOCK ROD PARTS 1 & 2" on Jan & Dean's DRAG CITY lp, was written by the combination of Don Altfeld-Jan Berry-Roger Christian-Dean Torrence. "SCHLOCK ROD PART 1" was also issued as the flip side to Jan & Dean's Top 10 hit "DRAG CITY" (Liberty #55641) in October 1963. Roger Christian's handwritten lyrics are featured here.

"SIMPLE SAILOR" remains a mystery although music exists.

PAGE 62:
"SURFIN' SCENE" remains a mystery although music exists.

"SING SANG A SONG", written by Jan Berry-Alan Wolfson-Jim Pewter, was recorded and released by Jan Berry for Ode Records (#66120) in March 1976.

"STREET MACHINE" with handwritten lyrics by Don Altfeld remains a mystery.

PAGE 63:
"SHE'S THE QUEEN OF THE SURFER GIRLS" subsequently became "HONOLULU LULU", appearing as Jan & Dean's third single for Liberty (#55613) in August 1963. Jan Berry-Roger Christian-Lou Adler shared the final songwriting credit.

"SOMEDAY" appeared as the flip to the previously mentioned "HONOLULU LULU". "Aldon Music" was an anagram of DON ALtfeld's name. Altfeld's lyrics are shown here ... Jan Berry wrote the music.

"STREET MACHINE" alternate lyrics.

TORRENCE OF BURIED TREASURES

PAGE 64: "TITLE SONG" subtitled "SURF SCENE" remains a mystery although music exists.

"TOTALLY WILD", written by Jan Berry-Alan Wolfson-Joan Jacobs, appeared under the Jan & Dean name as a single for Ode Records - #66111 in August 1975.

"TERRENCE WIPEOUT" remains a mystery.

PAGE 65: "THEY DO NOT KNOW" remains a mystery.

"TOTALLY WILD" alternate lyrics

PAGE 66: "TROPHY RUN" remains a mystery.

"TINSEL TOWN", written by Jan Berry-Joan Jacobs-Roger Christian, was recorded and released by Jan Berry (under the name 1 JAN 1) for Ode Records (#66050) in July 1974. "BLUE MOON SHUFFLE", the flip to Jan Berry's first Ode release "MOTHER EARTH" (#66023) released in January 1972 was in fact the instrumental track to "TINSEL TOWN". In addition "BLUE MOON SHUFFLE" as the flip to Jan's second Ode release "DON'T YOU JUST KNOW IT" (#66034) was a demo vocal version of "TINSEL TOWN". This demo version was issued in June 1973.

PAGE 67: "THOSE CALIFORNIA DRIVERS" with handwritten lyrics by Don Altfeld remains a mystery.

"TINSEL TOWN" subtitled "HITCH-A-RIDE TO HOLLYWOOD".

PAGE 68: "UNIVERSAL COWARD" written by Jan Berry-Jill Gibson-George Tipton appeared in November 1965 as a solo single for Jan Berry on the Liberty Records' label (#55845). It was also included on the Jan & Dean album FOLK 'N ROLL (LRP 3431/LST 7431) issued the same month.

PAGE 69: "WHEN IT RAINS IT POURS" remains a mystery.

"WHEN IT'S OVER", written by Don Altfeld-Jill Gibson-Horace Altfeld, was included as the flip side to Jan & Dean's national Top 30 hit "SIDEWALK SURFIN'" (Liberty #55727) issued in October 1964 and also on the duo's album THE LITTLE OLD LADY FROM PASADENA released the previous month. Altfeld's handwritten lyrics are shown lower left.

PAGE 70: "WHY DOES EVERYTHING GO WRONG" with handwritten lyrics by Don Altfeld remains a mystery although music exists.

"WHO CARES" remains a mystery.

PAGE 71: "WHAT'S HE GOT" remains a mystery.

"WHO PUT THE BOMP", written by Gerry Goffin-Barry Mann, appeared as a single by Jan & Dean in July 1962 (Liberty #55496) but failed to achieve any major chart success. In fact Barry Mann had released his own version of the song the previous year with considerable success.

"WAY TOO MUCH" remains a mystery.

PAGE 72: "WHAT NOW COBRA (BEWARE COBRAS)" remains a mystery.

TORRENCE OF BURIED TREASURES

PAGE 72: "YOUR SWEET SWEET LOVE", written by Jan Berry-Tom Sumner, remains unreleased although rhythm tracks were recorded at A&M studios in Los Angeles in June 1976. Musicians present at the session were Hal Blaine (drums), Mike Lang (piano), Ray Pohlman (bass), Tommy Tedesco and Ben Benay (guitars).

PAGE 73: Three untitled sets of lyrics which remain a thorough mystery. The Fred Weider-Don Altfeld composition is in Don Altfeld's handwriting.

PAGE 74: Two untitled sets of lyrics, both of which remain a mystery.

PAGE 75: Two untitled sets of lyrics. The lower set are in Roger Christian's handwriting and possibly bore the title "SURFIN' CRAZE".

PAGE 76: Two untitled sets of lyrics, both of which remain a mystery.

****

ODDS 'N ENDS - CONTINUED FROM PAGE 2

RIGHT FROM THE START	Words & Music, no author. Demo exists
SUMMER CASANOVA	Music only, no author
SHE SAY	Music only, no author
STANDING STILL	Music only, no author. Rhythm track demo exits, track cut by Hal Blaine (drums), Joe Osborne (bass), Mike Deasy, Ben Benay (guitars), Larry Knetchal (piano)
VEST & ASCOT	Music by Jan Berry, no words
WONDERFUL GUY	Written by Marie Gregory and Hal Davis
WHAT'S YOUR NAME	Lyrics only, no author
YOU GO YOUR WAY	Title only
YESTERDAY MAN	Title Only
YOU CAN'T BLOW MY MIND	Music only, no author

JAN BERRY'S NON JAN & DEAN SCREEN GEMS COMPOSITIONS

ACRE OF HEARTS	(UNRELEASED) (Berry-Diaz-Young-Zekley)
THE BOY WHO SAID HELLO	(UNRELEASED) ("no credits")
BROTHER SURFER	(UNRELEASED but RECORDED) ("no credits")
CINDY GO HOME	(UNRELEASED) (Berry-Jack Keller)
GUESS FOREVER ENDS TODAY	(UNRELEASED) (Berry-Jack Keller)
HE DON'T LOVE ME	(RELEASED by Shelley Fabares) (Berry-Altfeld Gibson)
I ADORE HIM	(UNRELEASED) (Berry-Artie Kornfeld)
I'M DYING TO GIVE YOU MY LOVE	(UNRELEASED but RECORDED) (Berry-Altfeld)
IT'S NOBODY'S FAULT	(UNRELEASED) (Berry-Lou Duhig)
JUDY LOVES ME	(RELEASED by Johnny Crawford) (Berry-Altfeld Kornfeld)
JUST BE YOURSELF	(UNRELEASED) (Berry-Willingham-Grantino)
LA CARRIDA	(RELEASED by The Matadors) (Berry-Minichiello Diaz-Sanchez)
LET THE LITTLE GIRL CRY	(UNRELEASED) (Berry-Lou Duhig)
LET YOURSELF GO	(RELEASED by The Matadors) (Berry-Kornfeld)
MY SWIMMIN' GIRL	(UNRELEASED) (Berry-Sloan-Barri-Christian)
SPOOKY TWISTS	(UNRELEASED) (Berry-Lou Duhig)

TORRENCE OF BURIED TREASURES

Cash Box

AUGUST 3, 1963

Two young men who are sitting pretty because of the nation's surfing craze as well as their swinging singing are Liberty's Jan and Dean. Having made a strong showing with their last effort, "Linda," the boys came into their own and soared up to the #1 spot with their smash hit "Surf City." And they seem to have a strong follow-up "Surf City" LP which this week broke onto the album charts in the #80 spot. Jan Berry, the Jan half of the boys, produces the J & D disks for Screen Gems, Inc., which releases all Jan and Dean product through Liberty Records.

JAN & DEAN TOUR BOOK

Page intentionally left blank
to match original
tour book layout

JAN & DEAN TOUR BOOK

JAN & DEAN TOUR BOOK

In the Beginning
and The Origin of J&D

JAN AND DEAN WERE BORN IN LOS ANGELES. JAN COMES FROM A LARGE FAMILY, WITH TWO SISTERS AND FIVE BROTHERS, KENNY, BRIAN, BRUCE, STEVIE, BILLIE, MELISSA, AND ALITA. DEAN'S FAMILY IS CONSIDERABLY SMALLER WITH ONLY ONE SISTER. THEY BOTH WENT TO EMERSON JR. HIGH, ALTHOUGH NOT MEETING UNTIL HIGH SCHOOL. THEY PARTICIPATED IN THE USUAL GARBAGE FIGHTS AND SITTINGS IN THE PRINCIPAL'S OFFICE. BELOW IS A PICTURE OF JAN AND DEAN ON THE SAME FOOTBALL TEAM AT UNIVERSITY HIGH SCHOOL IN LOS ANGELES. NOTICE IN THIS PICTURE HOW JAN'S HAIR IS LONGER THAN DEANS'. SINCE THEY WERE BENCHED CONTINUOUSLY, SINGING WAS THEIR FAVORITE PAST TIME. IT WAS IN JAN'S GARAGE THAT THEY RECORDED "BABY TALK", THEIR FIRST MILLION SELLER.

ASIDE FROM SCHOOL, JAN AND DEAN TRY TO WORK IN AS MANY PERSONAL ARREARANCES AS POSSIBLE. THEIR FAVORITE T.V. SHOWS ARE DEAN MARTIN, DICK CLARK, LLYOD THAXTON, RED SKELTON, HOLLYWOOD PALACE, AND THE CELEBRITY GAME. IN THE LAST SIX YEARS JAN AND DEAN HAVE BEEN IN EVERY MAJOR CITY IN THE UNITED STATES, AND PLAN ON VISITING JAPAN AND HONG KONG IN THE NEAR FUTURE, FOR THEY EVEN MANAGE TO BE POPULAR THERE TO!

THEY ARE BOTH SINGLE AND VERY AVAILABLE. THEY HAVE HIGH I.Q.'S, JAN IS A MEDICAL STUDENT, AND DEAN IS A GRADUATE ART MAJOR ATTENDING USC. THE DUO ENJOY FAST CARS AND FAST WOMEN; BOTH HAVE '66 STINGRAYS. BOTH ARE OVER 6' AND HAVE BLOND HAIR.

THEY ESPECIALLY LIKE HAWAII WHEN THEY DON'T HAVE TO WORK.

JAN & DEAN TOUR BOOK

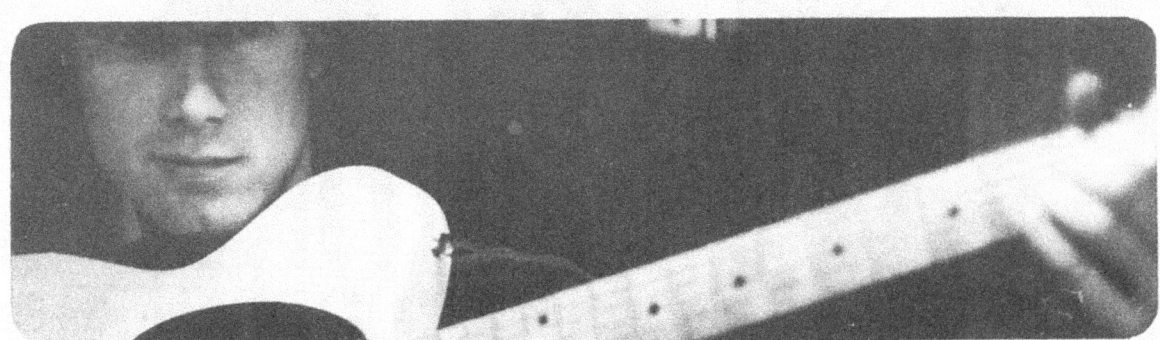

JAN & DEAN TOUR BOOK

An end... less world of recording

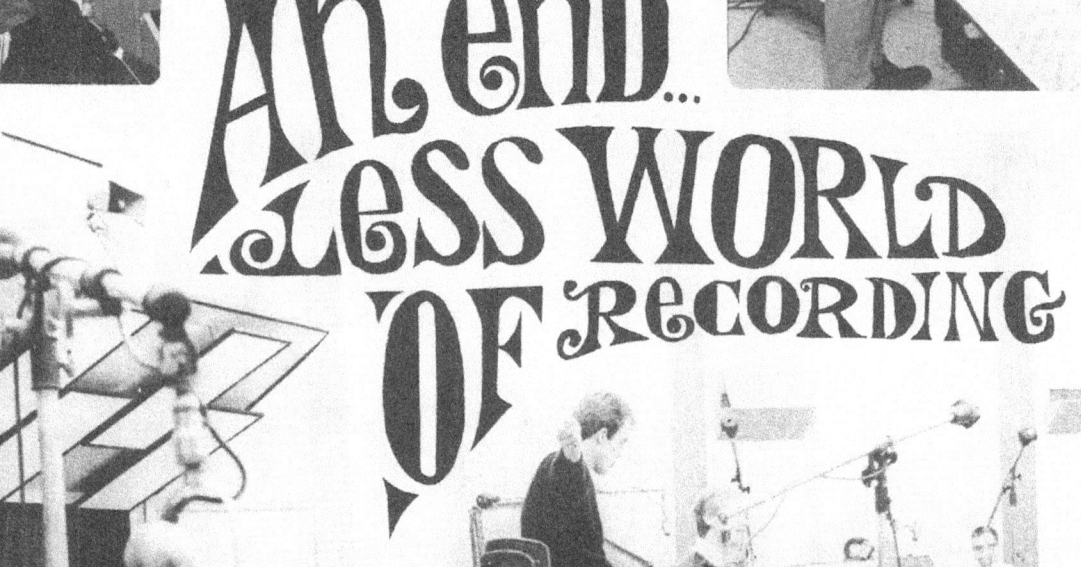

JAN & DEAN TOUR BOOK

DUNHILL STORY

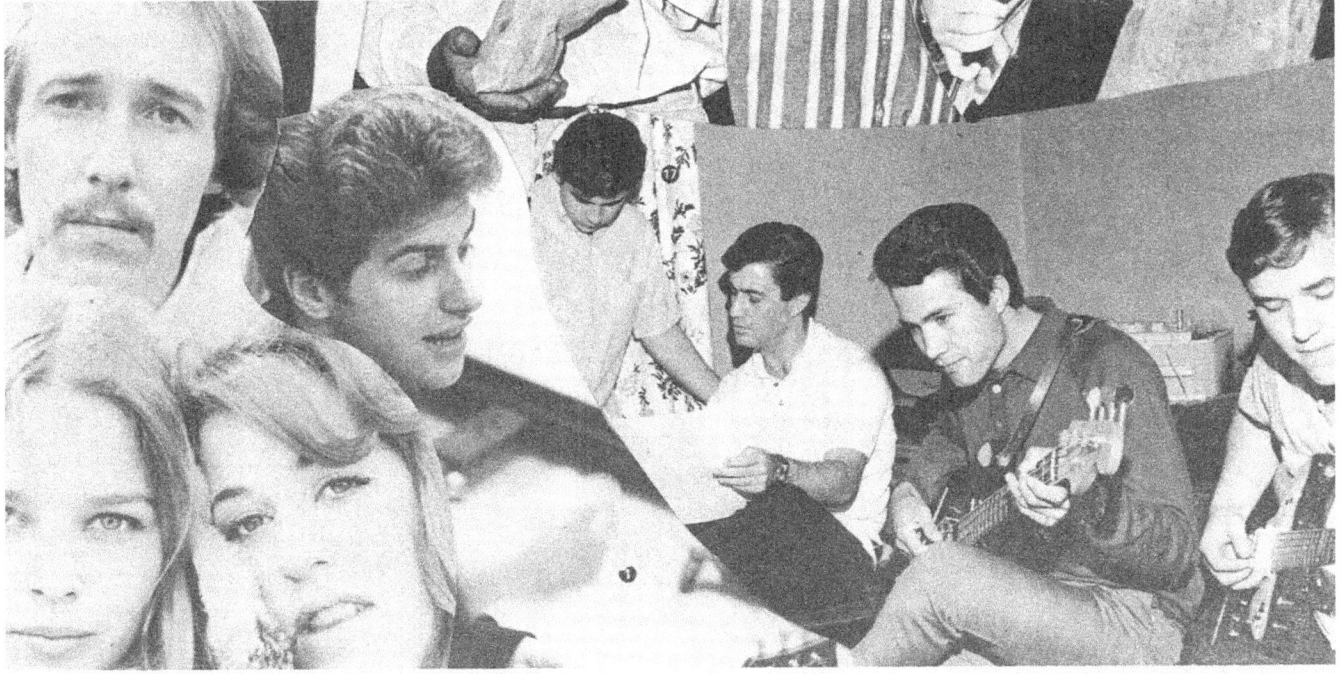

1. DEAN TORRENCE   7. JAN BERRY   10. ANDY WIPEOUT   13. JAY LASKER
5. SHELLY FABARES   8. HAL BLAINE   11. MAMAS & PAPAS   14. BARRY McGUIRE
6. LOU ADLER MGR   9. BONES HOWE   12. TERRY BLACK   15/16. SLOAN & BARRI

JAN & DEAN TOUR BOOK

wh<!-- cut -->
YOU DON'T HAVE ALL THESE FAN<!-- cut -->
(Well, now is the time to<!-- cut -->

JAN & DEAN MEET BATMAN • LST-7444/LRP-3444 • Lots of Battaculars (holy mirth and merriment!) and Bat-tunes (zowie!).

2 BRAND NEW ALBUMS —

"LIFE ISN'T WORTH LIVING WITHOUT<!-- cut -->

LRP-3431/LST-7431 • FOLK N' ROLL • JAN & DEAN • I Found A Girl; Hang On Sloopy (My Girl Sloopy); I Can't Wait To Love You; Eve Of Destruction; It's A Shame To Say Goodbye; Where Were You When I Needed You; A Beginning From An End; Yesterday; The Universal Cowboy; It Ain't Me Babe; Folk City; Turn! Turn! Turn!

LRP-3417 LST-7417 • JAN & DEAN GOLDEN HITS, VOL. 2 • Linda; Surf City; Honolulu Lulu; Drag City; Dead Man's Curve; The New Girl In School; The Little Old Lady From Pasadena; The Anaheim, Azusa And Cucamonga Sewing Circle, Book Review And Timing Association; Ride The Wild Surf; Sidewalk Surfin'; From All Over The World; You Really Know How To Hurt A Guy.

LRP-3403 / LST-7403 • COMMAND PERFORMANCE • JAN & DEAN • Surf City; Little Honda; Dead Man's Curve; I Get Around; All I Have To Do Is Dream; Theme From The TAMI Show (Here They Come From All Over The World); Rock And Roll Music; The Little Old Lady From Pasadena; Do Wah Diddy Diddy; I Should Have Known Better; Sidewalk Surfin'; Louie, Louie.

LRP-3377 LST-7377 • THE LITTLE OLD LADY FROM PASADENA • JAN & DEAN • One-Piece Topless Bathing Suit; Skateboarding, Part 2; Move Out Little Mustang; It's Easy as 1, 2, 3; Summer Means Fun; The Anaheim, Azusa & Cucamonga Sewing Circle, Book Review & Timing Association; Sidewalk Surfin'; Old Ladies Seldom Power Shift; Horace The Swingin' School-Bus Driver; When It's Over; Memphis; The Little Old Lady From Pasadena.

LRP-3368/ LST-7368 • RIDE THE WILD SURF • JAN & DEAN • The Submarine Races; Walk On The Wet Side; A Surfer's Dream; Down At Malibu Beach; Surfin' Wild; Sidewalk Surfin'; Skateboarding, Part 1; The Restless Surfer; She's My Summer Girl; Waimea Bay; Tell 'Em I'm Surfin'; Ride The Wild Surf.

JAN & DEAN TOUR BOOK

at?
TASTIC JAN & DEAN ALBUMS?
do something about it!)

FILET OF SOUL • LST-7441/LRP-3441 • Norwegian Wood, One Two Three, Hang On Sloopy, Michelle, Cathy's Clown, and lots more!

COUNT 'EM 2 (TWO, II, DOS)

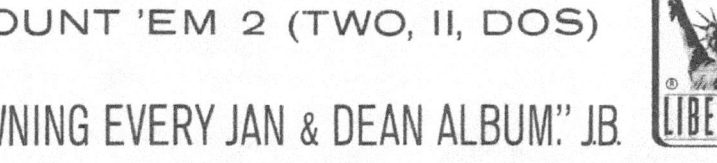

OWNING EVERY JAN & DEAN ALBUM." J.B.

LRP-3361/LST-7361 • DEAD MAN'S CURVE/THE NEW GIRL IN SCHOOL • JAN & DEAN • Dead Man's Curve; Three Window Coupe; Bucket "T"; Rockin' Little Roadster; "B" Gas Rickshaw; My Mighty G.T.O.; The New Girl In School; Linda; Barons, West L.A.; School Days; It's As Easy as 1, 2, 3; Hey Little Freshman.

LRP-3339/LST-7339 • DRAG CITY • JAN & DEAN • Drag City; I Gotta Drive; Drag Strip Girl; Surfin' Hearse; Dead Man's Curve; Schlock Rod (Part 1); Schlock Rod (Part 2); Popsicle Truck; Surf Route 101; Sting Ray; Little Deuce Coupe; Hot Stocker.

LRP-3314/LST-7314 • SURF CITY • JAN & DEAN • Surf City; Memphis; Detroit City; Soul; Tallahassee Lassie; Way Down Yonder In New Orleans; Manhattan; Philadelphia, Pa.; I Left My Heart In San Francisco; Honolulu Lulu; Kansas City; You Came A Long Way From St. Louis.

LRP-3294/LST-7294 • JAN AND DEAN TAKE LINDA SURFIN' • Linda; Walk Like A Man; Surfin'; Let's Turkey Trot; Rhythm Of The Rain; Mr. Bass Man; Walk Right In; The Best Friend I Ever Had; The Gypsy Cried; My Foolish Heart; When I Learn How To Cry; Surfin' Safari.

LRP-3248/LST-7248 • JAN & DEAN'S GOLDEN HITS • Baby Talk; We Go Together; Palisades Park; In A Turkish Town; Who Put The Bomp; Heart And Soul; Barbara Ann; Poor Little Puppet; Tennessee; Queen Of My Heart; A Sunday Kind Of Love; Jennie Lee.

JAN & DEAN TOUR BOOK

TIRED OF BEING JUST A FAN..... JOIN THE FRIENDS OF J&D

❀ BONUS....... SPOT JAN OR DEAN IN THE PICTURE BELOW AND WIN A BUNCH OF STICKY THINGS WITH J&D'S PICTURE ON THEM. THIS IS TO BE ACCOMPANIED WITH A COMPLETED APPLICATION TO THE FRIENDS OF JAN & DEAN

MAIL TO:
KATHY TORRENCE
2145 BENECIA AVE
LOS ANGELES CALIF
90025

DEAR KATHY, PLEASE SEND ME A MEMBERSHIP CARD TO THE FRIENDS OF JAN & DEAN ALSO I UNDERSTAND THAT I WILL ALSO RECIEVE TWO PERSONALLY AUTOGRAPHED 8X10'S AND A WALLET SIZED PICTURE AND THATS NOT ALL..... I WANT TO ALSO RECIEVE THE JAN AND DEAN NEWSLETTERS WHEN THE'RE ABOUT TO DO SOMETHING I SHOULD KNOW ABOUT...... AND THEN DON'T FORGET TO REGISTER ME SO THAT I CAN BECOME ELIGIBLE TO WIN ANYTHING FROM ALBUMS TO USED J&D CLOTHING...... ALSO IF I HAVE CLEVERLY SPOTTED J or D IN THE PHOTO BELOW, SEND ME THE J&D STICKERS.... AND FOR ALL THIS I AM SENDING YOU TWO DOLLARS

SIGNED _____
_____ STREET
_____ CITY _____ ZONE

JAN & DEAN TOUR BOOK

JAN & DEAN TOUR BOOK

JAN & DEAN TOUR BOOK

JAN & DEAN TOUR BOOK

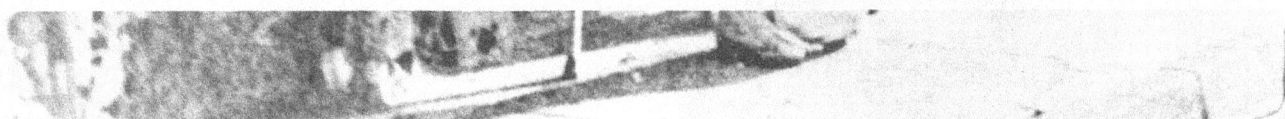

JAN & DEAN TOUR BOOK

DEAN IN OCEAN PACIFIC AD

SURFIN' AGAIN
THE MUSIC OF Jan & Dean — ISSUE 3

SURFIN AGAIN Issue 3

```
issue 3 - august 1984            danny bossard
                                 gotthelfweg 9
assistant : jacki dove           5o36 oberentfelden
                                 switzerland
contributors : (in alphabetical order)
                                 subscription rates
jan berry                        for six issues :
mike berry
william `bill` berry             uk,europe :    £  5
angelia fraser                   all other
lloyd hicks      the number on the envelop,    countries :us $ 8
paula moore      after your name,is the
dean torrence    number of the last issue      cash,bank draft
                 of your subscription.         or imo
```

READ ALL ABOUT IT...

having rummaged through many record sale lists in the last few months/
years,it seems that jan & dean records become very valuble as the
prices of the duo`s waxings have recently increased.

this is mainly the case because of the airing of the "deadman`s
curve" telemovie which made jan & dean catch a second big wave of
popularity and because of the renewed interest in surf music in
general.

the us liberty singles with picture sleeves sell for something
between $ 2o and $ 3o (jan`s "universal coward" was recently offered
for $ 8o);the sixties liberty albums go for about the same price as
the singles.

the jan & arnie 45s are priced around $ 15 ("jennie lee") and
$ 25 ("i love linda").the jan & arnie picture sleeve ep on dot records
recently changed hands for $ 2oo !

jan`s solo singles from the seventies vary between $ 12 ("fun city")
and $ 25 ("little queenie"),both stock copies,while the j&d rec co
singles from the mid-sixties go for around $ 25 too.

the prices revealed here are not obligatory but they show how the
trend is evolving.of course,there is always the chance of finding
bargains but these occasions get rarer.

the increment at least shows that jan & dean are in demand and it
is better to have it that way than finding all their records in the
record shops` junk boxes.

on september 15 th,the sixth annual beach boys fan convention will be
held at the harrow leisure centre,christchurch avenue,harrow,ha3 5bd,
england.the convention will commence at 12.oo noon.
as usual,a lot of records and other items will be for sale,and there
may be a video session,a raffle and an auction and you surely will
spend an enjoyable afternoon there.

SURFIN AGAIN Issue 3

MY HEART SINGS (THE COLLECTOR'S SECTION)

JAN & DEAN RELATED RECORDS PART ONE
****

during all the years jan & dean have been in the recording business, it happened that they sang on some records of their friends, contributed their writing talent or produced or arranged recordings by other artists than jan & dean.
below you will find a list of records jan & dean have been involved in. any additions or corrections are most welcome, however.

THE ANGELS
i adore him(berry,kornfeld)/(thank you and goodnight)-smash 1854,(1964)

the angels consisted of three sisters; peggy,barbara and jiggs.they had several hit songs in the charts with their biggest seller being "my boyfriend's back", recently covered by mike & dean.
jan berry co-wrote one song for the trio which was released as the a-side of a single in 1964."i adore him" also surfaced some time ago on the compilation album "my boyfriend's back"(raven 1oo3,australia)

THE BARONS
there in the night - beverly hills diner,(1983)

the barons were jan berry,dean torrence,arnie ginsburg,chuck steele, wally yagi and john saligman(the nephew of dinah shore)."there in the night" is the first song ever released with a jan & dean involvement and was available for the first time on the "jan & dean rarities" lp.

THE BEACH BOYS
fun fun fun/(why do fools fall in love)
   -capitol 5118,(feb 1964)
help me rhonda/(kiss me baby)
   -capitol 5395,(april 1965)
barbara ann/(girl don't tell me)
   -capitol 5561,(dec 1965)
sloop john b/(you're so good to me)
   -capitol 56o2,(march 1966)

there is no need to write big stories about the beach boys as they are well known.dean torrence sang background vocals on all the above singles except on "barbara ann" on which he sang lead with brian wilson.

THE BEL-AIR BANDITS
history of surf music vol.3 -rhino o54, (1982) incl. "summer"
the bel-air bandits-permanent 2,(1982)

the bel-air bandits during the above recordings consisted of jim armstrong, mark ward,gary griffin,chris farmer and danny de hart.both,the song "summer" and the 5 track 12" ep "the bel-air bandits" had dean's backing vocals. however,this group is not identical to the bel-air bandits that recorded with jan & dean the "batman" album.

CALIFORNIA MUSIC
why do fools fall in love/(don't worry baby)-rca 1o363,(aug 1975)

personell on the a-side were kenny hinkle,gloria grinel,terry melcher, brian wilson and dean torrence.

SURFIN AGAIN Issue 3

THE CALIFORNIA SUNS
masked grandma/(little bit of heaven)-imperial 66179,(may 1966)

the a-side is a takeoff on "the little old lady from pasadena",written by roger christian and carol connors.jan & dean are said to have contributed backing vocals to this one.

CAROL & CHERYL
(sunny winter)/go go gto(carol connors,cheryl connors,
    jan berry,terry melcher)-colpix 767,(feb 1965)

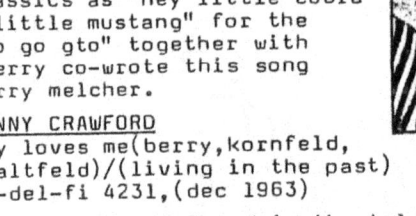

carol connors (aka annette bard) sang with phil spector in his group,the teddy bears,before she went into hot rod music and wrote such classics as "hey little cobra" for the rip chords or "run little mustang" for the zip-codes.carol recorded "go go gto" together with her sister cheryl and jan berry co-wrote this song with the two sisters and terry melcher.

JOHNNY CRAWFORD
judy loves me(berry,kornfeld,
    altfeld)/(living in the past)
    -del-fi 4231,(dec 1963)

johnny crawford played in the television series "rifleman" before he was discovered as a recording artist in 1961.during the next four years,he had eight hits for the del-fi label.one of the songs was "judy loves me",co-written and co-produced by jan berry and artie kornfeld.

SONNY CURTIS
(a beatle i want to be)/so used to loving you-dimension 1024,(1964)

sonny curtis has been the guitarist of the crickets,buddy holly`s band.he wrote songs like "i fought the law" which was a smash hit for the bobby fuller four and he now is more into country music. the b-side of his 1964 single was produced by jan berry.

DANTE & THE EVERGREENS
alley oop/the right time-madison 130,(may 1960)
time machine/dream land-madison 135,(july 1960)
yeah baby/what are you doing new year`s eve
    -madison 143,(1960)
think sweet thoughts/da doo-madison 154,(1961)
danté & the evergreens-madison 1002 (1961)

danté & the evergreens consisted of danté drowty,tony moon,bill young and frank rosenthall.they were pals of dean`s through his early years and after they had a big hit with "alley oop",which reached no. 15 in the charts,they had to put a group together.during their recording career,jan & dean always helped out on backing vocals,most notably on the single "time machine" which also was a hit.
though the songs were said to be produced by herb alpert and lou adler,jan berry was at least as much involved in producing their singles and the album.

WALTER EGAN
fundamental roll-cbs 34679,(1977) incl. "she`s so tough"
not shy,(1978) incl. "the blonde in the blue t-bird"

dean torrence contributed his backing vocals to the above mentioned songs,as well as designing the album cover of the "not shy" album.

SHELLEY FABARES
(football season's over)/he don't love me(berry,gibson, altfeld)-colpix 721,(march 1964)

shelley (born as michele) fabares had her biggest hit with "johnny angel" on colpix records.later on,she married jan & dean manager lou adler and so it was obvious that she got involved with the dynamic duo.jan co-wrote the b-side of her above mentioned single.shelley and jan & dean were to star in the "ride the wild surf" movie,but jan & dean got kicked out of the movie.however,shelley then wrote the liner notes to the duo's album of the same name.

THE FANTASTIC BAGGYS

tell 'em i'm surfin'/surfer boy's dream come true
 -imperial 66047,(aug 1964)
anywhere the girls are/debbie be true
 -imperial 66072,(nov 1964)
it was i/alone on the beach
 -imperial 66092,(feb 1965)
tell 'em i'm surfin'-imperial 9270,(1964)
ride the wild surf-imperial 374,(1966)
 (south africa only)

the fantastic baggys,phil 'flip' sloan and steve barri,sang on various of jan & dean's records and released records under the name fantastic baggys and some other pseudonyms.jan & dean are said to have sung on the baggys' songs.

JILL GIBSON
it's as easy as 1,2,3/jilly's flip side-imperial 66068,(aug 1964)
come on baby-beverly hills diner,(1983) by jill & judy

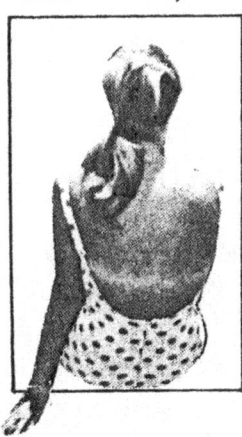

jill gibson was jan's long-time girl-friend,before they parted for good.jill co-wrote many jan & dean songs and recorded a solo-single in 1964 which never got beyond the promotional stage.the a-side appeared on the "jan & dean rarities" album together with "come on baby",a song jill recorded with dean's girl-friend at the time,judy lovejoy. both songs were produced by jan berry.jill appeared on some jan & dean records,most notably on "a surfer's dream" and the duo's version of "it's as easy as 1,2,3".you also can see her on the cover photos of "we go together","surf city" single,"jan & dean take linda surfin'" and the british "ride the wild surf - hits from surf city,usa" compilation.in late 1966, jill gibson joined the mamas & the papas for a very short time when michelle phillips left the group.one single,"look through my window"(dunhill 4055,sept 1966), featured jill as a vocalist.

DEANE HAWLEY
queen of the angels/you conquered me-liberty 55446,(march 1963)

jan arranged and conducted both sides of this single.deane hawley also was signed to the dore label during the time jan & dean were there,so the duo might have worked with him on his earlier singles as well.

next issue : jan & dean related records part two

A HOT TIME IN THE OLD TOWN - THE NEWS

after we got rhino records,hit bound records,radio shack and all the
other companies which brought us our favourite music,there is a new
name to add to the list and hopefully to our discographies and record
collections : JB RECORDS ! (and guess what `JB` stands for).

their first effort was the jan & alohas debut single "rock city",
still only available on cassette.but now that this new firm exists,let
us hope that the single,the long promised album and many more new
recordings will come out soon.

NEWSMAKERS

Move over, **Clara Peller.** Make room for **Ethel Sway**, 76, the newly crowned "Little Old Lady From Pasadena." To celebrate the 20th anniversary of their surf-sound hit, **Jan & Dean** are making a video version of the song, starring Sway in the title role. "You always think that all the good things happen to someone else," says the soon-to-be terror of Colorado Boulevard, who won her ticket to stardom by beating out 100 other aspirants with what judges called her "zaniness, energy, wisdom and zest for life." Those qualities will come in handy. "She'll be doing some drag-racing, some singing, and I guess she'll have to learn to break-dance," says Dean Torrence, adding that the **Beach Boys**—who have helped keep the song popular by playing it in their concerts—will also appear in the video, due for release in July.

newsweek, june 11 1984

'Little Old Lady' Sway with Jan & Dean

the new album by the group the association is out (hit bound 1oo5),
full of remakes of oldies and features guest stars bobby vee,mary
mc gregor and mike love.mike`s song is "stagger lee" but it is his
solo version and not by mike & dean as it long has been rumoured.

remaining in the can are songs by mike & dean like "please mr
custer","deadman`s curve" and "sidewalk surfin`".

SURFIN AGAIN Issue 3

while on the subject of mike & dean : dean contributes a song entitled "on the beach" to the soundtrack album of the film "the karate kid"(??). mike love sings the song in the movie but being a beach boy and having complicated contracts with even more complicated record companies, his version can't be used for the album. collaborator on the song is england's adrian baker, well-known from "rock 'n' roll city" and his gidea park records.

"the karate kid" is playing in the states now, so the soundtrack album should surface soon. hero in the film is ralph maccio ("the outsiders").

jan & dean appeared on american tv in a show called "on stage america" on june 2 1984. the show featured stars whose popularity and talent have made an impact on people all over the world.

and this issue's beach boys' hot gossip column : not only have the hawthorne boys recorded "the air that i breathe" with crooner julio 'hisPANIC' iglesias (just imagine jan & dean doing "are you lonesome tonight" with johnny cash !) but they also appeared with iglesias, michael jackson's sister la toya and drummer ringo starr on the us independence day concert in washington dc on july 4 th before a crowd of 530,000. after last year's 4 th july fiasco, they seem to have found their way back to washington.

julio, la toya and mike in washington on july 4 1984

"surfin' again" 's suggestion : brian and the boys had better return to the studio and put some work into the next album (is there anyone out there who still believes in a next album ?). but listen fans, it is only four years since the last beach boys' album. jan & dean fans have waited 18 (in words : eighteen) years for a newly recorded studio album by both of the duo and we are still very confident.

steve 'surf' dromensk, rhythm guitarist from papa doo run run, just has finished his first solo project. it is a four track ep featuring the songs "callin' me", "secret streets", "i gotta run" and "don't let the sun catch you cryin'". the first three songs were written and produced by steve with a little help from his friends, while the last song, "don't let the sun ..." is a remake of a favourite tune from the sixties, a top 6 hit for gerry and the pacemakers in 1964.

as suggested by one of our readers (thanks lynn !), here is the complete british jan & dean discography with release dates and values. if anybody else has a suggestion for future issues of "surfin' again", we will be glad to hear from you and will try to please you.

JAN & DEAN UK RELEASES

label/ number	title	date	value in £
singles			
london			
8653	jennie lee/gotta getta date	7/58	11.50
8936	baby talk/jeanette get your hair done	9/59	8.50
8990	there's a girl/my heart sings	11/59	11.00
9063	clementine/you're on my mind	2/60	11.00
9395	heart and soul/midsummer night's dream	7/61	6.00
liberty			
55397	a sunday kind of love/poor little puppet	1/62	3.50
55531	linda/when i learn how to cry	2/63	3.50
55580	surf city/she's my summer girl	6/63	3.50
55613	honolulu lulu/someday(you'll go walking by)	8/63	3.50
55641	drag city/schlock rod	11/63	3.50
55672	dead man's curve/new girl in school	3/64	3.50
55704	little old lady from pasadena/my mighty gto	6/64	3.50
55724	ride the wild surf/aaacscbrata	9/64	3.50
55727	sidewalk surfin'/when it's over	11/64	3.50
55766	from all over the world/freeway flyer	3/65	3.50
55792	you really know how to hurt a guy/it's as easy...	5/65	3.50
55833	i found a girl/it's a shame to say goodbye	10/65	3.50
55860	batman/bucket t	6/66	3.50
10225	norwegian wood/a beginning from an end	6/66	3.50
10244	popsicle/the joker is wild	66	3.50
10252	tennessee/horace the swingin' schoolbus driver	9/66	3.50
55923	school day/new girl in school	12/66	3.50
cbs			
202630	yellow balloon/taste of rain	3/67	8.50
united artists			
(1) 35542	gonna hustle you/summertime summertime	3/73	
35714	walk like a man/tennessee	7/74	2.50
35897	sidewalk surfin'/gonna hustle you	7/75	1.50
(2) 36142	surf city/sidewalk surfin'/summer means fun	7/76	1.50
36271	sidewalk surfin'/summer means fun(picture sleeve)	6/77	2.50
creole			
204	surf city/dead man's curve	7/80	1.50
extended plays			
liberty			
2213	surf 'n' drag hits(picture sleeve)	4/65	14.50
2258	the titanic twosome(picture sleeve)	6/66	14.50
coke			
1466	let's swing the jingle for coca cola	65	28.50
united artists			
602	remember jan & dean(picture sleeve)	10/73	7.00
albums			
liberty			
1163	surf city(and other swingin' cities)	12/63	17.00
1229	ride the wild surf	4/65	18.50
1279	golden hits vol. 2	12/65	11.00
(3) 83016	golden hits vol. 2		
1304	folk 'n roll	5/66	11.00

label/number	title	date	value in £
liberty			
13o9	jan & dean meet batman	6/66	11.5o
(4) 1339	filet of soul	1/67	11.5o
cbs			
(5) 63o15	save for a rainy day	3/67	----
sunset			
5o165	the very best of jan & dean	73	6.oo
united artists			
(6) 29987	ride the wild surf(hits from surf city usa)	8/76	4.oo
creole			
bftp 1	the jan & dean story	5/8o	3.oo
k-tel			
(7) 1o84	*the jan & dean story	9/8o	5.5o
emi/liberty			
(8) 2o11	*ride the wild surf(hits from surf city usa)	6/81	3.oo

* denotes still widely available

notes :

(1) released as the legendary masked surfers
(2) "summer means fun" by the fantastic baggys
(3) released with a light blue label contrary to the usual black label records from liberty records in england
(4) totally different track listing to the us version.tracks included : little deuce coupe/memphis/one piece topless bathing suit/school day/three window coupe/tennessee//popsicle/surf route 1o1/summer means fun/i gotta drive/schlock rod part 2/horace the swingin` schoolbus driver
(5) only very,very few promotional copies do exist,so it is impossible to state a concrete value but expect to pay a fortune when you can come across a copy.the album was credited to `jan and dean featuring yellow balloon`
(6) two songs from that album were performed by the fantastic baggys namely "tell `em i`m surfin`" and "when surfers rule" though only the latter was credited to the baggys.
(7) a re-issue of the creole album
(8) a re-issue of the united artists album on emi`s `green light` label

SURFIN AGAIN Issue 3

GOLDOGRAPHY:

JENNY LEE
BABY TALK
SURF CITY
HONOLULU LULU
DRAG CITY
DEADMAN'S CURVE
NEW GIRL IN SCHOOL
SIDEWALK SURFIN'
LITTLE OLD LADY FROM PASADENA
RIDE THE WILD SURF
BARBARA ANN

GOLD ALBUMS:

GOLDEN HITS VOLUME ONE
SURF CITY
DRAG CITY
DEADMAN'S CURVE
LITTLE OLD LADY
RIDE THE WILD SURF
GOLDEN HITS VOLUME TWO
JAN & DEAN ANTHOLOGY (1974)
SWINGIN' SIXTIES (1982)
BEACHBOYS / JAN & DEAN (1984)

LIBERTY

These two native Californians sold more than 20 million records worldwide between the years of 1960 and 1966. Their career came to an abrupt halt at its peak when Jan Berry was seriously injured and almost died in a catastrophic car accident in 1966. The very successful CBS-TV Movie "Deadman's Curve", which aired in prime time nationwide in February of 1978 and again in March of 1979, chronicled Jan's valiant fight to regain his ability to function as a human being.

A short time after the second airing of "Deadman's Curve", Jan & Dean embarked on their "Phase II" maiden tour as special guests of The Beach Boys. People magazine called it "The most heartening music tour of 1978."

Based on the success of The Beach Boy Tour, Jan & Dean went on to tour on their own. They toured summers 1979, 1980 and 1981. Their summer tour in 1981 was their most successful in their careers. They played 75 concerts between May and September.

Jan & Dean took 1982 off then played only a limited but very successful summer schedule in 1983.

1983	DATE	ATTEND
NATIONAL ORANGE SHOW	MAY 3	5,700
SAN DIEGO WILD ANIMAL PARK	JULY 1, 2, 3, 4	56,000
ORANGE COUNTY FAIR	JULY 12	14,000
CONCERT ON THE GREEN HYANNIS, CONN.	SEPT. 3	6,500
SIX FLAGS MAGIC MOUNTAIN	SEPT. 5	7,100
KNOTTS BERRY FARM	NOV. 25, 26	11,500

HEY LITTLE ~~FRESH~~POSTMAN - THE LETTERS

it's nice to hear that there are other jan & dean fans in europe. i've liked them ever since i saw the film in 1980.
   i've been lucky enough to receive a xmas card from jan and a post card from dean.
   at the latest count i have about 29 jan & dean albums (not including compilations of various artists) and about 3o singles.
     pat atkin,glenrothes,scotland

although i'm more a beach boys than a jan & dean fan,i enjoy reading "surfin` again" a lot.maybe i'll start a jan & dean collection, who knows ? it was a very good idea to print a jan & dean fanzine. i imagine that writing a fanzine must take quite a lot of time. anyway,the result is very satisfying.
     jean-pierre + philippe petit,charleville-mézières,france

i enjoyed reading "surfin` again" so much that i'm subscribing to another six issues.
   i have just received a copy of the latest "rarities" lp and on first hearing it is a great lp.
     ted warrington,astley,tyldesley,gt.manchester,england

i thought you may be interested in this letter i'm sending out.
   to let you know the connection between your magazine and myself, it's that i was the creator and leader of papa doo run run 12 years ago.i've been back with the band for 4 years and i have recorded some new tunes.
   my previous credits include : "sunshine music" on jan & dean album "gotta take that one last ride";"sunshine music/healthy lady" single released by papa du run da run in 1974 and "i've got to make it/another season" single released by g.t. shoes (former name of papa) in 1971.
     steve `surf` dromensk,san jose,california

thank you so much for issue 2 and for placing my ad in it ! can i have another ad placed in the next issue ? x-cept there's <u>13o</u> pages of script.i guess i was thinking about something else when i wrote 384 ! ah,that's how many jan & dean photos i have ! sorry ! (oops !!)
   oh,this photo of this strange-looking character here,with antlers, is the same person that wrote this letter.how ugly !
     paula moore,west falls,new york

if you'd like to see your picture here,send us a photo of your good side !
(the photo will be sent back if you'd wish it)

HEY LITTLE ~~FRESH~~POSTMAN - THE LETTERS

it's nice to hear that there are other jan & dean fans in europe.
i've liked them ever since i saw the film in 1980.
   i've been lucky enough to receive a xmas card from jan and a
post card from dean.
   at the latest count i have about 29 jan & dean albums (not
including compilations of various artists) and about 30 singles.
     pat atkin,glenrothes,scotland

although i'm more a beach boys than a jan & dean fan,i enjoy
reading "surfin' again" a lot.maybe i'll start a jan & dean collection,
who knows ? it was a very good idea to print a jan & dean fanzine.
i imagine that writing a fanzine must take quite a lot of time.
anyway,the result is very satisfying.
     jean-pierre + philippe petit,charleville-mézières,france

i enjoyed reading "surfin' again" so much that i'm subscribing to
another six issues.
   i have just received a copy of the latest "rarities" lp and on
first hearing it is a great lp.
     ted warrington,astley,tyldesley,gt.manchester,england

i thought you may be interested in this letter i'm sending out.
   to let you know the connection between your magazine and myself,
it's that i was the creator and leader of papa doo run run 12 years
ago.i've been back with the band for 4 years and i have recorded
some new tunes.
   my previous credits include : "sunshine music" on jan & dean
album "gotta take that one last ride";"sunshine music/healthy lady"
single released by papa du run da run in 1974 and "i've got to
make it/another season" single released by g.t. shoes (former name
of papa) in 1971.
     steve 'surf' dromensk,san jose,california

thank you so much for issue 2 and for placing my ad in it ! can i
have another ad placed in the next issue ? x-cept there's <u>130</u> pages
of script.i guess i was thinking about something else when i wrote
384 ! ah,that's how many jan & dean photos i have ! sorry ! (oops !!)
   oh,this photo of this strange-looking character here,with antlers,
is the same person that wrote this letter.how ugly !
     paula moore,west falls,new york

if you'd like to see your picture here,send us a photo of your good side !
(the photo will be sent back if you'd wish it)

the titanic threesome

album like "drag city".it may be because (a) you're a frustrated stockcar driver; (b) you received a self-hypnosis album for personal improvement but you're already satisfied with your personality so you exchanged it for "drag city"; (c) you were stocked with the album cover and decided it would look great over the family fireplace next to the moosehead; (d) you are just a stalwart jan & dean fan like me !

the grand high potentate and secretary of the jan & dean fan clubs, horace altfeld,cleared up the origin of captain jan and dean,the boy blunder,'scuse me,boy wonder,when he stated once and for all that jan & dean are not brothers.jan comes from a bunch of berrys and you might say dean came down in torrence !

another aspect is that there have been many quotes,sayings,etc. to depict a good time,such as "more fun than a barrel of monkeys","you're a barrel of laughs",etc. anyone who has been around jan & dean will not be too surprised if in the not-so-distant future someone says "you're more fun than a barrel of jan & deans" because anyone who has been fortunate enough to come in contact with these two slapstick kids from california knows that nothing could be more fun than jan & dean,except a barrel of them.

now that jan & dean's magical power,humour,had been discovered, they let themselves go totally and went straight into probably the most comical character ever in music,the little old lady from pasadena ! the very clean little old grandpa warned,"your grandmother will love this album,even if she's not from pasadena,and you will too,no matter where you're from.if you peek out your door about midnight,you may see old granny in a one-piece topless bathing suit doing the watusi and practicing speed-shifting (from 33 to 45),playing jan & dean albums and singles.but,if you do catch her,don't be too mad.she might not let you borrow her jan & dean skateboard."

meanwhile,jan & dean were a well-known and highly recommended live act.everyone who attended one or more of their concerts had no worries about boredom between tunes,because you heard some of the famous jan & dean humour.the slapstick jokers from los angeles have gained quite a reputation as the "laurel & hardy of the surf crowd".

dean torrence,who never had any say in which material was to be recorded,once got his big chance in the recording studio.he ramroded a session and all the musicians trebeled up when they saw the big t. the chertb was there on guitar,brian brought his favourite game,clue, to keep the musicians awake and blu was there to see that they were there.jan brought his pet hampster who was loaded on pills (breath mints).the background swingers were there to sing the bo-de-o-dos. boy,they were set to cup a smash."let the tape roll bones,turn up the tuba fankly".dean shouted orders left and right,wright and left then to the left again.he shouted loud so they could hear him cause its hard to hear someone who`s locked in the janitor`s broom closet !

dan said,"spleen,the next big craze will be protest music...", so green said "what ?" well,look,join the jan & dean potest train movement.here`s what you can do : go find sum railroad tracks and siton them.if you are a beachboy fan siton tracks only at night... but after all,it wasn`t their fault,it was yours.

but then,that stupid rat fink came up with these silly poems on the covers : ene mene minie moe / what exactly is filet of soul / blue eyed soul hum not quite it / rubber soul doesn`t really fit / soulful soul...please don`t snicker / country soul ? hinker hinker /

the caped crusaders

great scott what does it mean/ and then praytell who are jan and dean ?

but on the other hand,they knew exactly who jan & dean were and what they were all about : who knows what's next or in the air;one thing is for sure,j.&d.'ll be there. this little what-ever-it-is could go on and on,but very soon you'd wish i was gone.

anyway,he stayed and went into even more sophisticated rhymes ("without rhyme and reason !" i hear someone say),but look at the "popsicle" album and tell me what's next : hickory dickery lick,the mouse ran up the stick / one stopped at the rapper cause he was scared to death / he was a chicken / so actually hickery dickery lick a mouse and a chicken ran up a stick / (the mouse wore track shoes)(the rooster has pointed toes ya know) / the chicken stopped at the wrapper cause he's a yellow bellied sap sucker ! / so actually hickerey dickery lick / a mouse and a yellow bellied sap sucker ran up the stick / the mouse stopped at the wrapper cause wasn't sure the sap sucker wood / mouses as you shirley know don't sack suckers / as well as you or i. / mouses are stupid / some people used to watch mouses on tv / personally i couldn't see it ... get it / mostly because "top of the pops" was on at the same time / but after words i used to go out and watch ants.

everybody got that ?? well,it doesn't really matter ! because everybody who laughs last, everybody who,every... ,who,ha,ha ! ha,ha,choo !!

your fault again ...

(this article was borrowed from bill balance, roger christian,horace altfeld,shelley fabares, the little old grandpa,dean,jean,dan,ran, jean again and michael bryan kelly)

the dynamic duo

| something a little bit different - corrections to the last issue : |
| page 13 : the "brian wilson production" 2-LP set is <u>not out yet</u>. as usual,beach boys-related items are delayed. |
| page 14
page 16 : entry 19- has not "jan & dean take mr bass man surfin'" but <u>"mr bass man takes linda surfin' - jan & dean"</u> on the spine of the cover. |
| page 14
page 17 : entry 2o-,the paper picture disc of "linda/mr bass man" is on <u>columbia record club 33 1/3 rpm d4o</u> , and not on warner brothers. |

16

SURFIN AGAIN Issue 3

NEW WAX AND OLD WAVES

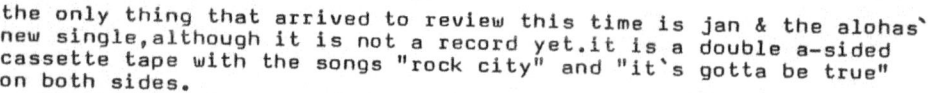

ROCK CITY/IT'S GOTTA BE TRUE
(JB RECORDS)
JAN & THE ALOHAS (cassette only)

the only thing that arrived to review this time is jan & the alohas'
new single,although it is not a record yet.it is a double a-sided
cassette tape with the songs "rock city" and "it's gotta be true"
on both sides.
   "rock city" is a superb up-tempo song starting with an intro/
chorus by the alohas.then jan takes over the verses and the second
chorus.jan's voice is stronger than ever since the sixties and the
whole song really moves during all its 3min 34 seconds.
   musically,it is somewhere between "fun city" and "blow up music".
jan & the alohas (marv allin-piano;shawn bryant-guitar;jim ebert-
drums;dave loe-guitar,vocals;jeff todd-bass) do work well together.
   "it's gotta be true" is a bit slower and is kind of a novelty
song about the `national enquirer`,a newspaper which has its
counterpart in about every country.the song was first mentioned in
stephen mc parland's excellent "gonna hustle you" in june 1981,
under the title "would the `national enquirer` ever lie to you",
written by jan berry,dean torrence,billy berry,roger christian and
jim armstrong.now,three years later it has surfaced.it is a
very nice song with jan on lead vocals,harmony by the alohas
and a saxophone bridge in the middle.the duration of the song is
a full 224 seconds.
   we can only hope that the single will be released as a disc and
that the announced album will follow very,very soon.
   now,woodn't that bee nice ?

Jan Berry is on the road again

by Julie Neal

Jan Berry

"Now here's the man who came all the way back from Dead Man's Curve."

Jan Berry, 43, a surf rock star of the 1960s, rushes onto the stage at Vidinha Stadium. One leg lags behind him. One arm is limp. One side of his face sags slightly — all the result of a gruesome crash near a Sunset Boulevard curve, made famous by a Jan and Dean song about a race between a Jaguar and a Corvette.

A mischievous grin spreads across Jan Berry's face. He obviously feels the music and his voice pours forth — the familiar voice of the old Jan and Dan hit songs — perhaps played even better by the seasoned Aloha Band.

The crowd starts to sing and dance.

It was after "Deadman's Curve" sold nearly a million copies that Jan barely survived his own tragedy there. The accident cut his medical school studies short and stopped his musical career for more than a decade — but it's now a part of his surf-revival show.

He's a hero, says the drummer in his Aloha Band, Jim Eberl, who says that working with Jan is much more than playing music. "Jan Berry's not a star, he's a hero."

"Take Last Vegas," says road manager David Flumano. "The sellout crowds remember "Dead Man's Curve." They remember the part where Jan says, 'Well the last thing I recall, doc, is I started to swerve. Then I saw the Jag slide into the curve ...'

"The lights dim. The spotlight's on Jan. Then he'll sometimes forget the words," Flumano says. "The crowd just about cries, but afterwards they give him a standing ovation."

Jan Berry is the only entertainer, Flumano says, who can forget the words and still get a standing ovation.

The 1966 accident left Berry in a coma for six weeks. It left his brain damaged, particularly those parts that govern speech. And he lost much of the ability to use words as symbols and to string together complex ideas.

He had to start from the beginning, recalls Stephanie Townsend of Kalaheo, a college classmate of Jan Berry's sister.

"He was a brilliant kid. He had a

(please turn to page 18)

17

★ Jan Berry ★
(continued from page 17)

printing outfit as a young teen, recording contracts in high school and then on to medical school."

AFTER THE ACCIDENT, she remembers, he had to start over — relearning simple tasks as if he were an infant.

She attributes his comeback to a will that never died and a kind of "extra sense" that's helped him to make right decisions despite his handicaps.

The barriers to Jan Berry's return to productive life, however, have been far more than his injuries. When he became well enough to move back to his house overlooking the lights of Los Angeles, he became a target for people who stole his time, his money and his gold records off the wall.

"THEY WOULD HANG AROUND," Berry recalled in an interview last Saturday. "But I needed them, I was lonely."

His father Bill Berry, who retired as a project manager for Howard Hughes to manage Jan's new band, said he was afraid Jan's wealth would be totally depleted. But for many years Jan refused to move home with his parents. He wanted to recover on his own.

In that house where Jan Berry decided to become an independent person, a wall full of medical school books and an electric piano were his favorite possessions. In 1972 he told me — I had been hired to help him learn to talk and read again — that he understood he could never become a physician.

THE ONLY THING LEFT, he said, as he fumbled on the keys of the piano and sang out in the slurred lyrics of a seemingly drunken man, was music. He could try to recapture the audience and the career he'd gained more than ten years ago when at age 17 he cut his first Number One song, "Jenny Lee".

The simple tunes of those teen hits he made, the simple words about going to Hawai'i to "Ride the Wild Surf" and meet up with his "Honolulu Lulu" were difficult for Jan Berry to relearn.

Afflicted with aphasia, and continually frustrated by his understanding of situations — only to mix up the order of words as he tried to talk or sing a song — Jan Berry faced a long and continuing ordeal.

IN THE LATE 1970S, after a television drama about the career of Jan Berry and Dean Torrence, however, it became obvious that surf rock fans across the country wanted to applaud Jan Berry for coming back ... and they wanted to hear the light hearted music.

Jan took to the road with Dean. "But Dean had his own ideas, his own band and way of running things," Jan recalled.

"I ONLY FELT like hiding."

Jan said he turned to drugs and alcohol, then dropped out of the Jan and Dean duo.

One-hundred-and-forty days of sobriety later, he said, he has his own band and a schedule that books Jan and the Alohas through the end of the year on the west and the east coasts and on to Australia.

And in September he will have a reunion concert with Dean at Magic Mountain in California.

"I can feel the renewal of Jan and Dean is going to start happening again," he says.

"So all I do is pray."

Says drummer Ebert, those prayers are being answered in many ways. Jan and the Alohas has been playing to sell-out crowds around the country, and Jan Berry once again has a successful career.

the garden island, hawaii august 9, 1983

```
whole lotta lovin`
*******************
(as recorded by jan & dean)
there`s a whole lotta colour in the rainbow
a whole lotta leaves in the tree
and it`s also true,now that i have you
there`s a whole lotta lovin` for me

there`s a whole lotta sand in the desert
many drops of water in the sea
what a wonderful world,now that you`re my girl
there`s a whole lotta lovin` for me

there`s a whole lotta pages in a book
that tell of a love so true
just like the ripples in a brook
it`ll last the whole life through

there`s a whole lotta people in a city
as lonely as they can be
but i have no fear,now that you are here
there`s a whole lotta lovin` for me

there`s a whole lotta pages in a book
that tell of a love so true
just like the ripples in a brook
it`ll last the whole life through

there`s a whole lotta people in a city
as lonely as they can be
but i have no fear,now that you are here
there`s a whole lotta lovin` for me
there`s a whole lotta lovin` for me
yeah a whole lotta lovin` for me
there`s a whole lotta lovin` for me
```

SURFIN AGAIN Issue 3

adverts adverts   (ads in "surfin` again" are printed free of charge)
****** *******

i have <u>surf records for sale</u> (45s,LPs,EPs,picture sleeves);for example :
jan & dean,beach boys,astronauts,hondells,hornets,rip chords etc.
write to : heimo vuorio,12640 jokiniemi,finland

<u>rare records for trade</u> ! jan & dean "rarities" pic disc;"studio out-
takes vol. 1 + 2";beach boys "hawthorne hotshots" eps (white cover);
"come go with me" metal acetate;"landlocked";"smile";gold wax and
pic disc copies of "new album","adult child","merry xmas","california
feeling",etc.   write : danny bossard,gotthelfweg 9,5036 oberentfelden,
switzerland

<u>california music</u>,the mag dedicated to the music of the beach,to
jan & dean,beach boys and more. 2 kentwell avenue,concord 2137,
new south wales,australia

<u>jan berry and the alohas newsletter</u> from bonnie hoyt,186 lakeview ave.,
apt. 1-2,new canaan,connecticut 06840,usa

<u>surfers rule</u>,the european surf music magazine,deals with jan & dean,
the beach boys,instrumentals,revival etc. available from:lilla
nygatan 16,111 28 stockholm,sweden

<u>sunshine music</u>,2817 crawford,parsons,kansas 67357,usa. the us jan &
dean magazine.

<u>don`t forget</u> the one and only "surfin` again" magazine,please !!

for $ 40 i`ll send you a xeroxed copy of <u>the first script of the</u>
<u>"deadman`s curve" telemovie</u>.130 pages all in all. paula moore,
33 short road,west falls,new york 14170,usa

for a copy of stevie surf`s debut solo ep,write to:ars productions,
p.o. box 9997,san jose,california 95157,usa. stevie is the creator
of papa doo run run and is back with his band now.

harmony beach -five track ep of acapella versions of beach boys
songs,sung by england`s finest vocalists.prices : £ 3.50 (uk);
£ 4.00 (europe);£ 5.00 (overseas),includes donation to `help
a london child`,so c`mon everybody and get a copy.kingsley
abbott,39 eglington hill,london sw18 3nz,england.the ep is
limited to 500 copies and comes with a numbered picture sleeve.

LATE NEWS   LATE NEWS   LATE NEWS   LATE NEWS   LATE NEWS   LATE NEWS
****
TOUR DATES :
```
aug 3,4,5    san diego wild animal park  escondido,ca      jan & dean
aug 8        san joaquin fair            stockton,ca       jan & dean
aug 10       riverside county fair       hemet,ca          jan & dean
aug 11-18    cruise ship                 miami,fl          jan & dean
aug 29       antelope valley fair        lancaster,ca      jan & dean
sept 16-29   concert tour                northwestern u.s. jan & alohas
```

thrilling news for those fortunate people in the land of the kangaroo :
in 1985,jan & dean are touring australia and new zealand,from january
21 - february 10!!!remains the question : will they come to europe
afterwards ?? stay tuned !

this issue`s beach boys` hot gossip column # 2 : for all those who
don`t know yet,brian wilson,yes <u>that</u> brian wilson,recently visited
london and spent some time in the studio together with steve
levine (and do we hear rumours of a new album ???).let`s hope that
steve won`t turn the beach boys into a second edition of culture
club,or can you imagine boy carl instead of boy george ?

DEAD MAN'S CURVE - THE MOVIE

JAN BERRY
E.M.I

DEAN TORRENCE
PAT ROONEY PRODUCTION

PRODUCER: PAT ROONEY
"DEADMAN'S CURVE"

SURF SCOUTS FAN CLUB

FIRST SURFSCOUT BOARD MEETING

Summer Coast-To-Coast

What do you do when you live in Rochester, NY where the biggest waves are made by fishing boats dropping anchor, and you want to record a song about summer waves? You either summon up your imagination or you do what Surfscout Mark Braccio did—pick up the whole operation and move it to Huntington Beach, California, home of the fabled "Golden Bear (major showcase club for surf music) and the OP Surfing Championships.

His single "Summer Days," backed with "Heaven In My '57" was recorded on the beach there and released back in Rochester on DRC Records. It comes in a spiffy full-color jacket showing Mark cavorting on the beach with a beautiful blonde. The record is dedicated to the summers of the early '60's" and Mark gives special thanks to "the Beach Boys for the inspiration and memories." Write to Mark c/o Surfscouts for information.

Number 2

SURF SCOUTS FAN CLUB

Surfscout Gazette

© 1983 SURFSCOUTS
SURFSCOUTS, PO BOX 240, ROSLYN, NY 11576

MEMBERSHIP NOTES

We're pleased to report that the response to SURFSCOUTS has been phenomenal! Less than six months from our birthdate we've already got members in 35 states and three countries! One drawback to the great response is that it's slowed down the machinery a bit—things like getting names onto the computer (yes, we're into the silicon age—have been ever since "Jenny Lee") and having to re-order T-shirts (a lot more extra-large than we anticipated—watch that extra tuna malt) have backed us up a bit. Thanks for bearing with us. But now that things are caught up every letter will get a prompt individual response.

In answer to several inquiries we can tell you that the Gazette will come out as often as there's something to say, no less frequently than quarterly. It'll depend on who's on tour and how much you decide to use the Gazette to communicate with each other, 'cause you are the Surfscouts!

A word about T-shirts—all "Ladies" shirts are "French Cut" in standard sizes—the same cut and sizes that Jan & Dean sold on tour—and they're cut to fit the form! If you have any doubts about the size fitting you, it might be a better idea to order a Men's shirt, which is a regular, traditional T-shirt cut.

For those who didn't include the optional photo on the membership form, you can send one along any time you decide your good side is showing. These two are clearly the best likenesses so far:

(l) Surfer Dan Ricketts, Flint, Michigan, "Some people say I look like somebody named Elvis," Mike Wirth, Seaford, NY

In the next Gazette we'll be revealing the startling results of the Surfscout Survey (those little boxes you checked off on the back of your membership form). Then later on in 1983 we'll be designating state representatives—keep watching for details.

REMEMBER TO INCLUDE YOUR MEMBERSHIP NUMBER IN ALL CORRESPONDENCE.

NEWS

GRINNING FOR GADGETS..Darned if right there inside the pages of **Rolling Stone** that wasn't a picture of **Mike Love** and **Dean Torrence**! Never mind that it wasn't the Cover, never mind that it wasn't a Revealing Interview, never mind (well, maybe just a little) that it wasn't even a Small Article, but there they were, the Sultan of Surf and the Maharishi of Maui gazin' and grinnin' right out from under a bright & shiny new **Radio Shack** stereo amplifier, Mike saying, "It's slim and trim like I am, and simple enough for Dean to use." If that wasn't enough to get you to shimmy on down to the local Shack and shell out some shillings for the latest stereo stuff, the folks from the Shack can top it—and will—any day now there'll be a special cassette album on sale exclusively at Radio Shack stores nationwide featuring Mike, Dean and a whole bunch of their friends singing some of their favorite old tunes—what better souvenir if you can't make it down to the South coast shows this month....**BEL-AIR BANDIT GARY GRIFFIN** appears on the next **Tony Sciuto** album. Gary went to Japan with Sciuto just before the Bandits got together....**PART-TIME BANDIT STERLING SMITH** can be seen, if you look closely, on the MTV video of **Randy Meisner**. He's the one with the jokes and keyboards....**YOU CAN'T TELL THE SCORERS WITHOUT A PLACARD**..Quick, what group comes to mind when you hear the names **Mark Ward, Jim Armstrong, Chris Farmer** and Gary Griffin? If you said Bel-Air Bandits you're right. If it's Saturday. But if it's Friday this must be California, because the night before the Bandits played a Saturday night show at **Knott's Berry Farm** (their summer home), the same foursome answered to the name of the **Bad Boys** at an LA area high school dance. Got that? But isn't the Bad Boys the new name for the band originally called the **Bangers**, made up of Mark, Jim, Chris, **Dave Jolley** and **John Stamos**, you ask? Why, yes. But Dave was busy with a previous commitment (he's an A.D. for Paramount Pictures) so Gary sat in on keys. Follow so far? So that meant Mark, Jim, Chris, Gary and John, right? Will..uh..not exactly, see, 'cause John's **General Hospital** shooting schedule kept him away, so **Rick Murphy** filled in on drums. So we've got Jim, Mark, Chris, Gary and Rick. The Bad Boys, right? Well, Friday, yes. The next night, that aforementioned Saturday night at Knott's, the same five answered to the name of the Bel-Air Bandits at

(continued on pg 2...)

SURF SCOUTS FAN CLUB

BLACKIE AND THE BANDITS
General Hospital's John Stamos stops backstage at Knott's Berry Farm to visit old pals, Southern California heartthrobs, the Bel-Air Bandits. (l-r) Mark Ward, Jim Armstrong, Stamos, Danny deHart & Gary Griffin. (back) Chris Farmer.

Membership Notes
(...continued from pg 1)

Knott's, Murphy sitting in for absent Bandit **Danny deHart**. So at least you know what band it is if Mark & Jim are in it, right? Weeellll...the two erstwhile **Surf Brothers** also have another band going that includes Murphy and two of the **Cowsills**. That one's called the **Blue Flames**. Bel-Air Bandits, Bad Boys, Bangers, Blue Flames. Got that? If you do, send us a card and explain it, will ya?....**ONCE IN EVERY EVEN-NUMBERED DECADE..With Jan & Dean** not doing any live shows in 1983 (it's official) Jan decided to hit the road with a new edition of his **Aloha Band**, and hit the road they did. One day, while traveling between gigs in their motor home, they hit a bump in the road. The motor home shimmied, caught Jan off guard and he fell on his shoulder, cracking his collarbone. Though Jan missed some starts and might not recover his fastball for a season, he's already back in the rotation, with new plans to get back on the road with a show called "the Music of Jan & Dean starring Jan Berry." One thing to watch out for—some less-than-scrupulous promoters might try to bill the show in a way that makes it look like both Jan and Dean will be there. It's the same thing they tried in 1978 before **Phase II** started. This is definitely not happening! Dean is busy with other projects....**SLOW, BUT STEADY**..There's talk in the wind of a special reunion of the **Turtles**. Dean's first album jacket design was a Turtles' album, plus the very famous Turtles picture disc shows 6 band members in the shot taken at the beach. Everyone knows there were only five Turtles! If you look closely, number six is..Dean! who was there taking the photos for an album and they tricked him into a picture! The reunion is set to include **Mark Volman, Howard Kaylan** (known to Jan & Dean fans as **Flo 'n' Eddie**) and **Jim Pons** (who now shoots game films for the **New York Jets**). If **John Barbata** (Turtle drummer, later with **Jefferson Starship**) is unavailable, there's talk that **Joe Stefko** might get the call. Stefko, once **Meat Loaf's** drummer, is a good friend of Jan & Dean's, in fact, they snuck in a picture of him doing a guest singing shot on "One Summer Night/Live."....**DEAN'S DESIGNS**..Look for Dean's design work on the next **Dirt Band** album. Dean has teamed with the Dirt Band for some pretty good stuff over the years including the classic "**Will The Circle Be Unbroken**" album which had its jacket nominated for a Grammy....**EVERYONE NOSE THE SOUNDEST HORN IS ON THE RHINO**..The folks at LA's **Rhino Records**, the same ones who brought you Jan & Dean's "One Summer Night/Live", the 3-record "**Anthology of Surf Music**," the "**Malibooz**," and the "**Turtles Greatest Hits**" should have the brand-new LP by the **Honeys** (with **Marilyn Wilson**, ex of Brian) on the shelves just about the time you read this. Believe it or not, many record stores are still not

(continued on pg 3...)

SURF SCOUTS FAN CLUB

FIRST REGATTA

Sorry, but entries are closed and the oars are in the water for the First Surfscout Gulfjump Regatta. Mike (Love) and Dean (Torrence) will kick off the festivities with a March 15 concert bash at Padre Island, Texas. The competitors will dive in the water immediately after "Barbara Ann" and swim to their boats. They'll push past the Mississippi delta and land in Fort Walton Beach, Florida 16 days later, where they'll be greeted by another Mike and Dean concert. Finishers get free tickets, as do non-finishers and spectators. While waiting for the competition, Love & Torrence will keep busy entertaining the tourists up and down the Florida coast (see schedule elsewhere in Gazette). Entries for the next Regatta are pending notification of next of kin.

Competitors line up for group shot at registration

(...continued from pg 2)
hip to Rhino. We can all help do the job by going to the local store's staff and asking them to get all these great records in stock. And keep going back until they listen! If they still don't order the records, drop HQ a line with the store manager's name. We'll get Rhino to call direct...**JAN BEEN BERRY, BERRY GOOD TO ME**..Bonnie Hoyt has started a "Jan Berry & Aloha Fan Club." You can write to her at 186 Lakeview Ave, Apt 1-2, New Canaan, CT 06840.... **CAUGHT IN THE CROSSFIRES**..Flo 'n' Eddie fans who went to see their New Year shows in New York were happily surprised to have the show open with a set by the **Crossfires**, six funny-looking characters dressed alike in red and white striped blazers! Of course it turned out to be Flo 'n' Eddie, who were doing a send-up of their own pre-Turtles LA surf band. After all those years these guys can still swim with the best of them!

SURF SCOUTS FAN CLUB

APPEARANCES

Mike & Dean
(all free admission)

Mar 15	Padre Island, Tx
Mar 17	Daytona Beach, Fla
Mar 23	Ft Lauderdale, Fla
Mar 24	Daytona Beach, Fla
Mar 31	Fort Walton Beach, Fla

Beach Boys

Mar 25	Rockford, Ill
Mar 26	Louisville, Ky
Mar 27	Chattanooga, Tn
Mar 28	Nashville, Tn
Mar 30	Savannah, Ga
Apr 3	Sunrise, Fla

Surfscout Needs Help

Surfscout Sue Kuntz of Massilon, Ohio has a sad tale to tell. Sue sings in a church folk group called "St. Mary's Folk Group." That's not the sad part, because the group is good. So good, in fact, that they recorded an album in 1980. Not knowing anything about the technical part of making a record, however, the record didn't come out sounding so good. Sue says, "The only way it sounds good is if you would have headsets on."

In April of 1982, a little smarter this time, they recorded their second album. The master tape sounded great and release only awaited the album cover design, which they decided to do themselves. During the cover's preparation, tragedy struck. Their group leader's house burnt down, with the tape stored in it. Fortunately no one was hurt. But the second album was gone and so was the money they'd borrowed to record it.

So now they have to borrow more money, and though they definitely will go back into the studio and re-record it, by Sue's figuring "we will have to sell three times the amount of albums to pay" for it all. The albums sell for $8.00 each.

Any ideas out there to help Sue sell those records?

Classified Ads

For sale: Beach Boys 1967 Concert Program, mint $5, Beach Boy song folio #3 (with 8 pages of color photos), mint $5. Prices include postage. Roland Coover Jr, 1537 E. Strasburgh Rd, West Chester, Pa 19380.

For sale: Jan & Dean Concert Book (Phase I), autographd by Dean. $25.00. PO Box 240, Roslyn, NY 11576.

Mackie - you're the dreamiest! See you again at Knott's next summer. Your Summer Secret.

Classifieds are free to Surfscouts. Send to PO Box 240, Roslyn, NY 11576. Include Membership Number.

SURF SCOUTS FAN CLUB

RECORD	UNIT PRICE	POSTAGE & HANDLING	NUMBER ORDERED	= AMOUNT
JAN & DEAN & Bel-Air Bandits ONE SUMMER NIGHT/LIVE (RHINO RNDA 1496)	$10.00	$1.25	__ × $11.25	$ ____

New York State residents add tax (7.25%) $ ____

TOTAL ENCLOSED $ ____

Please send check or money order
payable to "Surfscouts"
to: SURFSCOUTS, P.O. BOX 240,
ROSLYN, NEW YORK 11576.
Allow 4 to 6 weeks for delivery.

NAME _____

ADDRESS _____

CITY _____ STATE ____ ZIP ____

JAN & DEAN & the Bel-Air Bandits — ONE SUMMER NIGHT/LIVE

Surfscout Gazette

NUMBER ONE — 1982 SURFSCOUTS
SURFSCOUTS, P.O. BOX 240, ROSLYN, N.Y. 11576

WELCOME

Well, it sure has taken us long enough, but here it is! The answer to questions like "Is there a real Jan & Dean fan club?," "Did Dean really sing on Beach Boy records?," "Whatever happened to Roger Christian?" and all of the other questions you've got. The answer is SURFSCOUTS—a brand new club that you can join today. Much more than a fan club, Surfscout chapters will sponsor their own events, maybe even private concerts by some of your favorite people! Your mail will get priority treatment and get to your favorite people as fast as if you had their home addresses. You'll get the inside information on records in progress, concerts in your area, how to get T-shirts, pictures and up-to-the-minute news that's not available anywhere else on Jan, Dean, the Beach Boys, Bel-Air Bandits, and many more of your favorites through the Surfscout Gazette, a periodic newsletter that comes directly to your house if you're a Surfscout! And best of all, the Gazette's classified section (free to Surfscouts) lets you buy, sell, trade or just plain talk to thousands of others around the world who like the same things as you do, so don't delay—sign up today!

JUST BEACHED!

Summer of '82 was a Surfscout's paradise in California...the BEL-AIR BANDITS held fort all season at KNOTT'S BERRY FARM in Buena Park and were joined frequently by special guests JOHN STAMOS ("Blackie" from GENERAL HOSPITAL), members of PAPA DOO RUN RUN, and of course, DEAN TORRENCE...Dean and the Bandits headlined frequently at fairs in Southern California, while the Bandits 12" EP was featured in store displays all over Southern California and spawned a local hit "She Loves the Radio," (available in stores nationwide in a couple of months, or immediately by mail from Surfscout Headquarters)...the ubiquitous Dean (that means he's everywhere!) also turned up as a special guest at BEACH BOY shows in San Diego, Irvine, and Los Angeles and joined BB Mike Love unannounced for Mike's solo gigs at KNOTT'S and the SANTA CLARA COUNTY FAIR in SAN JOSE, where JAN & DEAN set attendance records in 1981...MIKE & DEAN's association is stepping up pace—their first shows together at Spring Break celebrations on Padre Island, Texas; Daytona Beach, Fla.; and Kansas City in early '83 were such smashes that sponsor BUDWEISER has put together a series of dates in Texas and Louisiana (schedule below) revolving around the theme "Be True to Your Bud" (after guess-which-song!) and they're thinking of going nationwide...while JAN & DEAN played no live dates in '82 (when would Dean have had the time?) JAN BERRY played some L.A. dates with his band ALOHA and in early October JAN & DEAN met to discuss the future. Meanwhile, just a shell's skip away, the final touches were being put on ONE SUMMER NIGHT/LIVE, a spectacular double album set that is J&D's first new recording since 1966! It's in stores now, or by mail from Surfscout HQ courtesy of RHINO RECORDS, the same folks who made waves earlier in '82 with their 3-volume SURF MUSIC ANTHOLOGY series, and in 1981 put out the MALIBOOZ, which featured WALTER EGAN and guested FLEETWOOD MAC's LINDSEY BUCKINGHAM and (who else?) Dean (cover by, who do you think...Dean). Also coming on RHINO any day is an all new record from the HONEYS...also coming, but not on Rhino, the second solo effort from CARL WILSON who's obviously decided that he can be both a BEACH BOY and a solo after 1982's Beach Boy tour was their biggest and best ever, no small reason being that Carl insisted on pre-tour rehearsals and re-auditioning long-time backup players...Bandits JIM ARMSTRONG, MARK WARD, and CHRIS FARMER doing hit & run local L.A. gigs as "The BANGERS" with John Stamos on drums...Bandit GARY GRIFFIN producing local heartthrob KATHY JONES...don't you wish you were in California?

If any part of your name and address is spelled or listed incorrectly, please let us know!

A NOTE FROM DEAN

Dear Folks,

Just a word to thank all of you who've taken the time to write to us over the past few years. Up 'til now I've only been able to personally answer a small fraction of the bags of mail we get, and that's just not enough. I'll keep on doing that, but after a year of planning, the Surfscouts has been set up so that no one's letters will go unanswered and your requests will get directly to me. I'm really happy that we'll finally have a way to stay in touch, because the few minutes we catch its mail, or onstage, or in a theatre hallway, just isn't enough time for me to find out what you've been doing and having fun at. I hope you'll be actively involved with the Surfscouts so we can spend more time together.

Keep the surf up.

P.S. Surfscouts has a New York address 'cause there aren't as many good beach days there and they've got less to do. Your letters get to us faster that way!

meet me here!

MON. NOV 8—8:00 PM
S.H.S.U. COLISEUM
SAM HOUSTON STATE U
HUNTSVILLE, TX
713-294-1841

FRI. NOV 12—8:00 PM
LUBBOCK MUNICIPAL COLISEUM
LUBBOCK, TX
806-742-3641

SUN. NOV 14—2:00 PM
U.N.O. BASEBALL FIELD
UNIV. OF NEW ORLEANS
NEW ORLEANS, LA
504-286-6368

TUES. NOV 16—8:00 PM
EWING COLISEUM
NE LOUISIANNA UNIV
MONROE, LA
318-342-4198

THURS. NOV 18—8:00 PM
U.T.E.P. SPECIAL EVENTS CENTER
UNIV OF TEXAS AT EL PASO
(TICKETMASTER—915-532-6661)

"MIKE & DEAN" appearing at:

SURF SCOUTS FAN CLUB

ALL YOU WANT TO KNOW ABOUT SURFSCOUTS

WHAT IS SURFSCOUT?

Surfscouts are people like you who live active lives, enjoy outdoor sports and activities and like to listen to outdoor music, especially surf music.

HOW DO I BECOME A SURFSCOUT?

You automatically become an official SURFSCOUT when your membership application is approved and you pay your dues and initiation fee (explained in detail in the membership brochure). You can be an individual member or join as part of a group. If you're part of a group of ten or more who join together your group can be certified as a SURFSCOUT CHAPTER and given an exclusive numerical designation and all the special privileges that go with being a chapter. Your present club activities can continue as before with no restrictions, plus you get all the advantages of being SURFSCOUTS.

I'M IN A JAN & DEAN OR BEACH BOY FAN CLUB NOW. CAN I STILL BE A SURFSCOUT?

Of course! Just join up as an individual. Or, even better yet, your fan club can be certified as a SURFSCOUT CHAPTER.

HOW CAN MY PRESENT FAN CLUB BE CERTIFIED AS A SURFSCOUT CHAPTER?

Have your fan club president write to SURFSCOUT headquarters (the address is on the membership brochure) for membership application. If you want to belong to a different chapter, if you move, or if you get ten new friends and would like to start a chapter of your own, your fan club will be certified as a SURFSCOUT CHAPTER and given an exclusive numerical designation.

IF MY FAN CLUB BECOMES A SURFSCOUT CHAPTER, MUST I STAY A MEMBER OF THE FAN CLUB TO STAY A SURFSCOUT?

No. Even if you join SURFSCOUTS as a member of a chapter, you are also considered an individual member. If you want to belong to a different chapter, if you move, or if you get ten or more fan club members for each member of the fan club. If ten or more fan club members sign up as SURFSCOUTS, your fan club will be certified as a SURFSCOUT CHAPTER and given an exclusive numerical designation and all the special privileges that go with being a chapter.

WHAT DO I GET AS A SURFSCOUT?

First of all, you get an offical SURFSCOUT multi-color T-shirt, available only to full-fledged SURFSCOUTS in good standing. You also get a membership card and a subscription to the Surfscout Gazette, the newsletter that gives you first-hand information about what your favorite people are doing and you get a direct line of communication open to them. Surfscout mail gets priority over all other mail. Many of these experts are becoming advisers to Surfscouts and you'll be able to ask them questions and get direct answers from them through the Gazette about questions in their areas of expertise. Also, you'll get priority announcements of concerts by your favorite groups in your area and sometimes you'll get to buy tickets before they go on sale to the public, sometimes even at special prices! You'll be able to buy a variety of merchandise at special Surfscout prices. The Surfscout Gazette will have a column about you, in which you can let the other Surfscouts know all about things you're doing. If you are given the names of Surfscouts and their chapters in your area so you can get together with them. You'll be able to sponsor Surfscout events and activities and even have private appearances by some of your favorite people when they're in your area!. And you can earn Surfscout achievement badges for accomplishments in many activities that will enrich your life. And much, much more!

NEW!!! DOUBLE RECORD SET
SPECTACULAR FULL-COLOR PHOTO COLLAGE OF JAN & DEAN AND THE BEL-AIR BANDITS ON TOUR

BEST PRICE AVAILABLE

1
HIDE YOUR LOVE AWAY • BACK IN THE U.S.S.R. • SURFIN' U.S.A. • HONOLULU LULU • DO YOU WANNA DANCE DANCE, DANCE, DANCE • RIDE THE WILD SURF

2
NEW GIRL IN SCHOOL • JENNY LEE
BABY TALK • LINDA • DRAG CITY
LITTLE DEUCE COUPE • SHUT DOWN

3
SIDEWALK SURFIN' • HELP ME, RHONDA
CALIFORNIA GIRLS • LITTLE OLD LADY FROM PASADENA
DEADMAN'S CURVE

4
GOOD VIBRATIONS • I GET AROUND
FUN, FUN, FUN • SURF CITY • BARBARA ANN

SEND FOR IT TODAY!

24 SONGS EACH ONE A HIT!

RHINO CATALOG

SURF MUSIC

CROSSFIRES "Out of Control"   RNLP 019
An album of rare, previously unreleased early material by the famed "Turtles." Prior to their name change, "The Crossfires" were known as the heaviest surf band on the West Coast. Album contains great cover pic and detailed liner notes. The historical importance of this LP, along with the renewed interest in surf music makes this album a must for all rock and roll collectors.

$7.98 List

THE MALIBOOZ   RNLP 100
A contemporary surf music masterpiece in the mold of the early Beach Boys, the Malibooz are led by Walter Egan (an artist who has had two national top ten hits in the past 2½ years) and John Zambetti. Among other "surfer buns and bunnies" featured are Lindsey Buckingham of Fleetwood Mac, Dean Torrance of Jan and Dean and Wendy Waldman

$8.98 List

HISTORY OF SURF MUSIC   RNLP 051
Vol. I - The Instrumentals
From 1961-63 surf music was one of the most important and dominant forms of American Music. Rhino has put together the only definitive collection of surf instrumentals with Top Ten Hits like "Pipeline" and "Wipeout", as well as cuts by all the important artists who shaped this form of music, such as Dick Dale, The Pyramids and an early configuration of the Turtles, known as "The Crossfires".

$8.98 List

THE HISTORY OF SURF MUSIC   RNLP 052
Vol. II - The Vocals
This album represents the best of the surf vocals with cuts by Jan & Dean, The Beach Boys, The Trashmen, The Tradewinds and many more.

$8.98 List

THE HISTORY OF SURF MUSIC   RNLP 054
Vol. III - The Revivals
Our four volume series was inspired by the tremendous resurgence surf music has experienced in the last couple of years. This volume contains songs by the groups that were responsible, including The Malibooz (featuring the legendary Dean Torrance) and local faves, Jon & The Nightriders.

$8.98 List

CHALLENGERS "The Best Of"   RNLP 053
The Challengers were one of the best of the surf bands, with a high visability due to numerous TV appearances. They sold an unheard of 200,000 copies of their first album in 1963. This 14 song collection was mastered from original tapes from the Vault Records catalogue.

$8.98 List

THE WEDGE   RNEP 509
Redondo Beach's the Wedge have taken the kind of instrumental surf music that was popular in the early 1960's, and have heavied-it-up with 1980's power, energy and recording techniques. Songs: Mr. Moto, Night of the Living Wedge, Penetration, Godzilla Stomp, Debbie.

$4.98 List

THE BEL AIR BANDITS   PERM 2
Southern California's legendary band, The Bel Air Bandits, release their first LP, distributed by Rhino Records. This dynamic record features Dean Torrance, of Jan & Dean fame, on vocals.

$5.98 List

JAN AND DEAN   RNDA 1498
"One Summer Night/Live"
Rhino is proud to announce the first ever live album by the immortal Jan & Dean. This two LP set, the first new recording by the group in over 15 years, is packaged in a deluxe gatefold sleeve, designed by Dean Torrence himself! The recording features Jan & Dean doing all their greatest hits as performed on their last tour of 1981. The sound quality is superb, and the backing of the incredible Bel Air Bandits lends an extra special punch to the surf sound that Jan & Dean defined in the '60's. This is sure to be the definitive Jan & Dean collection to have.
Also available on cassette (RNC 1498)

$14.98 List

SEATTLE TIMES

From Seattle Times (date unk.)

Jan Berry, left, and Dean Torrence on the comeback trail. "People assume that anybody who is a celebrity just never gets hurt..."

Rock 'n' Roll

Road Back From Dead Man's Curve

BY JAMES BROWN

SEATTLE TIMES

The last thing I remember ..doc I started to swerve. And then I saw the Jag slide into the curve. I know I'll never forget that horrible sight. I found out for myself that everyone was right. You don't come back from Dead Man's Curve..

• The intermingling sounds of sirens, screeching brakes and a resounding crash in the night. That was Jan and Dean's "Dead Man's Curve" a tongue-in-cheek odyssey of two cars culminating in the ultimate teen-age drag rumble off of the Sunset straightaway. But something went wrong. The satire and celebration of survival could no longer be considered a joke. The twisted irony of "real life" became too close a relative—a song became a reality.

It was in early April of 1966 and Jan Berry was in a hurry. It seemed to be always a matter of speed and saving time with him—a prisoner of things to do.

A Downhill Slide

Berry's career as half of one of rock music's most successful teams (with Dean Torrence) was on a downhill slide once again. It had been three years since "Dead Man's Curve," one of their last big hits, and the music business seemed to be passing them by.

No longer was California sunshine and Bikini Beach and Drag City and all of surfing's fantasyland a salable musical commodity. The kids—gremmies, hodads, Frankie, Annette, Shelley—they all grew up and so did the music. It was no longer fashionable to have fun. Music was serious business because the events of the day dictated so—things to get done, things to improve, an awareness of new freedom and responsibility—who better to sing of this social revolution than its underground poets, Bob Dylan and Joan Baez shouting that we're on the eve of destruction and dawn of creation.

Jan and Dean had joined the rock junkyard. But it was more than that speeding Jan Berry to his destination that day. A premed student at UCLA, Berry's studies were interrupted by a fractured leg incurred during a fall from a railroad car while filming a movie. Leaving school for six months, Berry received a call from his local draft board to do some explaining as to why his student exemption shouldn't be dropped.

Another pressure, another place to go just like it has always been. Going to school, performing and recording, personal appearances and plugs, making a movie, and now a trip to the draft board—a revolving door of automobile rides. There just never seemed to be enough time.

He came off of Sunset Blvd. to Whittier Ave. in his sleek Corvette Sting Ray—three blocks away from Dead Man's Curve—at a speed later estimated to be 90 m.p.h.

Losing control, he smashed into a parked truck on the side of the street. Since no one saw it happen, and Berry doesn't remember, it was purely conjecture from the police and witnesses who helped pull him from the wreck.

His Corvette was twisted and shattered. Compressed into a hideous abstraction resembling the work of some mad sculptor, it seemed inconceivable that anyone emerged from it alive.

Newspaper accounts were sketchy. 3 MORE DIE IN TRAFFIC; SINGER HURT said one headline on a three-paragraph story. When it became weeks, then months before any further information could be obtained, the story of Jan Berry was forgotten.

But Jan Berry did live. Pulled unconscious from his car, he existed for 10 months in a coma. There had been a few hazy rumors to that effect, but apparently no one really wanted to believe it. His life for close to a year was one of test tube oblivion.

Like Being Reborn

Initial hope for a partial recovery was rewarded when Berry awoke. But how much had he lost? How much could he get back? It was, in a very real sense, like being reborn. Learning to do again what a child takes for granted—walking, talking, reading, writing—all to be learned as a baby learns to take its first step.

Seven years later, the learning process continues—and Jan Berry is making a comeback. He and Torrence have renewed their partnership, this time to be known as the Legendary Masked Surfers. It is a step neither took lightly. But for Jan it was a chance to be productive again, to do something he enjoys doing. As for Dean, he hopes it will mark a continuation of Jan and Dean's kind of music—a sound both of them feel never got a chance to mature.

The Los Angeles public saw for themselves a few weeks ago when Jan and Dean appeared on KNBC's local Saturday night variety program, 90 Tonight. This particular show was entirely devoted to rock music's past, and Jan and Dean were part of the package. But Berry and Torrence did not go on the program to sing. They wanted to talk about what had happened—and get a reaction. •••

"It was an experiment," said Torrence from his Sunset Strip offices where he operates Kittyhawk Graphics, designing album covers. "We both wanted to see if Jan's story was interesting to someone else. We had done some radio interviews and the response was good. But we had to see if we could come across without having to sing, sell something or any of that other garbage we had to do for so long."

And then Torrence introduced Jan Berry... seven years later at age 31. Berry shook hands with his left because of a partial paralysis on his right side. He walks with a noticeable limp. He is deaf in his right ear and has a limited peripheral vision in his right eye.

He has suffered brain damage, saying that it was caused by the cells on the right side of his brain being destroyed. His speech is halting; he sometimes confuses names, dates, places and thoughts.

But he knows these disabilities and has learned to live with them. His conversation is intelligent, and his plans are directly one-dimensional, keyed entirely toward his desire to return to the music business.

"After the accident, I was completely out for 10 months and I guess people thought to themselves, wow! He's dead!" Berry explained. "After I did come out of it, the news was there but it didn't play. People just didn't want to know. Now, they see us and think to themselves, wow! He made it! It's a good thing.

"People just assume that anyone who is a celebrity just never gets hurt. They feel, I suppose, that by being a rock performer you are rich enough to buy your way out of being hurt . . . if they don't see you, you're OK . . . they assume you've made it."

But Jan and Dean, the Legendary Masked Surfers, will try that public one more time. The experiment goes one step further. "We don't want to be thrown in with the nostalgia craze," emphasized Torrence. "Our music never really had a chance to expand, it was cut short. The idea of what you might call 'surf consciousness'—enjoying the day, your girl, the weather, your car—anything. It's so simplistic that it sounds funny, but that's what our music was and is all about. Rock records should be made to listen to in your car."

Maybe they were right all along. The rock cycle has never been more in need of a new turn. Who knows? Surfing, little old ladies from Pasadena, sidewalk skateboards and recruising the endless boulevard may still have a moment or two left. After all, who would ever have predicted David Bowie?

But coming back means a new life for Jan Berry. He has worked hard these past seven years to get this far, and will likely work at it the rest of his life. "I've been exercising my hand two times a week for about an hour to get some strength back into it," he said. "The nerves were cut, and it will never be normal but I have to try . . . sometimes I get so frustrated with myself I think, Oh God! Why do I do this? But I've got to keep doing it. It's easier now because I'm back doing something I really enjoy again. I guess I'm pretty happy."

LOS ANGELES PHONOGRAPH July 1975

THE LOS ANGELES Phonograph
RECORD MAGAZINE

THE BEACH IS BACK!

Featuring:
THE BEACH BOYS
JAN & DEAN
JOHNNY RIVERS

DEAN TORRENCE & friends· photo by Neal Preston.

FREE FROM KMET

JULY 75/VOL 5; ISSUE 10/60¢

JAN & DEAN

Jan Berry — Dean Torrence

By KEN BARNES

Can you believe it? Third year in a row *Phonograph*'s run a surf revival story, as if it were a current event. Looks pretty suspicious to me, some kind of under-the-pier deal. Well, I want no part of it. I'm going to take up something completely different. Let's talk about...skateboards.

They're hot, all over the sidewalks again, at least in California—but can the rest of the country be far behind? Skateboards are frequently underfoot even in urban Hollywood, while out in the suburbs buns are being busted constantly. In land-locked San Jose (the relative incidence of sidewalks vs. oceans, incidentally, is a significant advantage to the propagation of skateboarding, according to Dean Torrence, "This store called Skateboard City opened up and did $7000 worth of business the first day."

Why the boom? Back to Dean: "It's right there. Everybody's got a sidewalk. And now the technology has advanced—you've got much better balance and they've got the wheels set up so when you're riding down a bumpy street it doesn't feel like you're rolling over a minefield. Plus the boards are more flexible now. But it's really caught on—I wouldn't be surprised if it's already sweeping the country..."

Dean Torrence should know. He's reasonably adept at skateboarding himself (recall the *T.A.M.I. Show*, during which he executed a modish quasi-quasimodo), and Jan & Dean's "Sidewalk Surfin'", (the Beach Boys' "Catch a Wave" amicably transported inland) is the one enduring classic of the skateboard genre.

Anyway, Dean figured the time was right to capitalize on the new craze, and what better vehicle than "Sidewalk Surfin'"—if 12-year-old Beach Boys retreads could hit, what was there to lose? But could the record company (United Artists, whose defunct Liberty division issued Jan & Dean's surfeit of surf hits) be convinced? Not without some effort, apparently.

"I think the record companies are lost these days. They should be picking up on trends, but they're insulated in their own little world and they don't know what to do any more. The music in the 60's developed so fast that the record people went crazy trying to stay on top of it, till they had lost their objectivity. I think the audiences are way ahead of the record companies now.

"These people would drive to work every day and see something moving out of the corner of their eyes and it wouldn't register. I had to tell them that what they'd seen out of the corner of their eyes were skateboards, and that just possibly they could figure out some businesslike thing to do about it. And then it dawned on them and they said, hey, we could put out a record! And I said, Right...good idea!"

The new "Sidewalk Surfin'" single (backed with the Legendary Masked Surfers' "Gonna Hustle You") features a few minor lyric changes and a bit of adjustment on the harmonies, courtesy of a Torrence studio revamp. "I figured if you've got 16 tracks, why not use 'em," a potentially peril-packed dictum which could have led to the dubbing in of a howling moog track or a ten-piece horn section, but in this case just enhanced the original. It sounds brighter than ever, and is already #2 in San Diego (where "Dead Man's Curve" did the same in late 1973).

If it hits nationally it could well lead to an interesting album, possibly including the two California (Dean, Bruce Johnston, Terry Melcher) tracks cut for UA in 1973 (incidentally, Daryl Dragon of Captain & Tennille fame plays keyboards on these) and other intriguing prospects. Absolutely nothing is settled now, though; Dean, understandably cautious regarding musical projects these days, considers any commitments to be premature.

His cautious demeanor extends to performances, too, but it's worked out quite well. He has a standing arrangement with a Northern California surf band, Pa Pa Du Run Da Run, whereby he can join them live at his discretion. "They've been playing this stuff for four years—at first they had things thrown at them once in a while, but about two years ago audiences started to go wild for it. Anyway, they know all the material; it's not like the pick-up bands everybody had to use in the 50's and early 60's. They gig all the time, so there's no pressure. If I had to keep a band together, well, I don't want to perform that often, and they'd get restless and leave. This way I can call them up and play anytime."

Dean's performed with Pa Pa Du Run Da Run several times now, up in Santa Cruz, in LA's South Bay area, to gratifying response everywhere. "The audiences are really young; I can't figure out where they come from. But I really like the smaller audiences, where people sing along and dance and have a great time. Back in Jan & Dean days, any crowd under 10,000 would have been a disaster, but I've scaled down. In fact I turned down a gig at Palm Springs where 10,000 were coming—too many people."

With the band Dean, entering midway, performs a few Jan & Dean hits and then joins an extended Beach Boys medley. "I enjoy singing the Beach Boys songs better than doing our own, and I can't figure out why. Maybe it's because I expect more from ours, that I'm too personally involved with them.

"A lot of people think I should be doing something new, but I figure if people still like the old songs, why not do them? Other people who were involved with the music in the 60's kept running away from their early records, put them down. But I've always been kinda proud of our records."

One group of those "other people" is enjoying staggering success with their second consecutive anthology of past hits, and Dean is watching with interest the progress of one track in particular. "Barbara Ann" is breaking out in Pittsburgh, and may become a Capitol single soon (currently it's "Little Honda"). Dean sang lead on that track (from *Beach Boys Party*), suggested its performance in the first place and rather wistfully hopes for some official recognition if it hits again.

On the other hand, he will soon be receiving some recognition that he hadn't quite bargained for. Jan Berry's forthcoming single, "Fun City," on which Dean added some harmonies, will apparently be released as a "Jan & Dean" record. "Jan had been calling me up for a year, asking me to do something with him, but I didn't want to do it unless it was right. I sang on 'Fun City,' and I don't mind getting a credit, but Ode hasn't even notified me. Singing on a record is one thing, but when they put my name on the record that becomes a business matter." However the situation is resolved, "Fun City" sounds like a record worth waiting for with anticipation; apparently its Jan's best recent effort, and everything Dean's been involved with has been a high-spirited delight.

Dean Torrence is still fully occupied with his design firm, Kitty Hawk Graphics, and wary of committing himself to music again, but there's no doubt he's avid for a hit ("I'll take a Top 50 record, even something in the eighties," he jokes, sort of). He's convinced of the continuing vitality of the music he and Jan Berry helped pioneer, citing California harmony influences in the Carpenters, Captain & Tennille, some of Bruce Johnston's upcoming productions and many more. And, while definitely not counting on "Sidewalk Surfin'" for a comeback smash, he's got hopes.

LOS ANGELES PHONOGRAPH July 1975

JAN & DEAN

"You know they're either out surfin' or they've got a party goin'..."

By Gene Sculatti

Jan & Dean take Linda surfin' for real! No one remembers her last name, but she had other qualities that will live on forever in pop legend....

"There have been many quotes, sayings, etc. to depict a good time, such as 'more fun than a barrel of monkeys,' 'you're a barrel of laughs,' etc. Anyone who has been around Jan & Dean will not be too surprised if in the not-so-distant future someone says, 'you're more fun than a barrel of Jan and Deans,' because anyone who has been fortunate enough to come in contact with the two slapstick kids from California knows that nothing could be more fun than Jan and Dean, except a barrel of them."

In her short-lived career as a liner notes writer, Shelley Fabares said it for Jan & Dean and for a lot of people. She and her husband both loved Jan & Dean and with good reason. The two slapstick kids were a barrel of laughs. And, if momentary lapses of activity have marred their career in recent years, there's plenty of reasons to count them in in '74.

While a barrel of false starts and no-go shows have thwarted many surf pioneers of late (whatever became of the Sunrays or the Surfaris after their one-shot professional return at last summer's Surfers' Stomp at the Hollywood Palladium? Whither Dick "Metal Man" Dale or the head Beach Boy?), Torrence & Berry have been working hard at having fun for over a decade.

Fans were distraught when Dean was drafted, but after two days they threw him out for saluting left-handed.

Last summer it was the Legendary Masked Surfers, Dean's brainchild by which he took existing surf music tracks and, with a little help from his friends, recorded new vocals onto them; with such luminaries as Jan, Brian Wilson, Bruce and Terry and even Leon "Call Me Fading" Russell in attendance, "Gonna Hustle You" and "Summer Means Fun" picked up national airplay and perked up all ears within range. A subsequently re-issued Jan & Dean single, "Dead Man's Curve" (all on United Artists) also graced a few turntables.

Jan himself went into the studio for the first time since his accident and came out with "Mother Earth," to be followed by a decent reworking of Huey Smith & the Clowns' "Don't You Just Know It" (both on Ode) a few months later. The two teamed up as well to perform at the Surfers' Stomp as well as guest on a number of TV talk shows.

Jan learns to walk with crutches on railroad tracks at L.A.'s Watts Towers, which wacky Dean later climbs.

Not until this summer, however, did it all come together. The long overdue double Jan & Dean anthology is here, Dean is involved with more LMS projects (and the rejuvenation of the California saga with Bruce Johnston and Terry Melcher, if the Jan & Dean set kicks off the hoped-for bonanza)—and Jan has gone and produced what may be the sharpest surf record in ages.

"Tinsel Town" (Ode) is a delightful summer song (composed by Jan with hotrod poet Roger Christian and Joan Jacobs); combining a strong melody with brisk harmonies, Jan sings a welcome to Hollywood for all contemplating the trip. It's Scott McKenzie revisited and sounds like the most convincing blend of classic California style and contemporary pop substance.

Together again, at the 1973 Surfer Stomp. Jan clutches his backstage pass—they don't get many, anymore.

Meanwhile, the duo are well represented by *Hang Ten*, the double shot of surf 'n' drag tunes from the vault. A priceless collection, as they say, it delivers the goods along the lines of "Little Old Lady From Pasadena," the twin cities of Surf and Drag, "Ride the Wild Surf" and many others. Extra goodies include the late period "Vegetables," "Honolulu Lulu," the unexpurgated "Gonna Hustle You" and the all new "Sunshine Music."

"Sunshine Music" opens up the latest chapter in the Dean Torrence story. Originally the track came Dean's way as part of a demo from the San Francisco area group, Pappa Do Ron, a real live, working band whose repertoire consists largely of West Coast hits. Dean cut additional vocals onto "Sunshine Music" and felt strong enough about the cut to include it in the anthology.

After setbacks, foldups, bad luck and a story in Phonograph Record, the two slapstick kids are still in the swim. As Shelley Fabares well knew, both are nuts about cars and surfing, and when their busy schedule permits, you'll find 'em out there zoomin'—on land or sea.

In his characteristic, barrel of monkeys manner, Dean recently left me with a meaningful message. "The message is, please support the double album. If it happens, then we'll be able to get more Legendary Masked Surfers and California stuff out. If you'll pardon me now, I have to get back to zoomin'." Wotta barrel of laughs, that Dean.

PEOPLE August 25, 1997

WHERE ARE THEY NOW?

▲ To learn a song, Berry (at home in Brentwood, Calif.) says, "I practice all the time, one line at a time, over and over."

SURF CITY SURVIVOR

Thirty-one years after a horrific car wreck, Jan Berry cuts a solo CD

ONCE THE DAREDEVIL HALF OF '60s surf-rock duo Jan & Dean—the beach-blond pair behind the classics "Surf City" and "The Little Old Lady from Pasadena"—Jan Berry was enjoying a tranquil family holiday last June in St. Catharines, Ont., when he lost his balance walking up his mother-in-law's drive. Unable to right himself, he toppled to the slate pavement. "He went into convulsions," recalls his wife, Gertie Filip, who ran to help. "His eyes started turning back into his head, his face was red. I just held his head and kept saying his name. I was so scared."

Berry, 56, recovered. He always does. But the most mundane tasks have presented constant challenges to Berry and his broken body since April 12, 1966. That morning, rushing to a business meeting, the singer and second-year medical student swerved into the left lane of a curved stretch of Whittier Drive in Beverly Hills and plowed his silver '65 Corvette Stingray into the back of a gardener's truck

▲ "He can write music," says Dean Torrence (right, circa 1960) of Berry. "Yet he'll have to ask you how to spell the words."

Photographs by Ann Summa

WHERE ARE THEY NOW?

parked at the curb. His head split open, paramedics thought he was dead until he stirred with a faint breath.

Though his right side is paralyzed and he suffers from brain damage that makes it difficult for him to translate his thoughts into speech, Berry has slowly, tenaciously rebuilt his life. Now, having battled physical disabilities and bouts of depression, he has marshaled surprisingly good spirits and his enduring musical instincts to produce his first solo album, *Second Wave,* a collection of reworked Jan & Dean classics and new material. "For him to pick up a pencil," marvels his producer Rob Kuropatwa, "and be able to score melody, chords, key signatures and lyrics, takes an excruciatingly long time. He did it all himself."

Making a cup of coffee, let alone a record, is a major challenge for the musician. "I get flustered," he says. Ask him a question, and his response may not make sense. Or come an hour later. "I'm kind of in the dark a lot," says Filip. Only when a tune pops into his head is there a hint that he's a founding father of the California surf sound. He can still capture a melody, on pitch and in rhythm, and, for good measure, toss in a few "bomps" and "um-wa-wawas."

Sadly, Berry comes from a family well acquainted with suffering. His parents, William, 87, a retired electrical engineer, and Clara, 77, a homemaker, raised 10 kids, three of whom died young (Carol drowned at age 2 in the family pool; Bruce died at 22 in 1972 from a drug overdose; and Steven, then 36, succumbed to AIDS in 1995). Jan fell out of a moving car at 2, then nearly lost a leg when he jumped off a speeding train while filming a Jan & Dean flick in 1965.

Growing up in L.A., Berry was a hell-raiser who was expelled several times from school and liked to pick fights with strangers. "And he gave great parties up in Bel Air at his dad's house," says actor Ryan O'Neal, a former schoolmate. "He was deejay." Always in love with music, Berry had his first hit in 1958 with "Jennie Lee," a pre-Dean Torrence effort first recorded for fun in his parents' garage. Teaming up with Dean, Berry helped shape the California sound with 1963's "Surf City," a No. 1 tune he cowrote with Beach Boy Brian Wilson. Jan & Dean had five more gold singles before the crash, which put Jan in a coma for a month and a half. "Doctors said he would be a vegetable," says Clara. "Well, he proved them wrong."

Nothing came easily, though. "I was a baby all over again," Berry says. Still he was determined to make music, and in 1978—given a chance to open for their old friends the Beach Boys—he and Dean reunited. Their tours are brief, but Berry always looks forward to getting onstage. "Jan would probably like to work more, but he's the only one," jokes Torrence, 57, who runs a graphic-arts business in Huntington Beach, Calif.

It was on tour in 1990 that a warm new light was shed on his life. He met Filip when she was a waitress in Ontario ("I put extra butter on his baked potato," she says). At their wedding a year later, onstage in the middle of a concert at the Stardust casino in Las Vegas, he serenaded her with "Chapel of Love" and answered the priest with a vigorous "Yes, sir!" Caring for Berry is a challenge, but Filip is as proud of his comeback as he is. "I can't believe how many people come up to me and say, 'I have a niece, I have a brother [who is handicapped],'" says Filip, "and they look up to Jan in awe."

■ KYLE SMITH
■ JEANNE GORDON *in Los Angeles*

▲ After the devastating accident in 1966, "I had tears in my brain," says Berry.

▼ Onstage, Jan (left, with Dean in 1979) is "extremely happy," says wife Filip.

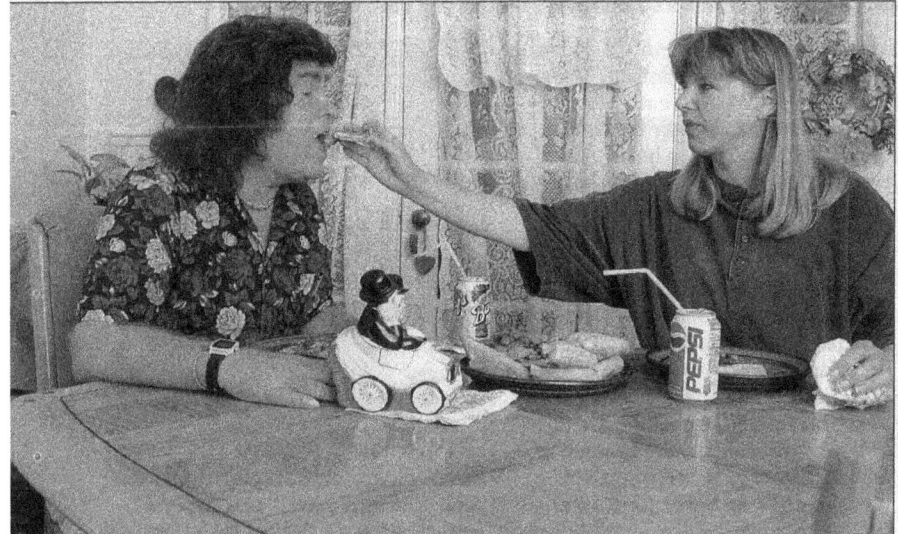

▲ Filip (feeding Jan in the kitchen) "watches out for him," says his mother, Clara.

Another Ride With DEAN TORRENCE

By CHARLES LUCAS

Dean Torrence rarely boasts. He hardly acknowledges the songs that Jan Berry and he made popular. Yet for two decades, teenagers have been smiling and tapping their feet whenever they hear a Jan and Dean (J & D) song on the radio.

Recently, a program called "The Roots of Rock and Roll" was televised. It featured most of rock's major artists, including J & D. Before the synopsis on their career began, Dean smirked briefly in front of the camera and said, "Our songs had heavy messages." Then he rolled his eyes and creased the smirk again.

Although J & D had replaced performers like Neil Sedaka, Fabian, and the Everly Brothers as top artists, Torrence appeared self-abnegating about his and Berry's accomplishments.

Jan Berry and Dean O. Torrence have crooned, cruised and surfed through rock 'n roll for twenty-three years. They met at West Los Angeles University High School in the mid-1950's. In 1958, they recorded their first hit, "Jennie Lee." Since then, the duo has sold more than ten million discs. Billboard Magazine has listed a total of eleven J & D singles in its weekly top twenty: between '63 and '64 that happened seven times.

SURF CITY
Jan and Dean

Jan and Dean's "Surf City" peaked at #1 nationally in July, 1963. The durability of their songs appeal is demonstrated by the fact that a dusted-off "Deadman's Curve" notched the fifth slot in a regional California all-time countdown less than five years ago.

Their songs' lyrics concentrate on surfing, racing cars and, for laughs, little old ladies from Pasadena. The melodies surge forward with driving rhythms overlapped by Dean's falsetto.

Rather than boast about Jan and Dean, Torrence defends. On the liner notes to the 1974 compilation album, <u>Gotta</u> <u>Take</u> <u>That</u> <u>One</u> <u>Last Ride</u>, he wrote, "Reviewers: No negative reviews please! These recordings are for fun and dancing only and not for the purpose of competing musically or artistically with any other artist's recordings."

Looking back, Dean remembers writing that and says he probably should not have. "Come to think of it, I did make a mistake," he recalls. "Once I took a logic course at USC, and the professor said that if you use a double negative, you're not saying anything." He does get the message across nevertheless.

Torrence must have been listening when gutiar great Jimi Hendrix sang "Third Stone from the Sun," renowned for the lyric, "May you never hear surf music again." He may have already accepted that J & D's type of music had little merit.

In 1966, before Berry's critical car accident, the duo was taping numbers for an album. During one of the between-song raps, Jan said, "We want to record 'Michelle' again because the engineer pressed erase instead of record." Dean interrupted, "...which is actually better on some of our stuff."

At this point in their careers, Jan and Dean considered music only one facet of their entertaining facade. Stand-up comedy and acting took up other portions. The comedy option offered them an opportunity to crack jokes, and Dean did not hesitate to joke about himself and his partner.

If Berry had not suffered paralysis and brain damage in his April, 1966 car accident, Screen Gems would have televised Jan and Dean, not the then unheard-of Monkees, as the stars of a weekly show. The production company planned to utilize J & D music and the "patter" routine the duo had developed on stage. The Beatles and the Dave Clark Five had done it in the movies, and J & D could have done it on television.

Jan produced J & D dialogues on various albums, using his talent to blend laughs and lyrics. (Berry had produced all of the duo's material since 1959, but he did not get credit until 1963 on Jan and Dean Take Linda Surfin'.)

Jan and Dean introduced contemporary rock to musical tracks overdubbed with marching bands, humans hawking and belching, cars crashing and bombs exploding. The Beatles released the unconventionally produced "I Am the Walrus" after J & D had used similar techniques on the original Fillet of Soul album.

JAN & DEAN'S GOLDEN HITS

Berry and Torrence were also among the first to break the standard of wearing suits and ties on stage. Torrence says, "We wore clothes like the people in the audience did. Fabian and other guys like him probably didn't actually want to get dressed up so they could sing. It didn't make sense."

Regardless of what J & D accomplished during their rock 'n roll years, Dean refers to the duo as clones of another surfing-racing group, the Beach Boys, rather than as innovative entertainers.

"Jan and Dean, the Beach Boys, and Bruce Johnston (composer of "I Write the Songs" and former Beach Boy) are like family," says the blonde Torrence. Brian Wilson wrote or co-wrote the majority of J & D's surf and car racing hits; Brian sings lead on J & D's smash, "Surf City;" and the Beach Boys recorded the instrumental tracks on some J & D albums.

Returning the favors, Dean sang lead on "Barbara Ann" - the Beach Boys fourth largest selling single - after suggesting that they record it for the Party album. He also sang on other Beach Boy cuts, including "Fun, Fun, Fun" and "Sloop John B." In the early seventies, the Beach Boys asked Dean to tour with them as a vocalist, but business and personal complications forced him to refuse.

After Jan Berry's tragic automobile accident in 1966, managers, distributors and friends wanted Dean to continue the duo. Accepting the responsibility, Torrence directed Jan and Dean's affairs for the first time. In October, 1966, he formed J&D Records.

"Before it was Jan's way or no way at all," Dean says. "Now things changed. I was in charge and proceeded to do everything that had to be done for the LP- I wrote, produced, sang and designed it."

This last Jan and Dean album of "new" material was titled Save for a Rainy Day. Though Billboard reviewed the album favorably, the record flopped commercially. J & D Records was unable to distribute and promote the LP nationally, and a major distribution deal with Columbia Records fell through.

Interestingly, writing credits on Rainy Day go to a Nat Ormsby, who happens to be Dean's mother. Legal technicalities and publication rights prevented him from using his own name. Earlier, Dean had helped write some J & D songs for which he had never received credit. He says, "I thought that the hit was more important than who wrote it. I wrote as much of 'Surf City' as Jan did, but I didn't get upset when he didn't put my name on the label as a writer. It'll all come out in the wash anyway."

After Rainy Day bombed, Torrence, a graduate of USC's School of Architecture, formed Kittyhawk Graphics. The company specialized in designing record album covers. Dean curtailed his musical involvement to devote his creative energy to his art work. In the early seventies, Torrence won a Grammy Award for designing the Air Pollution album jacket.

After an eleven year hiatus from the stage, Jan and Dean reunited for a concert tour with the Beach Boys in 1977. Prior to that, Jan had sung occasionally with the group, Aloha. Dean had sung with J & D clones, Papa Do Ron Ron. He says, "We did things like Disneyland and Magic Mountain shows. I'd come out after the guys did 'Surf City' to sing 'Help Me Rhonda.' I don't like Jan and Dean songs as well as I do Beach Boy stuff."

Torrence does not explain why he thinks so little of Jan and Dean efforts, but he does explain his dissatisfaction with record companies' sales and promotion departments. "'Baby Talk' (J & D's 1959 hit single) scaled to #1 on the west coast, but no one heard of it on the east coast," he says. "Jan and I went to Philadelphia to see Dick Clark with countdowns from California showing that 'Baby Talk' was a hit. He okayed it for airplay, but by this time it had passed its peak in L.A. The same type of thing happened with 'The Little Old Lady from Pasadena' six years later. Our stuff wasn't promoted nationally so that everyone knew about it simultaneously."

He continues, "If we had the guys who promoted Peter Frampton's live LP, which was trash, a couple of years ago, Jan and Dean would have had more number one hits. And I have also had trouble with United Artists/Liberty on royalties and album repackagings."

Torrence points out, "I didn't like the way they tried to cash-in on Jan's accident with the release of Jan & Dean's Golden Hits Volume Three. There were none of our hits on it - just covers and 'Batman,' a so-so spoof of the TV show.

By faulting record companies (whether or not justifiably), by attributing Jan and Dean's success to Brian Wilson, and by satirizing and making light of J & D records, Torrence takes the wind out of any critic's sails. He beats them to the punch.

A critic who read Torrence's liner notes to Gotta Take That One Last Ride could hardly fault Jan and Dean after Torrence had already done that for him. A writer's ego would not have stood the redundancy of saying what Dean Torrence had already said.

If Dean accepts that J & D songs encourage more teenagers to smile than someone like Jimi Hendrix's do, and that no one can judge the sublimity of lyrics anyway, then he may feel encouraged taking listeners to the beach or dragstrip again. The brightly lighted up faces of fans should reassure him of his worth.

(The above article was constructed from a series of conversations between Dean Torrence and the author in the late seventies.)
(Thanks to George Denham for additional information.)

RIDING THE TOP TWENTY WITH JAN AND DEAN   (Chart Action)

Year	Song	#
1958	Jenny Lee	#3
1959	Baby Talk	7
1963	Surf City	1
	Honolulu Lulu	9
	Drag City	10
1964	Deadman's Curve	5
	Little Old Lady from Pasadena	3
	Ride the Wild Surf	14
	Sidewalk Surfin'	20
1965	I Found a Girl	20
1966	Popsicle	18

RIDE THE WILD SURF

DEAD MAN'S CURVE / THE NEW GIRL IN SCHOOL

MIKE & DEAN PROMO PIC

MIKE & DEAN ROCK & ROLL CITY

RADIO SHACK AD WITH MIKE & DEAN

Now! Make High-Quality Cassette Copies in Half the Time with Radio Shack's Dual-Cassette Deck

High-Speed Dubbing. The exciting new Realistic® SCT-28 duplicates your tapes at twice the normal recording speed. You get professional sounding copies and you save time, too—no second deck or patch cords required.

Two Superb Decks in One. Deck-1 is designed for playback only, and features a special narrow-gap tape head. Deck-2 has full record/play capability and a wide-gap head for superior recording results. In fact, using Radio Shack's Supertape® Metal, the frequency response is an amazing 30-19,000 Hz. And both decks feature soft-touch controls for smooth, easy operation.

Continuous-Play Function. The SCT-28 can be set to automatically play two cassettes in sequence for up to two hours of uninterrupted music.

Auto-Search Music System. Deck-1 has ASMS to help you locate your favorite selections quickly. Each time you press the button the SCT-28 finds and plays the next or previous song automatically!

Features for Great-Sounding Copies. You get Dolby*B noise reduction for expanded dynamic range and dramatically lowered tape hiss. Selectors for noise-free normal, CrO_2/high-bias and metal cassettes and a fine-bias control. Two-color, five-step LED peak meters to indicate the signal level. And a normal-speed button so you can listen as you dub. Plus, mike and line inputs let you use the SCT-28 like a regular deck.

Come in for a hands-on demonstration today and discover high-speed dubbing for yourself. Only $339.95 at Radio Shack.

Here's Mike Love of the Beach Boys and Dean Torrence of Jan and Dean

"Dean uses the SCT-28 to make copies of my songs, so he can learn to sing."

Radio Shack
A DIVISION OF TANDY CORPORATION

Catch Mike and Dean's New Recording, "Rock'n'Roll City" Only $4.99 on Dolbyized* Cassettes—Exclusively at Radio Shack

Retail price may vary at individual stores and dealers.
★ TM Dolby Laboratories Licensing Corp.

# Jan & Dean:
The Sultans of Surf's Story of Survival

by Tom Lounges

If there is one thing the early '60s will surely be noted for aside from the British Invasion, it will be the hysteria of the "beach boom." It was an era of music that had its dawn in the rockabilly aftermath of the late '50s but one which didn't reach full force until the year 1960.

The beach syndrome was one of eternal youthfulness—an art form that reflected the innocence of falling in love and souping up deuce coupes for the strip. It had many heroes like Dick Dale & the Deltones, the Surfaris, the Rumblers, the Astronauts, the Marketts, and of course the immortal teen angels—Frankie Avalon and Annette Funicello. But of them all, the most prominent and enduring of the beach acts were the Beach Boys and Jan & Dean. These two acts lasted not only through the British Invasion, but have managed to transcend through the '70s and thus far into the '80s, as well. Such is not an easy feat when the music a group performs is all but extinct in the hearts and minds of the general public.

Of those two acts, the Beach Boys have received the most notoriety, due to consistent touring and recording. However, Jan & Dean were of equal importance in the creation of the surf sound. The story of the singing duo is both comical and tragic. The following is from a recent interview with Dean Torrence and Jan Berry.

Tom Lounges: When did Jan & Dean first get together?
Jan Berry: We went to the same high school together and got to be friends. We were on the football team together and used to sing doo-wop stuff while clowning around in the shower room.
Dean Torrence: We started a band as a way to meet chicks. The band was called the Barons, and boy did we stink. You couldn't even say we were a garage band, because we didn't even have a garage to practice in. We would sing in the washrooms and shower room because it had great echo. So I guess you could say we began (laughing) as a men's room band.
TL: Do you remember the first song you ever sang in public?
DT: Boy, do I! It was the old Silhouettes' tune "Get A Job," and man was I ever scared.
TL: How did you first get into the musical field? Had you played an instrument as a child?
DT: No, we were really more interested in vocals and harmonies. It seems that nowadays young people tend to pick up an instrument first; the guitar players and keyboard players are the stars these days. When we were starting out there weren't too many stars that were instrumentalists; the big hits were all by vocal groups. That was the era of doo-wop music and there was a

GOLDMINE April 1982 and ROCK n ROLL CITY POSTER

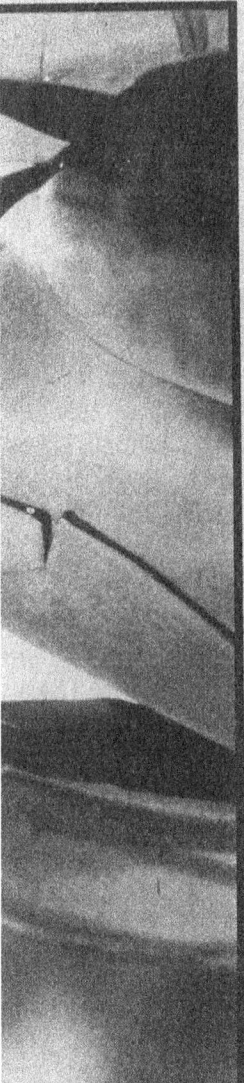

Courtesy of Peter Kanze

groups. That was the era of doo-wop music and there was a minimum of instruments present on any of the hit records at that time.

TL: I understand that Herb Alpert aided you greatly in the early days of your career. Enlighten us on his involvement.

JB: One of our early hits was "Baby Talk," and it was on the Dore record label which was owned by Herbie Alpert and Lou Adler. Herbie produced that record and helped us on some other ones, but we eventually did more ourselves.

DT: Herbie evolved into his own situation. He was a jazz musician per se and that is what interested him. After a while he pursued those interests. We worked together rather closely for maybe two or three years and then Herbie went his own direction. Lou stayed with us basically throughout our whole career.

TL: Lou Adler did a lot of work with the Mamas and the Papas. Was he still helping you guys out at that time?

DT: Yeah, he was working with both of us and right about that time Jan had his accident. (Berry was in a crippling auto crash in 1966.) So from then on Lou spent most of his time with the Mamas and the Papas and Spirit and a few others.

TL: How did you first get together with Adler? Did he approach you?

DT: Jan had met Lou through doing concerts with Arnie Ginsberg, who was Jan's singing partner before he and I got together. They had a record out at the time called "Jenny Lee" and they were doing some concerts with Sam Cooke. Lou and Herbie were involved with Sam Cooke at that time. So when it came time for us to look for someone to help manage and produce our records, Jan gave Lou a call because he had always been impressed by him.

TL: How did you tie in with Jan, and what happened to Arnie?

DT: Arnie just got tired of the whole thing. He just wasn't cut out for the whole thing. He did "Jenny Lee" and two other singles on the Arwin label called "Gas Money" and "I Love Linda," and after that he got tired and split. He's in the Navy now, he's a career man.

JB: Arnie only sang on the single recording of "Jenny Lee." The song was included on our second album I believe, but that version of the song had Dean singing.

TL: There has been a lot of interweaving between yourselves and the Beach Boys. Who was around first?

DT: We had known them, but we were doing records first. Their first record was in 1962 and our first record was in 1958, so that speaks for itself.

TL: Brian Wilson gave you the song "Surf City," is that correct?

DT: Well . . . yes and no. Brian had it partially finished and to be truthful, I think he was tired of playing around with the song. He gave it to us when it was about half done; the melody and the title were there and a few of the lyrics. Brian was always writing and he had tunes upon tunes upon tunes lying around. His publishing company was called Sea of Tunes for obvious reasons. He was tickled pink that someone else wanted to record one of his songs, because in those days people weren't exactly beating a path to his door.

TL: Speaking of collaborations with the Beach Boys, you (Dean) sang the lead on "Barbara Ann" for them. What brought that about?

DT: Originally the Beach Boys were going to record a party album, with a bunch of their musical friends. Because we were on different recording labels I was not credited with singing on the record because legally we couldn't swing the whole thing. But the whole thing was a lot of fun.

TL: Jan, you wrote most of the songs. Did you have a formula for writing? Where did the subject matter for the songs come from?

JB: I usually wrote the lyrics first and then built a melody around the syllables. "Little Old Lady From Pasadena" was inspired by a television ad we saw about this little old lady who drove around in a souped-up Dodge. "Jenny Lee" was written about a stripper that a friend of ours in high school had developed a crush on. "Honolulu Lulu" was inspired by an old Laurel and Hardy movie I saw where the two were supposed to have been at a business convention and instead went to Hawaii on a vacation without their wives. The wives saw them on television in Hawaii somehow dancing with a Hawaiian girl who I called Honolulu Lulu. Many of the songs have similar stories.

DT: The song "New Girl In School" was originally called "When Summer Comes, Gonna Hustle You." It was the same melody and the same chorus of "Papa do ron de ron," but the lyrics were much more suggestive. We wrote it at the same time we wrote "Surf City," but had to re-write it because it was called "dirty" and "suggestive." What's funny, is the lyrics groups can get away with nowadays. So we canned the song, rewrote the lyrics later and released it as "New Girl In School."

TL: Of all the songs you've done, which is your favorite?

DT: That's an interesting question because there are different songs for different reasons. Recording wise, we both agree that "Dead Man's Curve" is our favorite because it has all the elements. It had a great melody, it was satirical, we loved all the vocal parts, it's got a harp and strings in it, and Jan arranged some super horn parts . . . it was just a great song to record.

RADIO SHACK AD WITH MIKE & DEAN

Radio Shack's Mach One® Speaker Sale

3-WAY SYSTEM WITH POWERFUL 15" WOOFER NOW $100 OFF!

Our Mach One Liquid-Cooled Speaker System is a bass lover's dream. You can actually <u>feel</u> the punch of its powerful 15" woofer and massive 2-pound magnet.

We match our rock-solid bass with exceptional clarity in the mid and high frequencies—made possible by sectoral mid-range and heavy-duty tweeter horns. A ferrofluid cooling system helps control voice coil travel for a lifelike response and increases the system's power handling capacity to 160 watts.

And with its genuine oiled walnut veneer finish, you've got a 3-way speaker system that looks and sounds like a million.

Radio Shack®
A DIVISION OF TANDY CORPORATION

Take it from Mike Love of the Beach Boys and Dean Torrence of Jan and Dean. Dean says . . .

"I'm putting a pair in my studio. Mike wants a pair for his Bentley."

On sale at 42% off now through June 26. So don't delay, run down to your nearest Radio Shack, and experience the excitement of bass you can actually <u>feel</u>.

Mach One Speaker System
Reg. 239.95 **Sale 139⁹⁵** each

Catch Mike and Dean's New Recording, "Rock'n'Roll City", Only $4.99 on Dolbyized* Cassettes—Exclusively at Radio Shack

* TM Dolby Laboratories Licensing Corp.   Prices may vary from store to store.

MIKE AND DEAN TOUR PROMO

"BE TRUE TO YOUR BUD"

MIKE LOVE
DEAN TORRENCE
GARY GRIFFIN
© IRVING/ALMO MUSIC

WHEN SOME LOUD BRAGGART
TRIES TO PUT ME DOWN
AND SAYS HIS BEER IS GREAT
I TELL HIM RIGHT AWAY
NOW WHAT'S THE MATTER BUDDY
AIN'T YOU TASTED MY BEER
IT'S NUMBER ONE IN THE STATE

('N PROBABLY THE WORLD)

    SO BE TRUE TO YOUR BUD
    JUST LIKE YOU WOULD
    TO YOUR GIRL OR GUY
    BE TRUE TO YOUR BUD, NOW
    LET YOUR COLORS FLY
    BE TRUE TO OUR BUD

THE KING OF BEERS
IS WHAT THE GANG ALL CHEERS FOR
WHEN WE'RE OUT HAVIN' FUN
LET'S HAVE ANOTHER ONE
THE OTHERS TAKE THE BACK SEAT
TO THE NATIONAL CHAMP
BUDWEISERS NUMBER ONE

    SO BE TRUE TO YOUR BUD
    JUST LIKE YOU WOULD
    TO YOUR GIRL OR GUY
    BE TRUE TO YOUR BUD, NOW
    LET YOUR COLORS FLY
    BE TRUE TO OUR BUD

WE'LL ALL BE WORKIN ON A
SIX PAC TONIGHT
BECAUSE OUR TEAMS GONNA WIN
WE'RE GONNA ROUT 'EM
AND THE ONLY WAY TO PARTY
IS TO DRINK THE RIGHT BREW
THAT'S WHY BUDWEISERS IN
THAT'S WHY WE'RE SHOUTIN'

    SO BE TRUE TO YOUR BUD
    JUST LIKE YOU WOULD
    TO YOUR GIRL OR GUY
    BE TRUE TO YOUR BUD, NOW
    LET YOUR COLORS FLY
    BE TRUE TO OUR BUD

RAH, RAH, RAH BE TRUE TO YOUR BUD
RAH, RAH, RAH BE TRUE TO YOUR BUD
RAH, RAH, RAH BE TRUE TO YOUR BUD
RAH, RAH, RAH BE TRUE TO YOUR BUD
(RE-PEAT)

MIKE AND DEAN TOUR PROMO

University of Budweiser
STARTING LINEUP

Name:	Pos.	Hgt.	Wgt.	Class:	High School:
MIKE LOVE	LS	6-1	165	Sr.	Dorsy High, Los Angeles
DEAN TORRENCE	LS/RG	6-1	175	Sr.	University High, Los Angeles
ADRIAN BAKER	LG/RG	5-11	155	Fr.	Liverpool High, Liverpool
CHRIS FARMER	B	6-0	188	Fr.	Livonia Stevenson High, Livonia
JEFF FOSKETT	LG	6-0	190	So.	Willow Glenn High, San Jose
GARY GRIFFIN	KB	5-10	145	Jr.	Oak Hills High, Cincinnati
MIKE KOWALSKI	D	6-0	170	Jr.	Hollywood High, Hollywood

Coaching Staff:

TOM THOMAS

GEORGE BLYSTONE

WINSTON SIMONE

RICHARD CASARES

SUSAN VOGELBERGER

Mike Love, University of Bud's talented two year letterman has a very quick release and also has great touch. Mike has that natural born ability of having great field vision. He can spot a potential pass receiver even in a crowd and no matter their size. Some of his pass completions are legendary. Among Mike's sports heroes are Terry Bradshaw, quarterback for the Steelers, "I like his hairstyling" says Mike. Joe Namath, former quarterback for the New York Jets is also one of Mike's favorites. "I appreciate a family man like Joe."

Mike also kicks all the extra points and he truely enjoys his all purpose roll. "Moving through the field, heading towards that goal then finally scoring is indeed a real thrill but then to cap it all off by kicking one thru the uprights is the ultimate for me. Then when the last ones been kicked thru the uprights there's nothing I like to do better than to have an ice cold Bud and reminisce the conquest with my buddies.

Dean Torrence, University of Bud's scrappy defensive captain covers the field from sideline to sideline from his roverback position aggressively searching out potential pass receivers. His aggressiveness has led to quite a few pass interference calls. Critics have accused him of even being to defensive. "Hey, the way I look at it is that I have been doing my job for a very long time now and I have enjoyed every minute of playing time that I have been lucky enough to be involved in. Then when I hear critics say once again, "Well that's definitely their last season", I wonder when they will finally understand that our teams philosophy is totally built on the "spirt of fun" and this spirit will always endure. Sure, maybe some of the present team members may retire someday then ultimately ending up in the Hall of Fame, but new players with the same spirit will be there to take their places. My main goal every year is to make it to at least one more Spring break."

When asked if there were any changes in the game he would like to see. Dean answers with a twinkle in his eye, "Yeah bring back tear-away jerseys."

MIKE AND DEAN TOUR PROMO

BUDWEISER
PRESENTS

MIKE AND DEAN TOUR PROMO

NEW "Rock'n'Roll City" Dolby* Cassette

Only **4.99**

Starring Mike Love Of The Beach Boys And Dean Torrence Of Jan and Dean

Exclusive! 12 new rock'n'roll recordings. With special guests: The Beach Boys, Paul Revere & the Raiders, the Association and more! **51-3009 .. 4.99**

*TM Dolby Laboratories Licensing Corp.

MIKE AND DEAN TOUR PROMO

SPRING BREAK 1983

SPRING BREAK 1983

SPRING BREAK 1983

SPRING BREAK 1983

Mike & Dean

SOLD OUT

Sunshine Flockers Meet West Coast Rockers in a Beach–Music Blow–out!

After all, what good is the beach without the sounds of surf? And keeping surf music alive and kicking, are two legends of the sound—Mike Love of the Beach Boys, and Dean Torrence of Jan and Dean. Together with the Endless Summer Beach Band, Mike and Dean have been leaving Spring Break student audiences breathless and shouting for more. SRO in Daytona Beach. Twenty thousand fans in South Padre Island. Swaying and stomping to *"Surfin' U.S.A.", "Ba-Ba-Barbara Ann",* and *"Little Old Lady From Pasadena."*

"I can't wait to be back," exclaims Mike Love, "I'm really just a life-long student." Love has been the leader of the Beach Boys since the groups inception in the early 60's. Not only the band's leading singer and spokesman, he has also contributed to the group's popularity—by writing or co-writing such hits as *"Good Vibrations", "Fun, Fun, Fun", "California Girls", "Do it Again".*

Additionally, Mike has recorded his own solo album, "Looking Back With Love," performs on tour with the Endless Summer Beach Band, and still plays an important role in the present Beach Boys.

Dean Torrence burst upon the music scene in 1958 teamed with Jan Berry. Better known as *Jan and Dean*, they were early collaborators with the *Beach Boys*. Their careers were halted abruptly when Jan was involved in a near-fatal accident. The television movie, "Deadman's Curve" recounted the story of the duo's fame and misfortune.

Subsequently, Dean turned his attention to design and spawned Kittyhawk Graphics, specializing in music-industry merchandising. He has designed album covers for the Beach Boys, Steve Martin, Nitty Gritty Dirt Band, Nilsson, Anne Murray, Linda Ronstadt and Walter Egan.

"But I can't stop performing for the college crowd," glows Dean. So he joined forces with Mike in 1982, and Budweiser sponsored a Spring Break tour. The results were spectacular: "Everyone was in a party spirit... and the band delivered," reported the Daytona Morning Journal. The Dallas Morning News gave front-page coverage to the cheering crowd: "The perfect culmination..."

To keep warm through the winter, Mike and Dean and the band are engaging in a "Be True to Your Bud" college concert tour, again sponsored by Budweiser Beer.

Needless to say, Spring Break 1983 will find Mike & Dean, searching out those special places where the priorities are sand, sun, and fun. Delivering two hours of non-stop entertainment to aficionados (and who isn't) of the sounds of surf rock.

If you're planning a Spring Break vacation, you'll find Mike & Dean rocking through South Padre Island, Texas, on March 15 (raindate—March 16); double-teaming in Daytona Beach March 17 and the 24th; riding in with the tide in Fort Lauderdale on March 23; and taking the plunge in Destin Beach on March 31. All brought to you, FREE, by Budweiser, the King of Spring.

If you do see Mike & Dean, say, "Thanks guys," for keeping the *"Good Vibrations"* happening.

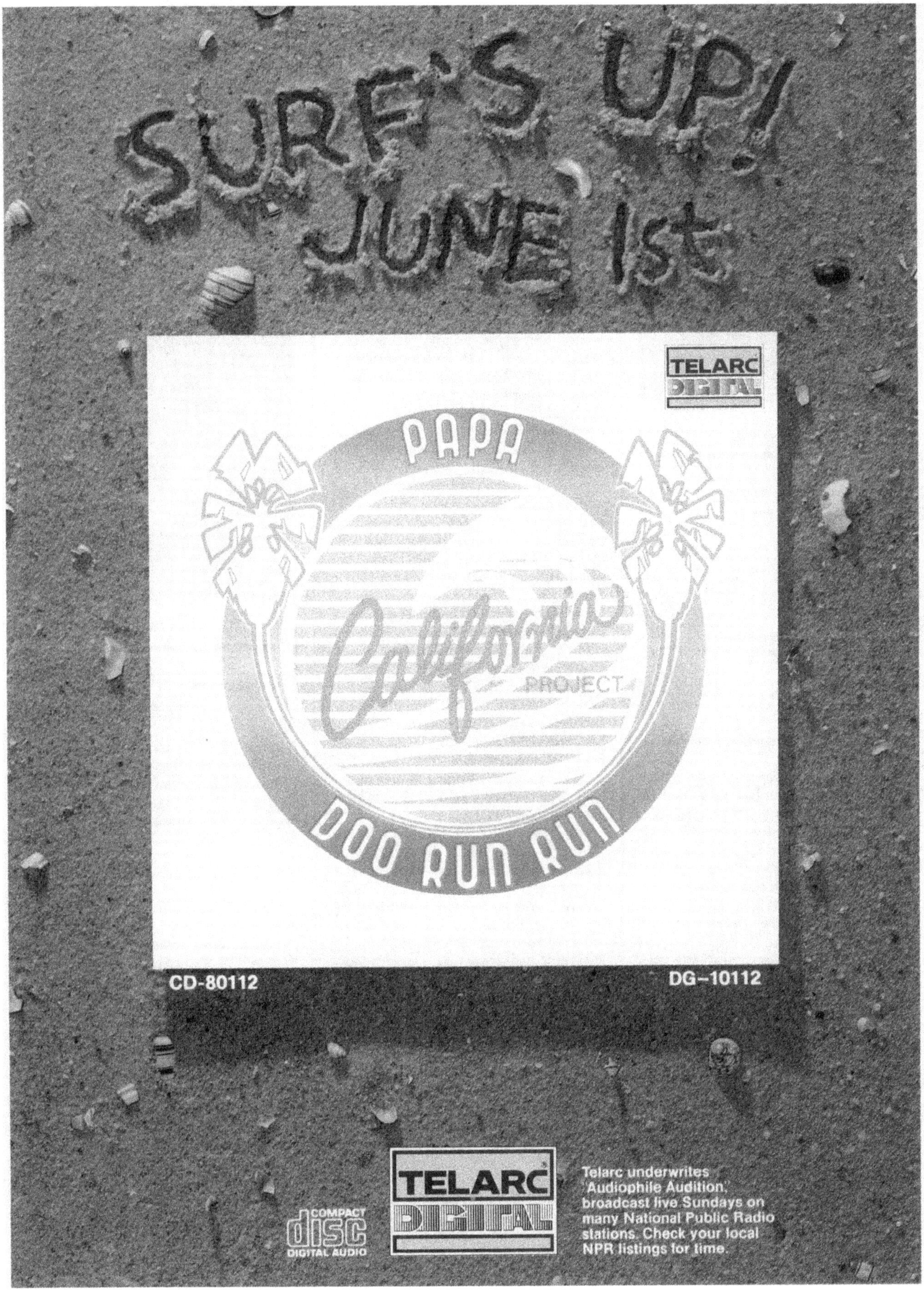
SURF'S UP!
JUNE 1st
TELARC DIGITAL
PAPA
California
PROJECT
DOO RUN RUN
CD-80112
DG–10112
COMPACT disc DIGITAL AUDIO
TELARC DIGITAL
Telarc underwrites 'Audiophile Audition,' broadcast live Sundays on many National Public Radio stations. Check your local NPR listings for time.

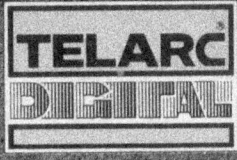

JAN & DEAN IN CONCERT

JAN & DEAN IN CONCERT

GOLDEN SUMMER AD

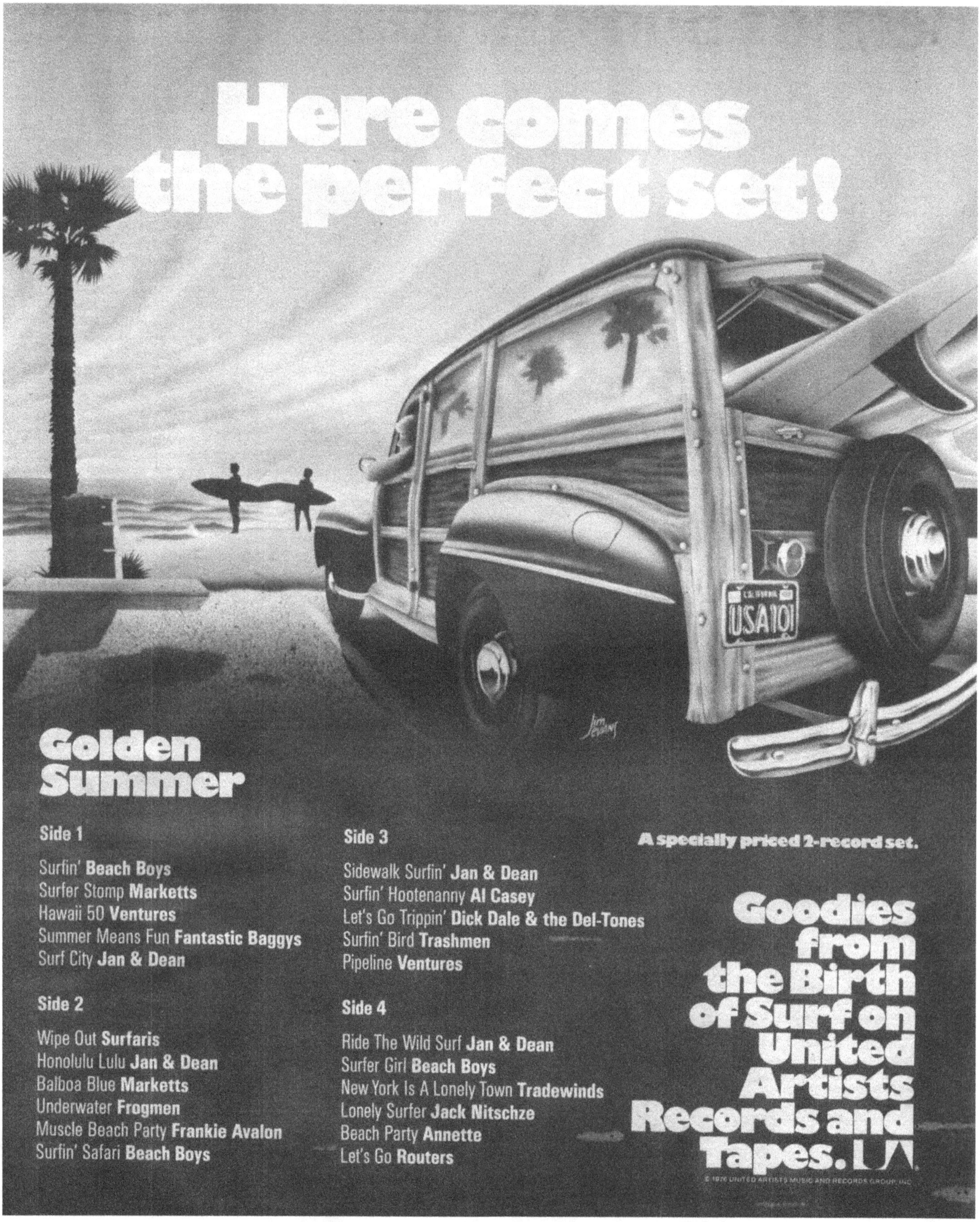

Here comes the perfect set!
USA 101
Golden Summer
Side 1
Surfin' Beach Boys
Surfer Stomp Marketts
Hawaii 50 Ventures
Summer Means Fun Fantastic Baggys
Surf City Jan & Dean
Side 2
Wipe Out Surfaris
Honolulu Lulu Jan & Dean
Balboa Blue Marketts
Underwater Frogmen
Muscle Beach Party Frankie Avalon
Surfin' Safari Beach Boys
Side 3
Sidewalk Surfin' Jan & Dean
Surfin' Hootenanny Al Casey
Let's Go Trippin' Dick Dale & the Del-Tones
Surfin' Bird Trashmen
Pipeline Ventures
Side 4
Ride The Wild Surf Jan & Dean
Surfer Girl Beach Boys
New York Is A Lonely Town Tradewinds
Lonely Surfer Jack Nitschze
Beach Party Annette
Let's Go Routers
A specially priced 2-record set.
Goodies from the Birth of Surf on United Artists Records and Tapes. UA
© 1976 UNITED ARTISTS MUSIC AND RECORDS GROUP, INC

DISCOVERIES JULY 1996

DISCOVERIES
FOR RECORD & CD COLLECTORS

JULY 1996 ISSUE 98

Jan & Dean
The Dore Years

Inside...
The Buoys
Serenaders

THOUSANDS OF RECORDS and CDs FOR SALE INSIDE!

DISCOVERIES JULY 1996

At Long Last!!
Jan & Dean
Coming Soon From Era

Jan & Dean's historic debut album is now available on compact disc.

Before Jan & Dean exploded on the surf scene, they recorded some great doo wop influenced sides for Dore Records. This new release contains Jan & Dean's entire Dore output (12 album tracks plus 6 bonus sides) and has been mastered by noted producer Bill Inglot. This Era reissue also features the original artwork and extensive liner notes by Michael "Doc Rock" Kelly who interviewed both Jan & Dean.

Experience Jan & Dean before they took Linda surfing.

- Original Dore lp sells for hundreds at collector shows
- Original artwork integrity maintained
- Extensive liner notes by Michael "Doc Rock" Kelly
- 18 tracks
- 3 chart hits
  - Baby Talk #10 (1959)
  - We Go Together #53 (1960)
  - Clementine #64 (1960)

A Great ERA For Music

1. Clementine
2. Judy
3. My Heart Sings
4. Rosie Lane
5. Oh Julie
6. Baby Talk
7. You're On My Mind
8. There's A Girl
9. Jeanette Get Your Hair Done
10. Cindy
11. Don't Fly Away
12. White Tennis Sneakers
13. We Go Together
14. Gee
15. It's Such A Good Night For Dreaming
16. Baggy Pants
17. Judy's An Angel
18. Clementine (Single Version)

Reserve Your Copy Now.
Call 1-800-328-6640 ext 418
Or visit us at:
http://www.k-tel.com

Available at Music Retailers
Coast to Coast Or Call 1-800-328-6640 ext 418

More Classic Reissues From Era

- 5001 • Aztec Two-Step
- 5002 • Evil Woman-The Best Of Crow
- 5005 • Roy Buchanan-My Babe
- 5006 • Michael Bloomfield Living in The Fast Lane
- 5010 • Upper Mississippi Shakedown The Best Of The Lamont Cranston Band
- 5011 • The Wayward Wind The Best Of Gogi Grant
- 5016 • Paul Davis-Cool Night
- 5019 • Best Of The Castells
- 5020 • The Birds And The Bees -The Best Of Jewel Akens
- 5021 • Best Of Dorsey Burnett -The Era Years
- 5025 • The Brill Building Sound
- 5027 • Marshall Tucker Band -Best Of The Capricorn Years
- 5028 • Bobby Vee & The Shadows -The Early Rockin' Years
- 5030 • John Kay & Steppenwolf-Live At 25

Member of NAIRD

Distributed in USA by K-tel International (USA), Inc.

DISCNEWS

paul petersen

Trashmen ("Surfin' Bird"). Apparently these tracks were all recorded in 1988 and finally released late last year. Despite the useless re-recording of some Trashmen staples like "Surfin' Bird" and "King of the Surf," the title track of this record is one killer rockin' song with as much a tip of the hat to rockabilly as surf music. These are all vocals, however, so don't expect any of those wild Trashmen instros.

Los Straitjackets: *Viva! Los Straitjackets* (Upstart). Another fine collection of guitar-dominated instros that doesn't blaze any new territory from their dynamic debut effort from last year. Still tight and rockin'! Highlights include the moody and whammy bar-drenched "Wrong Planet," the rockin' "Outta Gear" and the cute "Venturing Out."

In the reissue department:

One-Way Records in New York continues their somewhat ambitious surf and hot rod reissue schedule with three Jan & Dean "two-fers": *Surf City* and *Folk 'n Roll* are together on one disc, while *The Little Old Lady From Pasadena* album has been paired with *Filet of Soul*. The better release for surf music fans, though, joins Jan & Dean *Take Linda Surfin'* (with the Beach Boys playing backup on "Surfin'" and "Surfin' Safari") with *Ride The Wild Surf*. It's nice to have these albums, digitally mastered from original tapes, in their original track sequence.

Gary Usher: *Greats Volume 1* (AVI 5018). This essential Usher reissue combines two impossibly rare albums, credited to The Kickstands and The Knights, that he produced in 1964 using nearly the same group of studio musicians. Many of these musicians contributed to other, more well-known Usher projects such as The Super Stocks and The Hondells. Here, both albums – The Kickstands' *Black Boots and Bikes* and The Knights' *Hot Rod High* – are combined in their original track sequence and digitized from the original Capitol Records tapes. The detailed and historically pertinent liner notes are by noted Usher biographer Stephen McParland.

Various Artists: *Rare Surf Volume 3* (AVI 5017). Unlike the previous two amazing volumes in this series, this one features only two artists – **Johnny Barakat & The Vestells** and **Johnny Fortune**. Like the two previous volumes, this one's also a killer for surf instrumental purists. The liner notes are appropriate and well-written by surf historian Robert Dalley and the music is nothing short of incredible. Johnny Fortune's entire *Soul Surfer* album is here (taken from the original master tape which was thought to have been lost until only recently). The real magic, though, lies in the tracks (most previously unreleased) by the maniacal Johnny Barakat & The Vestells. Just listen to his take on Dick Dale's "The Wedge" for a lesson on how to play a fast tune even faster. Don't miss this. It's great stuff!!

Forthcoming:

The new **Jon & The Nightriders'** album is called *Fiberglass Rocket* and will be released nationally on Atomic Beat Records (a division of AVI) on July 23.

By the time you read this, Rhino Records' much anticipated *Cowabunga – The Surf Box* will have been in the stores for several weeks. Watch for a detailed review coming up in *Discoveries*.

Awesome.

Elvis Still On the Air

The "Elvis On the Air" program is shooting for a bigger audience – with the help of Elvis Presley Enterprises, which just officially licensed it.

The program, hosted by Steve Christopher and based out of Montgomery, AL, has been featuring Elvis tunes and arcana since the late 70s, with Christopher challenging the audience to come up with a legitimately released Elvis song that he can't play. If they do, they win a car... and they apparently haven't yet.

With help from the EPE agreement, Christopher and Creative Radio Network, a Southern California company, will be attempting to promote the show nationally in the upcoming year.

Dots On a Screen

Credit VH1 with a neat idea for its Archives series. The show features artists' appearances on TV from the pre-cable years. The first show, for example, included Janis Joplin's 1969 appearance (including an interview and performances of "To Love Somebody" and "Try (Just a Little Bit Harder)") on the "Dick Cavett Show." A second show featured Elton John in an in-studio performance for "BBC in Concert" in 1970. The show's schedule calls for episodes featuring Jimi Hendrix, John Lennon, James Taylor, Paul Simon and Sly & the Family Stone.

The PBS "Rock & Roll" miniseries won a Peabody Award, a high-culture version of an Emmy.

Folkie legend Richie Havens scored the new theme for the NBC show "Real Life."

If there's any current talk show worth watching, it's the Cartoon Network's "Space Ghost Coast to Coast." A recent show included appearances by Marshall "Duh" Staxx of weirdball heavy metalists Green Jelly (once known as Green Jello) and yodeler Wylie Gustafson interacting with the cartoon superhero.

Cyber Dots On a Screen

Pioneer Artists has released "Chuck Berry & Bo Diddley's Rock 'n Roll All-Star Jam" on laser disc. Filmed in 1985, the concert includes help from the Rolling Stones' Ron Wood, Carl Wilson of the Beach Boys, Ronnie Lane of Faces, a host of others and even John Lodge of the Moody Blues?

Graphix Zone, the company that recently released a Bob Marley CD-ROM and turned Aerosmith into a computer video game, plans to work its magic on Willie Nelson and some classic rockers. The Nelson disc promises unreleased songs, interviews with the singer-songwriter and his friends (i.e. Johnny Cash, Waylon Jennings), hundreds of photos and a compendium of his lyrics. The company is also working on a disc featuring the stories behind old hits from the Doors, Eagles, CSN&Y and such.

Graphix Zone also recently bought another interesting internet site, WILMA (Worldwide Internet Live Music Archive). It claims to have info on bookings at over 5,000 music venues and on over 1,700 artists. Its address is http://www.wilma.com.

Tori Amos' live performance at a new Virgin megastore in Manhattan May 13 was picked up for internet "broadcast" by Atlantic Records' "Digital Arena" (http://www.atlantic-records.com).

Paul Petersen, who was a kid star on the "Donna Reed Show" on TV and went on to have pop hits like "She Can't Find Her Keys" and "My Dad," appeared on the live, real-time Eliot Stein talk show on the internet May 1. Beatles expert Jim Berkenstadt (author of *Black Market Beatles: The Story of the Lost Recordings*) and Monkee member Peter Tork have also appeared on the Stein show. As with many things online, these can be retrieved to your computer. The address is http://www.audionet.com.

Blues and roots piano player Marcia Ball appeared on AOL's House of Blues Forum April 25; trumpeter (and record biz figure) Herb Alpert was on AOL April 28; old punks Bad Religion were on Prodigy April 29; would-be stadium rocker Tom Cochrane was on AOL April 30; Randy Newman was on Prodigy May 2; Latin bandleader Tito Puente was on AOL May 5; Paul Westerberg was on AOL May 6; former Pixies member Frank Black was on AOL May 6; B52 member Fred Schneider was on Prodigy May 8; DJ Casey Kasem was on AOL May 8; alt rockers Smashing Pumpkins were on AOL May 11; jam rockers the Dave Matthews Band were on AOL May 11; jazz sax player Boney James was on AOL May 13; ska band Goldfinger were on Prodigy May 14; soul legends the Isley Brothers were on AOL May 14; 80s techno popper Thomas Dolby was on CompuServe May 14; slide guitar bluesman Roy Rogers was on AOL May 16; surf guitarist Dick Dale and singer Dean Torrence were on AOL May 23; soul great Curtis Mayfield was on AOL May 24; and the current version of the Turtles were on AOL May 31.

Timed with the release of their latest record, *Electriclarryland*, the Butthole Surfers are out there in digital-land at http://www.buttholesurfers.com. Check it out for yourself and see what type of problems they're causing.

Around & About

It could be 1966 all over again. The Who, Bob Dylan and Eric Clapton are slated to headline a charity concert at London's Hyde Park June 29. The show for the Prince's Trust is expected to draw up to 150,000 people.

Former Crosby, Stills, Nash & Young drummer Dallas Taylor is suing the now non-existent band, according to media reports. He says he hasn't been paid his royalties from the band since he wrote his tell-all book, *Prisoner of Woodstock*.

The Ryman Auditorium, legendary former home of the Grand Ole Opry in Nashville, is the site for the stage show "Lost Highway – The Music & Legend of Hank Williams" this summer.

Hey, the Beach Boys know country music sells today. Presumably that's why they were booked for Nashville's Fan Faire country extravaganza, with help from Lorrie Morgan, Sawyer Brown, Ronnie Milsap and James House. Not so coincidentally,

MORE»

DISCOVERIES JULY 1996

JAN & DEAN SAVE FOR A RAINY DAY

Save For A Rainy Day
on CD & double LP!

That Rainy Day has finally arrived! A little masterpiece concocted by Dean, while his partner, Jan Berry, lay recuperating in the hospital from the automobile accident that almost cost him his life, this is the trippy project that took the legendary Los Angeles duo beyond their surf 'n' drag roots into the peppermint and dayglo world of 1967 pop. Two sets of liner notes, including an interview with Dean himself, and tons of extras make this package...too cool for words.

JAN & DEAN "Save For A Rainy Day"
All on one CD: SC 11035 • List Price: $13.98
or a 2-LP Set: LP 5022 • List Price: $15.98

Jan & Dean — Dore Doo Wop

by Michael "Doc Rock" Kelly

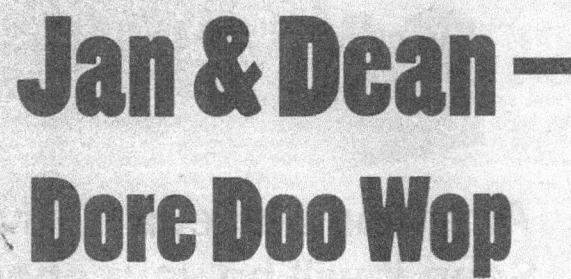

To fans of the first decade of rock 'n' roll, the names Jan & Dean are indelibly associated with Surf music. But hits like "Surf City" and "The Little Old Lady (From Pasadena)," as well as car songs including "Drag City" and "Dead Man's Curve," in reality represent only one facet of the Jan & Dean career.

Before Jan & Dean did Surf and Drag, they did Doo-Wop. Before Jan & Dean, there was Jan & Arnie. And before there was Jan & Arnie or Jan & Dean, there was Jan & Don!

Don Altfeld

Jan Berry, youthful rock 'n' roll addict, attended University High in LA in the late 50s. Don Altfeld, youthful music writer for a national teen magazine as well as for the Uni High school newspaper, also attended Uni. Puzzled by the way the "pick hit of the week" in his column seemed to change each week between the time he submitted his copy to the school paper and the time the paper hit the school corridors, Don went down to the school print shop one day to look into this matter. There he ran into a boy with printers' ink all over his hands and face. It was Jan.

Young Jan Berry was so in to music that he had been resetting the news type to reflect his own choice of hit of the week. Don forgave Jan; "From that point forward, Jan and I used to hang out in the garage daily."

The garage?

The Garage

Yes, young Jan Berry had converted his parent's garage into a makeshift recording studio. Jan's tape recorder was an Ampex reel-to-reel machine, used on the movie "The Outlaw," and given to his father Bill Berry by his employer, movie producer Howard Hughes. Jan's microphone was a specimen "borrowed" from the Uni High school auditorium.

Exactly what did Jan and Don record in that garage? Once, they recorded/"produced" a girl group singing a song called "Apollo." The group included Mary Sperling (who later became DeeDee in Dick and DeeDee of "The Mountain's High" fame) and three other girls from a school club called The Flairs.

Jan's own school club was The Barons. In the garage, the Barons recorded DJ shows, little radio programs on tape for school parties, with Jan and Don and other club members as the DJs. Over time, Jan and Don became fast and life-long friends. Don even ultimately earned composer credit on at least 30 songs that Jan & Dean recorded ("Dead Man's Curve" for one), as well as songs for other artists such as Johnny Crawford and Shelley Fabares.

Don Altfeld recalls those days with vivid and extreme fondness. "The second time I met Jan after the print shop incident was when he forged the vice principal's signature on a note saying to report to the principal's office. There was Jan waiting for me. We cut school, ended up drunk for the first time in my life; went to a drive-in movie; then down to the beach. We found a black group there singing a song called 'Stranded In The Jungle.' This was a group that was later known as the Jayhawks.

"Jan also stole an M-1 rifle from the armory of the ROTC. Jan was walking trouble. He had the FBI and the whole world looking for him. He punched a cop down at Pacific Ocean Park, an amusement park that no longer exists. Jan was trouble.

"Late at night, Jan would throw stones at my window on Montana and then he would climb in the window and work on songs. It was a devastating blow to me what happened to him, and there is no telling what he would have done had he not had the crash. He was so advanced.

"Jan even printed up stationary for our garage, calling us KJAN Radio, 'The Voice of Bel-Air.' There were a bunch of Baron Club brothers on the letterhead. Jan was the owner, I was D. Donald Adler the program director. We sent a letter to all of the record companies saying that we were a new radio station and we were breaking in records in Bel-Air, California and we would get tons of records. At one time we had about 8,000 45s."

The Barons' tapes featured largely R&B waxings, including obscure classics such as the Monotones' "Book of Love," Duane Eddy's "Movin' and Groovin'," Wee Willie Wain's "Travelin' Mood," the Teen Queens' "I Miss You," Bill Bodaford and the Rockets' "Tear Drops," the Avons' "Bonnie" and "Baby," the Clairemonts' "Angel of Romance," the Lovers "Let's Elope," the Junior Misses' "Never Never," Sugar Pie and Pee Wee's "Let's Get Together," and the Moonglows' "Soda Pop," "Sincerely," and "I Knew from the Start."

Every couple of weeks The Barons would take the surplus 45s up to a hill overlooking the Bel-Air golf course and play frisbee, going for distance and height. Somewhere up there in a little canyon there are thousands of old 45s.

"In fact, it was music that straightened Jan out," assures Don. "When I met him, he was stealing hub caps – not because he needed the money. Just for the thrill. He'd steal them, then throw them away. Girl's pocket books... He legitimized himself by stealing songs! Safer, and more rewarding!"

"Jennie Lee"

The Barons' membership included Jan, Don, Arnie Ginsberg, Dean Torrence, Wally Yagi, drummer Sandy Nelson, and Jimmy Bruderlin (later known as James Brolin). The Barons sang songs like "In the Still of the Night," "Get a Job" and "She Say."

Arnie wrote an original song for the Barons called "Jennie Lee," inspired by a local burlesque queen. The Barons sang it, Jan recorded it, and spliced the song into their DJ tapes. Finally, tired of splicing, Jan went to a real studio to have the "Jennie Lee" tape transferred to an acetate disc. There, he was "discovered" by record vet Joe Lubin, who had Jan re-record "Jennie Lee," without Dean (who was going into the Army reserves that week) and the rest of the Barons, except Arnie, who started the whole "Jennie Lee" affair. But Jan was the spark plug for the record.

Don explains Jan's fire this way. "One day when we were in Wallich's Music City, Ricky Nelson was there. I don't believe that Jan had recorded up to that point. When he saw Rick Nelson, who was great looking, and Jan was also great looking, Jan saw Ricky and said, 'If he can do it, so can I.' And that was the beginning of Jan seeing himself as a star. That was the turning point in Jan's life."

Jan & Arnie

"Jennie Lee" was released on Arwin Records by Jan & Arnie. Don Altfeld helped Jan get the song on the charts.

"'Jennie Lee' came out in Los Angeles, and Jan and I did about every kind of hype thing we could think of. We'd go into Wallich's Music City music store, where Jan would steal some, smuggling them out of under his Barons jacket. He would also hide copies around the store in other records' slots. Sometimes he would actually pay other kids to go in to the store and buy 'Jennie Lee.'"

Jan and Don also organized 40 friends to meet after school every day and call in requests on Wink Martindale's radio show. In one afternoon, "Jennie Lee" became the #1 requested, and was soon a Top 10 hit nationwide.

Two disappointing follow-ups later, the kids quit *buying* Jan & Arnie records, Arwin Records quit *releasing* Jan & Arnie records, and Arnie quit *making* Jan & Arnie records.

With Arnie gone, Jan needed a new partner. Don Altfeld, a logical choice, ruled himself out. "I couldn't sing, and I was way too shy. So, instead, in the interim between Arwin and Dore, Jan and I produced a record with a group called the Matadors called 'Jumpin' the Line' that Lou Adler placed on Liberty Records for us. It didn't go anywhere, but it was nice, we made some money."

Jan & Dean Torrence

With Arnie gone and Don incurably shy, Jan needed a new "&" man. (The act is invariably billed as "Jan &..." never "Jan **and**...") Jan chose Dean Torrence, an ex-Baron who had sung "Jennie Lee" (the song, not the record) and had now returned from the reserves during Arnie's reign. And, as Jan explains today, "I chose Dean because I liked his harmony, and I really liked his falsetto."

As Dean recalls, Jan used the subtle approach to recruit his services.

"Jan didn't say, 'Arnie is out, you are going to replace him,'" reflects Dean. "It was kind of innocent and non-committal. We'd just played some football together, and Jan said, 'Yeah, if you're not doin' anything, come by the house and I'll play you some songs that I've been working on.'

"As I drove up to his house, I went through all the scenarios of what he could mean. I thought that maybe he was asking me to come and listen to something that Jan and Arnie had done and see what my opinion of it was. He did kind of talk in there about him and me doing a song together or something, but it was so loosey-goosey that I remember being totally confused about what it was he said. But the bottom line was, he said, 'Come on up and listen to some stuff.'

"So I thought, 'What the hell? I don't have anything better to do.' So I went and did it.

"I can't exactly recall if we sat at the piano right away, or just listened to some songs. Somewhere in there, I likely said, 'Well, where is Arnie? Why aren't you doing this with him.' Or, I probably wouldn't have been quite that direct in those days. I probably said, 'Well, gee, where's Arnie?'

"Jan said, 'Arnie's more interested in surfing than working on songs.'

MORE»

ABOVE: Jan (right) & Arnie (left)

DISCOVERIES JULY 1996

Ironic, *surfing*, this Jewish guy, while the blonde guy who would later sing 'Surf City' wants to work on music. It still was not clear to me if Jan meant that Arnie was out from that moment on, if his absence was temporary, or what. Maybe Jan did not even know himself, and he was testing the waters without getting committed."

Finally, the team was official. At first, Dean thought Jan & Dean would be on Arwin, and there would be no worry about finding a label. Then he learned that Arwin was no longer interested in Jan's songs. "At that point, it was like starting from scratch. And if it weren't for Jan's remembering a couple of guys that he had met when he and Arnie had done a show with Sam Cooke, guys whom he was impressed with, who knows what would have happened."

The two guys? Herb Alpert, later of the Tijuana Brass and the "A" in A&M records; and Lou Adler, later to marry Shelley Fabares and found Dunhill Records (Mamas and Papas, Barry McGuire, Grassroots, et al).

Dean still marvels' at Jan's awareness. "Somehow, Jan realized, at age 17, that you needed a manager. I was scratching my head saying, 'What do you need a manager for when you don't have a career?' But he realized that strong management could help you get that deal. We were used to making the demo tape ourselves and literally dropping in on record companies, knocking on their doors, sitting down in their offices, and getting them to play our material.

"So Jan called Lou and Herb after we had not made any headway with Arwin. I don't remember ever going to Arwin myself, Jan must have. I don't even remember meeting the Arwin producer, Joe Lubin, who at the very least should have come up and checked us out to see what we had. It wouldn't have taken him very long to find out. Maybe he was being squeezed out of Arwin and was more worried about paying the rent that month than trying to predict the future. For whatever reason, I never saw Joe Lubin.

"When Jan saw that he didn't have Joe Lubin and didn't have Arwin and didn't have anything going particularly, we were still doing what Jan & Arnie had done, trying to come up with good songs, and we just weren't finding any. We weren't writing anything that was very exciting, and we were listening to other people's demo records and listening to new releases that were on small labels and weren't hits. But we just couldn't find anything that was very exciting. We knew that was the regular process that we had to go through, so we just kept plodding along.

"Somewhere in there, Jan did make the call. Next thing I knew, these guys, Lou and Herb, were showing up at Jan's place to meet me. They were about 24 or so. To us teenagers, they were men. Men. I mean, they wore *suits*. They were *cool*. They were *real men*. They were grown up. They didn't live at *home* like we did. We considered them grown ups, they were mature men to us. These were guys who had been involved in a career of someone that we really respected. Sam Cooke."

At Keen Records, Lou and Herb were the equivalent of junior executives. They were being brought along by the people in their 40s who held the power for themselves. And Lou and Herb wondered how long it would be before they had their chance. Did these older guys have to die first? Or did Lou and Herb need to move along. "When they came up and met us, and heard some of the things that we had done, then they pretty quickly committed to our careers and gave Keen notice that they were moving on. So it was Lou and Herb who found 'Baby Talk.' They delivered the song to us, probably on a 45."

Lou Adler

As Lou recalls, it wasn't just Jan & Dean who lured Herb and him from Keen Records. "Herbie Alpert and I were writing partners working for Keen records, which had Sam Cooke on it. We decided to leave Keen and I took a job for a management company guy named Lenny Poncher who was managing a lot of Latin acts in and around LA. Kim Fowley, who was a University High student with Jan & Dean, and also was on the edge of the music business as everyone in LA was at that time, since there was no real *contemporary* music business to speak of, it was just starting up, everything was in New York).

"One day, Kim came to me and told me that Jan, who had had a hit with Jan & Arnie, had a new partner and that I might be interested in talking to them. Either Jan or both of them came to the office I had that was actually an auto parts store in front and the management company in the back of the storefront.

"The first thing that struck me about Jan, and later Dean, was how great these guys looked. They both looked great. Also how different they looked, compared to most people who were having hit records at the time. The established artists were all dark haired, sort of Italian/ethnic looking guys out of Philadelphia. I hadn't recalled ever seeing a picture of Jan & Dean or a picture of Jan with Jan & Arnie, but here was this All-American surfer guy. He played me some Jan & Arnie records, said that Arnie was no longer with him and it was going to be him and another friend from University High, and they were out of their record deal and for some reason they had heard about me.

"Herb and I had only worked with Sam Cooke and Keen artists at that time, but we hadn't had any real success. But we hit it off with Jan & Dean really well, so we thought we'd take a chance."

Even with Lou and Herb, the garage remained Hit Central of Jan & Company. "The story is absolutely true that 'Baby Talk' was recorded in a garage. Jan had an old Ampex that he had hooked up in order to give him some echo. That is how he got all the 'Jennie Lee' echo. He had the tape going through the head twice. It sat up on top the piano, the dogs ran through, the kids cried, it was wild."

Dore Records

Dean credits Lou and Herb with finding Dore Records (pronounced "Doree") for Jan & Dean's recordings. In fact, Jan & Dean were never actually signed with Dore records proper. Jan & Dean were under contract to Herb and Lou. Herb and Lou signed with Dore. Dore was not one of their A or B lists. They didn't even consider Liberty where we had our first hits years later, which, like most of the majors, was still doing what they thought was not rock and roll. Also, they went to the smaller companies because, probably, there were more of them on the East Coast than in LA, but

ABOVE: Jan & Dean circa 1963. Photo courtesy W. L. Berry.

we didn't have the wherewithal to fly to the East Coast and shop our product. That would have been a smarter thing to do, because then we could have been on a real, big, player label.

"But Dore was only a mile from the recording studio, two miles from the garage, and had just had a number one record with the Teddybears' 'To Know Him Is To Love Him.' They had credibility, they'd proven that they could handle a major, national hit. It was as good as we could do at the time, and it worked out OK."

Did Dore have studios?

"No. All they had was one little office on Vine. What they did have was a distribution system already in place and a name and an old record guy who was running it. That was all you needed then."

"Baby Talk"

In the 8,000-record music library at the KJAN garage, no one had noticed a little record on the tiny Spring label called "Baby Talk." Lou chalks up that discovery to partner Herb.

"Herbie had some contact with a publisher who had given him some material, including 'Baby Talk' which was written by Melvin Schwartz. Everyone always thought that was a fake name, but he was a real guy. Herb had that piece of material before Jan & Dean came along. Herbie was always looking for material, even for himself... I found out later... to record.

"Although we had cut some demos which got us the job as associate A&R men at Keen we hadn't been in the studio yet on our own, we hadn't really produced anything before Jan & Dean came along." But Lou and Herb knew musicians and had contacts from working with Sam at Keen Records.

"Herb was a trumpet player, for Bar Mitzvahs and weddings, but he had enough musical ability to arrange, so we put the session together. Herbie jotted out some charts and we went into Western Recorders.

"First we cut the basic tracks, which were very different from what you would call 'basic tracks' normally. Ordinarily, you would record the instruments, then put the voices on later. We switched it and cut the voices and piano at Jan's garage, a la Jan & Arnie, and then took that into the studio and added the music to it."

Getting a full take of "Baby Talk" was not easy, in those days of one microphone, one track, and no mixing boards or re-takes. "We were on mono and did, I guess, hundreds of splices. Because we'd have to take the take, and we weren't overdubbing at the time. And that was how we got 'Baby Talk.' On the back, we put a song that they wrote called "Jeanette, Get Your Hair Done."

From Lou's point of view, then, getting the vocals on "Baby Talk" was the challenge. Dean, on the other hand, recalls how hard it was to add the instruments.

"We did the two vocal parts and the piano at Jan's garage, as we normally did. Then we went to a studio that Lou and Herb had booked. Herb had made charts and arrangements for the four or five studio musicians, and they sat down with earphones on and listened to our original track of just piano and vocal and simply played along with it. These were old black blues-type players, it was the Ernie Freeman Quartet. Not the wrecking crew, but within the musician's community, these guys were famous, and they were very good players.

"Good as they were, they had a hell of a time playing along with our tape. They were used to making an instrumental tape then having the artist sing along with their track, multiple times, until they've got it. But we did the vocals first, and *they* had to match *us*!

"These guys were real musicians and conscious of meter. When we recorded our vocals, we didn't have a drummer or a metronome to check ourselves. To our laymen ears, it didn't sound like there was any radical change in tempo. To these guys, our track was very uneven in tempo, like going back and forth between a rock song to a ballad – radical changes in the meter.

"Eventually, after eight or nine takes, they learned where the places were that we changed tempo and they sped up or slowed down with us."

"Baby Talk" is figuratively drenched in echo. Dean reported that "the echo or reverb, a delay echo we got off of Jan's tape recorder, was already there from the garage. In the studio, Lou and Herb dumped maybe a little bit more of a chamber echo on top of the instrumental track to compliment our track."

Lou also remembers that echo fondly.

"Jan used two tape recorders. He figured out how to wire things up so that your vocal went in one way, went to one tape, then he passed it on to the other tape machine and made it a little out of sync. So that it is not a real echo, but is a delay effect. So there were two tracks, one a little behind the other, and it sounded like an echo. It was a kind of different sound, a lot crisper than a chamber echo. A very distinctive sound. Whenever we tried to get that kind of echo in a studio, it never worked.

"So we actually brought that machine into the studio. It wasn't a professional machine, but it had a certain echo sound to it that we wanted. It was an Ampex 701 or some such. It was reel to reel and the first step up in recording. It was much better than a home recorder. But you know, Jan was and is an amazing guy. There is no telling what this guy would have done had he not had the accident."

Once the voices and instruments, and splices were in the can, all that was left for Jan & Dean to do was wait for their managers to find a label. Dean: "Lou and Herb, as managers, what would be today called a producer, paid for the studio and musicians, and then they took the tape recording out and they knocked on the doors as a management team."

And they ended up at Dore Records.

"Jan and Arnie" on Dore?

The names "Jan & Dean" fall so easily to our lips today, that it is difficult to imagine the name "Jan & Arnie" being attached to songs like "Baby Talk" or "Little Old Lady." But it almost happened that way, even without Arnie.

"There was a push to keep Arnie's name," sighs Dean. "After all, they'd had hits. We were actually negotiating with Arnie's dad to give Arnie a piece of the pie for the use of his name. But, thank god, Arnie said no. I had no say in it, I was just gonna hang in there,

MORE»»

JAN and DEAN

be called Arnie, and have a piece of it. Luckily, it went away. I remember seeing an Arnie label once – I was very glad it went away! Came that close! Whew!"

The Jan & Arnie Dore pressing of "Baby Talk" is very rare. Only a handful came off the line before Arnie himself nixed the notion; so few that Lou has forgotten them. "I don't remember any records pressed as by Jan and Arnie. But knowing Jan's sensibilities, he might have been ready to change Dean's name to Arnie."

Speaking of changing names – Herb Alpert was so taken with the name of this record company that, for live performances with his trumpet, and for a couple of vocal releases, Herb billed himself as "Dore Alpert" for a while, and named his new son Dore!

On Tour With "Baby Talk"

"Baby Talk" hit LA fast, but the rest of the country was a lot slower to catch on. "Originally, we weren't getting national exposure on 'Baby Talk,'" laments Lou. "So I took Jan & Dean to Philadelphia to do record hops, one of which I knew would be a Dick Clark record hop. And thereby having a chance to show Clark the response kids gave to Jan & Dean, so that we could start getting play on 'American Bandstand.' The response was unbelievable at the hops. They had never seen 6 foot 2, blonde haired guys in matching sweater outfits with white shoes at these hops. They went literally crazy for these two guys."

"Baby Talk" peaked at #10 on Billboard's national Hot 100. "But," explains Dean, "it was really a #1 hit. The problem was that Dore's distribution system was not as good as it could have been. The song hit #1 everyplace, but consecutively, not simultaneously."

After "Baby Talk" was a national hit, Jan & Dean were on the road on the weekends and during school vacations and breaks. And although they were a hit on the radio, in those pre-MTV days, few people knew what Jan & Dean looked like. Dean still laughs about the way that played out.

"When we had 'Baby Talk' and a few other tunes, we were booked just on the basis of these records, with the promoters figuring we must be a black group. That was how we ended up as the only white act on the bill!

"The first night of the tour, we still had no idea that nobody in the audience knew we weren't black. So, we were introduced, and we were standing off stage with guys like Bobby Day ["Rockin' Robin" and "Over and Over,"

1958], Little Willie John ["Fever," 1956, and "Sleep," 1960] and the backup band for everyone on the tour, the Little Richard Band.

"They introduced us, and the crowd went crazy! Just crazy! Until we walked out on stage. Then it went suddenly silent! They were shocked. When we came out they were screaming for the record they'd heard and thought a black group was singing it. And it was really surprising to them when the two whitest people they'd ever seen in their entire lives walked out!

"We were singing live with the Little Richard Band, which was a damn good band. And they really helped us out! They got the people enthused again, because the initial response to our color was... quite noticeable! Then, about half way through the first song, they started to get over the shock. By the time we finished the second or third song, they were into it again with us. But that initial gasp was, well, kind of funny.

"That was a very weird tour. We couldn't stay in the same hotels as they could. And we played mostly the South, which made it all very strange. They'd usually have to sneak us into their rooms, most of the time we did that because it was much harder to sneak all of them into our rooms! Very weird, like eating. We'd all eat together, but we got absolutely terrible service. Nobody would wait on our tables. Well, that's show biz!"

The Legendary Dore Album

Exactly when Jan & Dean's Dore album was recorded is a fact lost in the mists of time. Apparently, it was after the follow-up to "Baby Talk" was made. Lou Adler is sure of one thing. "It wasn't an album market at that time. Nobody was cutting albums unless you had a hit single. So we put the single out and it went up the charts very quickly in Los Angeles.

"We did do the album prior to releasing all the singles. We came out with the second single, 'There's A Girl,' which Herbie and I wrote, but we didn't wait until all of the other songs were done to do the LP, I think. I'm not sure."

Don Altfeld remembers writing songs for the album. "We started writing a lot of songs for the Dore album, most of them based on girls' names."

And Dean remembers a little more. "We continued to record in the garage for a while. I am sure we did not think of making an album, so I am sure

ABOVE: Jan with Glenn Ford, 1958.

we sat down and thought of an album as a testing ground for your next single or two. Hopefully, as you do the album you find tunes for your follow-up.

"'Baby Talk' took some time to become a hit, because it broke in regions. By the time Dore figured out that it was indeed going to be a legitimate hit, it had probably almost peaked. By the time we got an album, the song was long off the charts. We hoped the follow-up, 'There's a Girl,' would be strong enough to be a hit, and with two strong singles, you could sell an album."

Initially, every side that was on a 45 was later put on the LP. Eventually, every cut on the LP also appeared on a 45.

The Poster

The original pressing of the Dore album contained a rare bonus – a full-color, autographed, 12-inch poster of the Duo (which was reproduced for the first time in 35 years in KTEL's Jan & Dean CD released February 1996).

"That poster was pretty progressive," says Dean, who later earned a graduate degree in commercial design and won many awards for LP covers executed by his company Kittyhawk Graphics. Even in the 50s, Dean was very conscious of the visual end of the business. "[Record companies] were starting to understand that the visual stuff was merchandisable as well and added some kind of value. It was signed so you got an album, an autograph and a picture. That was a cool idea and probably came from Lou. That was what he and Herb were very good at. Good managers brought that kind of thing to the table, they were reliable liaisons between you and the company. It takes strong management to always be on top of everything and be sure that the record company does what you tell them to do. Often the company thinks that they know better so it is a constant give and take between what you want and what they do.

"Lew Bedell, the president of Dore, had not done a poster with anyone else, so it had to be our management who talked him into it. Like the picture sleeves. If you go into a record store, you'd like to be able to afford to buy maybe a hundred records. But if you can only get one, and one comes with a color picture and one does not, you're gonna buy the one with the picture and put the other one back and buy it next time, and then 'next time' never happens. The picture sleeve wasn't going to sell a dog of a record, we knew that, but getting a little extra something the consumer would want would help."

Lou confirms that the poster was his doing. "Yeah, it was something that I wanted to try because of their look. All of the packaging and marketing ideas at that time were mine. The picture sleeves were my idea, because I knew about their good looks and wanted their faces out there as much as possible. One of those girls on the picture sleeves went on to become a working actress."

Jan & Dean liked being successful, and Dean liked having the art work accompany the music but he explains, "We did not go out of our way to become teen idols, but they had picture sleeves with their records, so we needed to compete. The visual appearance became pretty damn important. Later, the visuals became even more important, whether you were visually pleasing or not. But at that time, the pretty guys had full-face pictures on their album covers."

As shown on their photos of the Dore era Jan & Dean had the duck tails which were expected for young singers of the day.

"I didn't get into that as much as Jan did. We got close. But it was too much trouble and we could see that the surfer look was something entirely different. And we were quick to realize that the other look was getting old and it was time to move on."

Certainly, the suits of the Frankie Avalons and Bobby Darins did not really fit the California lifestyle that was to sweep the whole country in a few years. So Jan & Dean wore things like sweat shirts, shorts, white jeans and tennis shoes whenever possible.

Dean saw a change coming. "Kids were tired of the suit-and-tie, gold lame, holier-than-thou attitude. We saw that kids did not want untouchable singers, but someone they could relate to. They wanted to be able to identify with artists in pretty much every way. To us, that seemed like a lot more fun. And probably a lot more powerful, although that had not been proven yet. We had no models who had already done that. We experimented and got feedback that we could get away with the non-traditional attitude, people bought it.

"The first Liberty album was done the old way, before we got a hold of our own destiny. The old pros, the guys at the record company, made those decisions. Quite frankly, Lou and Herbie also came from that school to a

certain degree. But then they were talented enough and had enough vision to be able to move on from there and not get stuck. They were flexible enough to change, they never fought us."

Even so, for the poster photo session, Jan & Dean were dressed in blazers and straw hats. Fortunately, the shot that they settled on was minus the straw hats! The back of the album showed Jan & Dean and Lou and Herb in the recording studio called Western Studio wearing their regular clothes.

About the Songs – the Album

"Clementine"

The first cut on the LP was a reworking of the old public-domain folk song from 1884, "My Darling Clementine." A great novelty number with a hot sax break, this rocker happened to be released on a 45 the same month as Bobby Darin's Atco Records 45, a Mack-the-Knife-ish version of the same old chestnut! It must have been Jan's idea to record it, as Dean never liked the record much.

In fact, Dean theorizes it happened to chart on Billboard by mistake. He says it took six weeks for Billboard to tumble to their mistake, at which point they correctly attributed the sales to Darin's version, which peaked at #21. "Since the song entered the chart so fast and left so quickly, I assume that is prob-

ably what happened," is Dean's wide-eyed summary. Was he serious?

Lou Adler disagrees with the mistake theory. "That sounds like a 'Dean Story.' No, we were selling records."

On the Dore LP, Dean's introductory "Oh my darlin'" was presented in single voice. For the 45, that same introduction was replaced on some copies with a mix that had a second track of Dean's voice, delayed a second or two, giving the weirdest Jan & Dean echo effect yet! Jan handles the lead. There is an eerie, faint, female soprano during the sax break. The singer of this part was session vocalist Sally Stevens. Ms. Stevens, and a group that varied between two and four girls, later sang on a great many hit records, including the hits of James Darren ("Her Royal Majesty," Paul Peterson (including "She Can't Find Her Keys," and Shelley Fabares (including "Johnny Angel," generally attributed erroneously to Darlene Love's Blossoms).

"Judy"

A slow number about an angel of a girl, with Dean's falsetto replaced by Sally Stevens voice, and Jan's bomps replaced by Dean's La-la-las.

Don Altfeld, who penned this dreamy doo wop tune with Jan & Dean, noted that there were "a lot of girls'

MORE

names on that album. This could have been written about Judy Lovejoy, who was Frank Lovejoy's daughter and Dean's girlfriend at the time. Or she could have been Jeanette Anderson's sister Judy, who was Jan's girlfriend, as in "Jeanette get your hair done." Again, Sally is in the background.

"My Heart Sings"

More bomps from Jan, and a lead from Dean, made this Alpert-Adler ditty a perfect follow-up for "Baby Talk." In reality it was the flip side of that follow-up! Obviously, the vocals were not recorded first on this one, as the drum beat figures too prominently for that.

"Rosie Lane"

Jan, Dean, and Don co-wrote this tasty if bomp-less song about another real girl, Rosie Lane Halprin, who was Baron Jimmy Bruderlin's girlfriend. On the cover of the Dore album, her name was spelled as two names, "Rosie Lane." While on the label of the LP inside the cover, it was one name, "Rosilane," without the "e." Apparently the two-name version is the correct spelling, although there are 45 labels with both variations.

The intro is by Jan, with the same delay-echo effect of Dean's intro on "Clementine." Lead vocals are shared with Jan predominating, the drum beat is strictly from "Baby Talk," and the ever-present Ms. Stevens is back. And listen to that weird, funeral march excerpt played on the chime at the end.

"Oh, Julie"

A little faster tempo, with Dean providing a cool lead, which is echoed by Jan.

Listed as simply "Julie" on the 33 1/3 label but as "Oh, Julie" on the album cover, this was a Top 5 hit for the Nashville one-hit-wonder quintet called the Crescendos a year before "Baby Talk" was recorded. It was the last of the LP cuts to come out on a single. In fact, it was issued by Dore after Jan & Dean left Dore and in the hopes of cashing in on the success of their Top 20 hit "Heart and Soul" on Challenge records. Lou Adler: "I liked that one, it was a nice record. And I don't remember that it came out after 'Heart and Soul,' and I didn't realize until you told me that we had left Dore any masters when we left the label. It was smart of Dore to put that out."

Interestingly, while the Crescendos original featured a female high voice in the background, Jan & Dean's track didn't bother with that vocal part, although a similar female soprano appeared all over the rest of this LP!

"Baby Talk"

The hit. That is Jan on the bomps, Dean on the lead, both drenched in echo. A true doo wop classic. Besides Jan & Dean, two other artists had 45s of this song. First was the original version by the Laurels on Spring records (Spring 1112), which Jan & Dean covered. The third was a cover version of Jan & Dean's cover version, by Tom and Jerry ("Hey Schoolgirl"), later better known by their real names, Art Garfunkel and Paul Simon (Bell Records 45-120).

"You're On My Mind"

Side two of the LP kicked off with the flip side of "Clementine." This cute number was written by Jan and Don Altfeld, who testifies, "That was a title my Dad, Horace [Altfeld], gave me. He later wrote Jan & Dean liner notes and was president of the Jan & Dean Fan Club.

The Fan Club address on the Dore album cover, 1307 Brinkley, was our house, and my dad was the subject of 'Horace, the Swingin' School Bus Driver,' a 1964 Jan & Dean album cut. 'You're On My Mind' was a little more legitimate type of song." Dean sings lead and falsetto, Jan adds the "dum dum dum" at the end. And Sally – she's back!

"There's A Girl"

Written by Lou and Herb as the perfect follow-up to "Baby Talk," it barely charted, stalling at #98. It was bigger in LA, of course, but marked the end of the garage as a studio. Dean takes the lead again with Jan harmonizing. The ending especially, is pure "Baby Talk" revisited. If you listen very closely to the very end, you can hear Sally Stevens singing "Da da da da" with Jan!

"Jeanette"

...Or as it was titled on the 45, "Jeanette, Get Your Hair Done." This is the most fun cut on the album, hinting of the fun to come in Jan & Dean records of the mid-60s. Jan takes the lead, with Dean harmonizing, even on the bomps. Don Altfeld remembers how this flip side of "Baby Talk" was conceived.

"At that time, Bobby Freeman was coming off a really big record with 'Do You Wanna Dance.' He was either coming to see Jan everyday, or he was living in the garage with the tape recorder. One day, he showed Jan a song called 'Betty Lou Got A New Pair of Shoes.' So we did a twist on it, and it became 'Jeanette, Get Your Hair Done.' Jeanette was Jan's girlfriend, whom we used to kid all the time about her hair, 'Jeanette, get your hair done,' because it was always a curly-haired mess! Jan and Bobby worked together a lot and Jan learned a lot and was inspired a lot by Bobby Freeman who was a real pal."

It is ironic that Jan & Dean are complaining here about how sloppy Jeanette's hair and clothes are since they were the ones to introduce the casual look to the world of rock. If that piano playing at the opening sounds familiar by now, then you've recognized another of Jan's trademarks on this LP.

"Cindy"

Dean starts the vocal off, with Jan joining in on the chorus, and, of course, providing his trademark bomps to excellent effect. "Cindy was a girl from high school, a blonde whose last name I have forgotten," according to Don Altfeld. Lou Adler remembers it as the flip side of "White Tennis Sneakers," although it is always considered to be the "A" side of that 45. Instead of a song about a classmate, Lou notes that, like "Baby Talk," it was also written by Melvin Schwartz, who came back in hopes of getting another hit with the Dore duo. Lou describes this song as "the same formula as 'Baby Talk.' Schwartz was not in the group the Laurels. The Laurels were a black group. Our only contact was with the publisher of the song, we never met Schwartz," and presumably Schwartz never met any of the classmates. Never mind who it was about. Cindy is a classic!

"Don't Fly Away"

Jan kicks off this medium tempo tune with Dean taking lead. Of all the songs Jan & Dean recorded at Dore, perhaps this was the most likely to score a hit. Why? For the simple reason that this treasure was written by the legendary song writing team of Doc Pomus and Mort Schuman, whose voluminous song writing credits include Elvis' "Hound Dog," Andy Williams' "Can't Get Used To Losing You," and Dion and the Belmonts' "A Teenager In Love," to name but a few. Ironically, it shares the dubious honor of last to be released off the album, and as a flip side yet!

"White Tennis Sneakers"

Jan & Dean are hardly known today as ballad singers. Yet this LP was mostly slow numbers, with "Clementine," "Jeanette," and this final LP cut the only true rockers of the bunch, and all three are novelties! This ode is a complaint about a girl who purposely dirties her white tennies, and seems to be a zesty conglomeration/synthesis of

ABOVE: The Jan & Dean Dore album and poster instert.

"Betty Lou Got A New Pair of Shoes" and "Jeanette."

That's Jan at the intro and Dean on lead as they give the "Baby Talk" formula one last variation. Three slightly different mixes of this recording have surfaced over the years. First was the original Dore vinyl. Jan & Dean lip-synced to a second version when they appeared on the "Dick Clark Beachnut Show" in 1960. And a cassette released around 1990, featuring poor reproductions of a few of the cuts from this LP, included a third version of "Sneakers" which has the instrumental break just before the fade out. It is in a slightly different form from the original vinyl. The cassette version, also used on the K-Tel CD, is missing two measures of guitar work at the start of the break.

The Other Dore Sides

After almost all the LP cuts had been issued as 45s, a return to the studio was scheduled to record some new 45s of material that had not been on the LP. The first to be released was a remake of another duo's old record.

"We Go Together"

Lou Adler takes credit for this wonderful Jan & Dean love ballad. "That song comes from a genre that I would have been closer to because of my leanings toward R&B or black music. I believe the first record on that was Marvin and Johnny, which was a hit in the R&B market. It stretched Jan & Dean a little bit, I think, vocally. Ernie Freeman did the string arrangements for 'We Go Together.' He was a piano player and an arranger. We pretty much stuck with the same rhythm section for as long as we could."

Dean was also proud of this recording. "This proved that we could do ballads and it would be accepted by our fan base." It charted at #53, their highest national placement since "Baby Talk." The flip side of "Together" was the LP cut "Rosie Lane."

"Gee"

Both sides of the next 45 were from post-LP sessions. Here, both Lou Adler and Don Altfeld felt they were tapping the roots of rock 'n' roll. Lou: "Like 'We Go Together,' this was from my very early days in high school. That was something that I listened to on the radio with Hunter Hancock. There were no national charts on it. It is not like it was a big hit. I remember it as the first rock 'n' roll record that I ever heard."

Don: "'Gee' by the Crows is my all-time favorite record. Lou may have suggested recording that one, but I introduced Jan to the song. In my life, it was the first rock and roll record. That was the one that did it for me. I couldn't believe that record. I absolutely remember suggesting they record that. Jan and I were very heavily influenced by black music. Jimmy Reed, the Spaniels, Little Walter, all those records on Veejay.

"Two songs had a great influence on me, 'Gee' and 'Come Go With Me.' Jan knew one of the Del-Vikings. 'A Sunday Kind of Love' was a Del-Vikings song that Jan & Dean recorded as their first 45 for Liberty in 1962."

These newer recordings have a much more – well, for want of a better word – "modern" sound to them. Dean: "Yeah, we were just starting to find better players, better songs, better technology, two-track machines and three-track machines so we could do some overdubbing, some fattening of the vocals, we were just coming into that realm of recording technique. We were probably right on the edge of doing breakthroughs like 'Barbara Ann' and, later, 'Linda.' The extra work really paid off; these are great recordings!

"Such A Good Night For Dreaming"

Here is another song by a legendary song writer, Barry Mann ("You've Lost That Lovin' Feeling"). Lou Adler brought this song from New York when he became the West Coast representative for Aldon Music (Al Nevins and Don Kirshner). It is probably the most musical song ever recorded by Jan & Dean to this day. Dean surprisingly responds, "I liked that song. In fact, that is my favorite song of ours from that era. It was another ballad, another step from 'We Go Together,' except that 'Dreaming' had not been recorded before and 'Together' was an old R&B hit." A truly rare 45 today is an early 1963 revival of "Such A Good Night For Dreaming" on Herb Alpert's A&M Records 45 #708 by the Kenjolairs.

"Baggy Pants (Read All About It)"

The final release of any new material on Dore came out a mere 18 months after "Baby Talk." The "A" side was a delightful two-and-a-half-minute situation comedy about a boy "born in the poorest part of town" who is dating, and embarrassing, a girl from the "rich upper class," and the whole fiasco gets written up in the society column of the Daily News. "Baggy Pants" was the only song on the LP written by Bob Roberts. No one remembers much about him today, including Lou Adler. "Bob Roberts was an East Coast writer. I don't recall where that song came from. I don't know how we got that song. They lyric is probably more contemporary today," he comments, referring to the current style of really baggy pants!

As a novelty tune, "Baggy Pants" both followed in the tradition of "Clementine," "Jeanette" and "Tennis Sneakers," while also foretelling of future Jan & Dean comedy/satire such as "Little Old Lady" and "Sidewalk Surfin'" on Liberty Records, which led in part to Jan & Dean's being nicknamed "The Laurel and Hardy of Surf." Dean, especially, enjoyed the comedy. "'Baggy Pants' was a novelty record and we were contemplating doing humorous things. I guess we were doing some humor on stage. It was not overt, but at that time any humor on stage by a musician was different, any at all. Because (speaking with sarcasm) those singers are pretty damn serious! Frankie Avalon, Fabian, they were real serious characters, boy! Bobby Rydell, boy, they were out there singing their hearts out. This business was nothing to be making fun of!

"Once again, you can see that we were thinking about taking it some other directions, and were willing to try it. We knew that somewhere along the line it would fit, that we would be able to do more tongue-in-cheek stuff."

By the mid-1960s, Jan & Dean had fully embraced humor, especially in their stage shows, which contained as much comedy as music. And it all started here!

BELOW: Jan & Dean on Llyod Thaxton's tv show circa 1965.

"Judy's An Angel"

Jan & Dean's swan song for Dore was unique, the only example of a re-working of a song off the LP, where the Berry-Torrence-Altfeld composition was called simply "Judy." The new version is more dramatic and heartfelt, as well as more elaborately produced. Don: "The new 45 version was a case of Jan's thinking he had something and went back to improve on it. Yeah, Jan was always tinkering on the songs." And he would do it again. The 1964 hit "Dead Man's Curve" was a major revision of a 1963 Jan & Dean Drag City album cut. This 45 is a great way to end Jan & Dean's Dore Doo Wop Days.

Leaving Dore

In all, between the summer of 1959 and January, 1961, Jan & Dean recorded and Dore released 12 tracks on both LP and 45s, and an additional five sides were released on 45s only.

Lou Adler saw the end of the Dore connection as a good thing: time to move on again. "The time on the contract ran out and we were just glad to make a move. We felt that a new company would put new vibes in the records. It wasn't a falling out or anything. This is interesting, because it starts to get into record history. About the same time, we met Jerry Moss, Herbie and Jerry became very friendly and Herbie and I split up. Basically, as the story goes, he took the tape recorder (and created the Tijuana Brass and "The Lonely Bull") and I took Jan & Dean."

Dean welcomed the change, as well. "Our involvement with Dore just tapered off. The real distribution was not there. Record companies were just barely beginning to get real hip that rock was a real business. It was not yet dawning on them that this music was not temporary and that Doris Day and Perry Como would not be back on the charts. It was very obvious in the way that they conducted business that they were not yet serious about rock music. To them, it was totally disposable, 'We'll do it for now because everyone else is doing it, but as soon as it starts to wane, it is back to the same old guys. Rock 'n' roll's a fad, like hula hoops.' I am sure that record people thought that it would go away and they'd be back to business with their tried-and-true. Mitch Miller, Frankie Lane, Roger Whittaker.

"For our part, we knew that we needed to upgrade. I don't think it was a matter of Dore letting us go. It was a matter of, we'd reached the end of our contractual agreement. I don't remember Dore even pitching us, because I am sure they felt that it was fait accompli, we were moving on.

"We wanted to go to Liberty. And the Liberty folk were interested enough in general, but they were not interested is some of the ideas we had. So we said, 'Take us and our ideas, or no deal.' That was the 'Heart and Soul' situation. They flat didn't want 'Heart and Soul.' They thought it was stupid. They even said, 'When you get that 'Heart and Soul' out of your system, come to us and then we will really get you some hits.'

"We proved them wrong. 'Heart and Soul' was a hit on our next label, Challenge. After that, Liberty took us, and the first year at Liberty they didn't get us anything that came even close to the success of 'Heart and Soul.'"

After Dore

After recording 17 tracks and charting five times on Dore, Jan & Dean's Challenge Records, scored one hit, then on to Liberty Records and 16 more chart records. Over the years, Jan wrote, arranged, and/or produced most of their recordings, as well as records for other artists. Unique among rock 'n' rollers, both men juggled music and school, graduated from college and even went on to graduate programs – Jan in medicine, Dean in commercial design. By 1966, they had filmed one episode of their own network TV series due to run in the fall. Then, on the way to a meeting to set up their own record company, Jan ran his Corvette Sting Ray into a pickup truck illegally parked on Whittier Boulevard and phase one of the Jan and Dean story abruptly ended in brain damage and par

MORE»»

tial paralysis on April 12, 1966.

Name another 50s doo wop act that had over a half-dozen hits, stayed in high school, shifted gears to a 60s sound, went to college, had another string of even bigger hits, and is still touring in 1996 with the original members. Can't, can you. Can nomination to the Rock 'n' Roll Hall of Fame for Jan & Dean be far away?

Jan & Dean's Dore Discography

Jan & Dean Dore LP #101

Side 1
Clementine (Jan Berry, Dean Torrence)
Judy (Jan Berry, Dean Torrence, and Don Altfeld)
My Heart Sings (Herb Alpert and Lou Adler)
Rosie Lane (Jan Berry, Dean Torrence, and Don Altfeld)
Oh Julie (Noel Ball and Don Moffat)
Baby Talk (Melvin Schwartz)

Side 2
You're On My Mind (Jan Berry and Don Altfeld)
There's A Girl (Herb Alpert and Lou Adler)
Jeanette (Jan Berry, Dean Torrence, and Don Altfeld)
Cindy (Jan Berry and Dean Torrence)
Don't Fly Away (Doc Pomas and Mort Schuman)
White Tennis Sneakers (Melvin Schwartz)

Jan & Dean Dore 45s

All 45 sides, unless otherwise noted, were also on the LP. Composer credits are listed above for the LP tracks.
7-59 Dore 522 Baby Talk/Jeanette Get Your Hair Done #10

10-59 Dore 531 There's A Girl/My Heart Sings #98

1-60 Dore 539 Clementine/You're On My Mind #65

4-60 Dore 545 Cindy/+White Tennis Sneakers

7-60 Dore 555 *We Go Together/Rosie Lane (aka Rosilane) released with picture sleeve with 2 girls #53

10-60 Dore 576 *Gee/*Such A Good Night for Dreaming (Davis-Watkins-Norton)/(Hunter-Mann) released with picture sleeve with new fan club address on Sunset Strip #81

1-61 Dore 583 *Baggy Pants (Read All About It)/@Judy's An Angel (Bob Roberts)/(Berry-Torrence-Altfeld)

7-61 Dore 610 Julie/Don't Fly Away

* Not on the Dore LP.

+ Released on a cassette circa 1990 in an alternate mix on a Neon label release "in association with K-Tel Holland."

@ Newly recorded version of LP cut "Judy."

For more information about Jan & Dean, send a self-addressed, stamped envelope to "Sunshine Music," c/o Michael "Doc Rock" Kelly, 3724 Woodmont Road, Toledo, OH 43613.

Thanks to Lou Adler, Don Altfeld, Jan and Gertie Berry, Alan Clark, Jill Gibson, Elliot Kendall, Frank Kisko, Rip Lay and Dean Torrence.

DISCOVERIES JULY 1996

 **VARÈSE SARABANDE** *Varèse Vintage* presents

DEAN TORRENCE

LEGENDARY MASKED SURFER UNMASKED

THE DEAN TORRENCE ANTHOLOGY 302 066 349 2
This collection brings together for the first time the best of Dean Torrence's solo recordings, created in the sprit of Jan & Dean. This is the first official release of many of these legendary tracks recorded by Dean Torrence, recorded over a thirty-year period, with an assemblage of friends including **Brian Wilson**, **Mike Love** and **Flo & Eddie** as well as **Gary Griffin**, and some of the best studio musicians of the era, including Joe Osborn, Mickey Jones, Larry Knechtel and James Burton). Jan & Dean fans have asked for an official release of these tracks for years. This release also includes a new 2002 version of "Barbara Ann" with The Vertikals, recorded especially for this package.

JAN & DEAN Teen Suite *A Varèse Vintage Classic Re-Release* VSD-5590
It's almost too easy to underestimate the importance of Jan & Dean in the history of rock & roll. The mere mention of their name today evokes images of suntanned California teens dancing and surfing on the beaches of Malibu. The ultimate good-time music act of the early '60s, who had many gold records, including "Surf City," "The Little Old lady From Pasadena," and "Dead Man's Curve" among others. Jan & Dean get credit for inspiring lots of smiles and providing the soundtrack to countless parties. This collection explores the early recording career of Jan & Dean during their formative years with hits like "Jennie Lee" (Jan & Arnie), "Baby Talk," and "Heart & Soul." Through the collective efforts of Jan & Dean and their producers (Herb Alpert and Lou Adler (Johnny Rivers, Mamas and Papas, Carole King), their management and their fans, these songs ascended the charts and brought a welcome smile to the music world. They also provided a solid foundation for a career that was soon to rocket forward, with tunes that described a carefree attitude and a brand new West Coast lifestyle. At 21 tracks this is the ultimate collection of early Jan & Dean hits and singles rarities. This release features many songs that have never appeared on any other Jan & Dean compilation. This collection was conceived and compiled by Dean Torrence, who also designed the original artwork.

ALSO AVAILABLE FROM VARÈSE VINTAGE
Jan & Dean *Golden Summer* VSD-5727
Beach Boys *Surfin'* 302 066 085 2
The Warmth Of The Sun *Songs Inspired By The Beach Boys* 302 066 117 2
The Ventures *Play The Greatest Surfin' Hits Of All-Time* 302 066 275 2

AVAILABLE AT BETTER MUSIC RETAILERS,
BY PHONE AT 1-800-VARESE-4 (1-800-827-3734)
OR ONLINE AT www.VareseSarabande.com
To join our new release update list, send your e-mail address to vintagelist@varesesarabande.com

Dean Torrence

Interview by Gary James

When you think of Fun in the Sun, and California rock, you just have to think of Jan and Dean. Between 1958 and 1966, they charted 13 Top 30 singles and sold over ten million records (a conservative estimate) worldwide. In 1966, Jan Berry was involved in a serious automobile accident which left him with severe brain damage. The duo began live appearances again in 1978, and continues to perform select dates around the country. EMI released Jan and Dean's greatest hits in a package, *Surf City*.

We talked to Dean Torrence about the history of Jan and Dean and what they're doing today.

DISCoveries: Dean, I know you and Jan still tour the country because you made a stopover in Syracuse, at the New York State Fair, not too long ago. When you're not touring, what do you do with yourself?

DEAN: That's a good question (laughs). I had my first child at 50, actually 49, I have a two-year-old, so during the off-season that keeps me pretty busy. I spend a lot of time with her. Up to eighty percent of the 55 concerts we do a year are done from May through half of October. Most of the 55 are kind of plunked in there, so, we're real busy. During the off-season we probably average working every other weekend. So most of our weekdays are available to do anything else we care to do.

DISC: What a great life!

DEAN: It's pretty neat. I like it a lot, although during the off-season you always kind of wonder whether or not it's gonna happen again. You don't really have any indication. I guess it probably feels that way for anybody. You wonder whether anybody's gonna be interested again. So, we just cross our fingers every year. But I've been quoted as saying that I've been doing that since 1961. I thought it was all over in '61. So, it's just the nature of it.

All my band members write music, so I'm involved with their side careers. I dabble a bunch in real estate. I own four homes, and I'm juggling those all around. I graduated from the School of Architecture at USC back in the '60s. I ended up getting a degree in advertising/design. I had a graphics business for 12 years. I'm involved in lots of things. I'm interested in almost anything, which actually gets in my way a lot, because I can't totally focus on one thing. (laughs)

DISC: What kind of venues are Jan and Dean performing in?

DEAN: Our perfect venue is the Fair circuit. For the most part it's a free stage. We draw families not just the over 40s. We draw a wide demographic spread. If you take out any one of the demographic pieces, it doesn't work. We just don't seem to do well when we go to a place that is geared only to over 40s. We're more a rock and roll dance band whereas many over 40s want to see a Vegas act. Our presentation doesn't lend itself to theaters particularly or clubs.

DISC: What album covers did you design with your Kitty Hawk Graphics business in Hollywood?

DEAN: I did the Nitty Gritty Dirt Band, all of their covers, from their second cover on. That was about 14 years worth. I did a couple of Michael Nesmith covers. I did Harry Nilsson covers, a string of maybe six. And just one or two apiece for everybody from Linda Ronstadt to Anne Murray, the Supremes, the Beach Boys.

DISC: That's almost a second career.

DEAN: Yeah, it would have been had I been better at collecting money from my clients. I was always looking for something else to do even though graphics-wise I got nominated four times for Grammys, and won it once for an album cover. I never got nominated in the music business.

DISC: What album cover did you win a Grammy for?

DEAN: It was a piece of junk that I didn't really want to take credit for by a group called Pollution.

DISC: Do you know how many records you have sold?

DEAN: (laughs) I have no idea.

DISC: Would it be ten million?

DEAN: I would say that ten million was conservative. If you're talking worldwide, and bootleg, it would have to be three to four times that amount. I run into stuff almost every time we go out on the road, another package that I wasn't aware of. That only tells me that somebody's interested enough to keep repackaging the stuff. Obviously it must be selling.

DISC: I doesn't hurt when your records are being played on the radio all the time.

DEAN: That sure helps. It's almost like having another hit record. I could almost turn on the radio and hear one of our songs a couple of times a day. That's almost like a hit.

DISC: Your success, and this is not to take away from your talent, was based in part on being in the right place at the right time with the right stuff. Had you been in Syracuse, maybe your career wouldn't have happened. Do you ever think how fortunate you are?

DEAN: Very fortunate. On the other hand we helped to create that. We were probably one of the first artists in California to make it. When we first started, we probably looked at it just the opposite. We wished we were in Syracuse. We didn't know where Syracuse was, but we knew it was on the East Coast, and Dick Clark was back there. All the hits were coming out of the East Coast. Most all of the teen idols were back there, in the late '50s; Murray the K, all of those radio and TV personalities, were all on the East Coast. We didn't have any out here. All the record companies were on the East Coast. We had a bunch of independent labels out here or middle of the road labels, that were pumping out Dean Martin records, or Pat Boone records. There weren't any progressive rock and roll labels. So, when we first started, we thought we were in the wrong place.

DISC: I've read that you and Jan played clubs at night when you were still in school. How did that work? Did you have a band that went with you?

DEAN: We never played clubs because there weren't any. (laughs) We wouldn't have been old enough to play in clubs. They probably naturally assumed we played clubs. How else does a band get started, except in clubs. In 1957 or 1958, we wouldn't have known enough to have a band. We don't play our own instruments. Jan was an adequate keyboard player, maybe. Besides, what clubs are you talking about? There weren't rock and roll clubs in the '50s, only high school hops. We played a few of them, mostly our own high school, 'cause we didn't know any other high school. Why would any other high school want us? If you had your own band, you played you own high school. That was the first gig we ever did, and probably the only thing I ever did was one talent show at our high school.

DISC: You played or play piano?

DEAN: I played a little piano, but not well enough to play live.

DISC: And Jan played keyboards?

DEAN: Yeah, he played well enough to be able to play live. But, he also was smart enough to know that you could hire somebody for $200 who was a genius.

DISC: Since you guys wrote some of your own music, is that how you composed the songs, on keyboard?

DEAN: Yeah. Jan's dad pretty much converted the family garage into a studio for Jan, and bought him a couple of tape recorders, microphone, a turn-table, stuff like that. It was a great room, up in Bel Air, with a beautiful view. It was a great place to work. The two of us would sit on the piano bench with a microphone between us, and just work on music.

DISC: How did Challenge Records hear about you?

DEAN: Just from beating the bushes. Challenge was Gene Autry's label. By the time we got to Challenge, sounds like a song, we were pretty involved with Lou Adler and Herb Alpert. They came up with the Challenge connection. It was just a matter of shopping our record around. We didn't particularly want to be with Challenge. We didn't think they were big enough.

DISC: Is it true, that prior to Jan's accident, you two were thinking of breaking up the act?

DEAN: No. A lot of people assume most groups don't get along that well, and I had to remind Jan that if we didn't get along I certainly wouldn't have been living at his house at the time of his accident. He asked me to move in. He and his girlfriend lived in this really big house and had plenty of room. For partners who had been working together for six, seven years, we got along very well. Jan wanted to start our own record label, but I didn't think it was a very good idea. So I was probably about to have a problem with him, or at least a disagreement. Whether we would have worked it out like we did every other problem, I don't know, but he crashed and we never had to work on that issue.

DISC: How accurate was the TV movie made about the life of Jan and Dean?

DEAN: It was pretty accurate. I even put in the part about the record label and all that, where Jan wanted to pay me a salary for working with him, and not make me a partner. That was something else we talked about. We never really had a fight over that issue, but, in the movie, it looks like we were about to. I tried to make that accurate. Had the accident not happened, we probably would have had a problem, 'cause I wasn't going to accept that. In the movie, it looks like I confronted him with it, but I hadn't quite done that. I was a month away from doing it. Whether it would have changed anything...we probably would've worked it out.

DISC: You guys hosted the TAMI show in 1964. That had to be one of the high points in your career, but did you know it at the time?

DEAN: Yeah, it's funny how you put that. When you start saying it was the high point of your career, we certainly didn't know that. We just thought it was another gig you got paid for. It did give us the opportunity to meet some of the other artists we didn't know. I think we realized the concept was a neat one. Whether or not it was gonna work, we had no idea. Had that group of people gone out and done a stadium or two, that would have really been fun. We should've probably done that. The people who produced it wanted to put it into theaters, which we thought would have been a mistake. As it turned out, I don't think it was all that successful, in the form they had created it which was a theatrical theater. I don't think it did well, until it was in syndication and on TV. I'm sure they ended up

DISCOVERIES OCTOBER 1992

making a good chunk of money on it.

DISC: What do you think made, and still makes Jan and Dean so special?

DEAN: Certainly the timing. There are probably so many elements, it's hard to name them all. But I think the fact that our music was pretty well defined in terms of what we were saying. And, it wasn't all that hard to grasp. We were just talking about having a good time. Nothing social. Nothing all that relevant, just the basics. Almost anybody can relate to the basics. Plus, there's always been a universal fascination with what goes on in California. I know that sounds kind of snotty, but that's the reality, and it always looks good on TV and in the movies. We were exporting the California kind of thing. At first we didn't do it consciously. It was the only thing we had to think about. (laughs) After that, we realized people were very interested, so we just kept it up. It's all pretty well defined.

DISC: I can't let you go without asking, how is Jan's health these days?

DEAN: He's well enough to do 55 dates a year, and get asked back a lot. He got married for the very first time about six months ago. I don't know if we'd put that in and say he's well. (laughs) Some people would say that means he's sick. He seems to be doing OK given the problems he has, in terms of brain damage. He started with an IQ of 185, a real ego, and a lot of chutzpah that helped him get by. Anybody else with as much brain damage as he has, wouldn't have been able to do as well.

DISC: I know this is probably an impossible question to answer, but had Jan not been involved in that accident, what do you think would have happened to Jan and Dean?

DEAN: That's an interesting question. We had just finished a pilot for ABC-TV. The Monkees were shooting their pilot at the same time; I think they were on NBC. We were gonna go at one another, except we probably would've been on different nights, and wouldn't have been in direct competition. The networks were figuring we would help each other. We had just sold the pilot, so it was gonna go on. Recordwise, the records were changing, but Jan was pretty creative. I think he probably would have been able to keep up. But, what was more important is, we would've had the TV show. A TV show would've overcome almost anything that was happening musically, as proved by the Monkees. The Monkees were right in the middle of the psychedelic era when no other middle of the road artists were making it. The Monkees had one of the biggest selling albums of all time. It was odd because the buzz wasn't about the Monkees. The buzz was about Jefferson Airplane and Quicksilver Messenger Service and Bob Dylan and the Grateful Dead. That's all you ever heard about. Nobody every mentioned the Monkees, yet you'd pick up the charts and say, who are these guys? I never met anybody who admitted they had a Monkees album in their collection, but somebody was buyin' 'em.

DISC: Was you TV pilot similar to the Monkees?

DEAN: It wasn't quite as goofy. Their pilot was more like *A Hard Day's Night*. Ours was more like *Route 66*. ❑

Jan Berry - Jim Pewter - Dean Torrence

Jan & Dean — The Fantastic Baggys

DISCoveries writer Steve Ramm has provided some related reviews that may be of special interest to surf music aficionados. Steve recently up with Jan and Dean on the concert trail. He also reviews the new issue on CD of the 1964 Imperial LP by the Fantastic Baggys.

CONCERT REVIEW
JAN AND DEAN
KOKOMO BAY CAFE
PHILADELPHIA, PENNSYLVANIA

Philly is no Malibu and the Delaware River has no surfers, but for an hour or so on August 19th the surf was up. In a rare club appearance, Jan Berry and Dean Torrence, introduced as "the Messiah of Malibu and the Sultan of Surf," gave a non-stop 70-minute performance under trying conditions. The night started with an unexpected rain storm which caused problems for the management of this outdoor riverfront cafe. One sound system blew and another was immediately rigged up. The opening act, a band from Philly, never went on. But just before the main act was to go the rain stopped and the fans arrived. The sound system never fully cooperated (dead microphones, booming speakers), but the guys and their band worked hard to give those who came a retrospective of their hits and a high energy show.

Jan and Dean are known for their 13 Top 30 singles and many of these were played both as separate numbers and parts of medleys. After sustaining brain damage in a car crash in 1966 at the peak of his career, Jan Berry made a triumphant comeback with his partner in the late 1970s. He is still partially paralyzed, but performs lead vocals (wearing his trademark blue shirt with white stars) on many of the songs (he wrote most of their hits). Dean played guitar and they performed with a capable four-piece back-up.

When it comes to surf music (*Ride the Wild Surf*) and car songs (*Drag City*), Jan and Dean are synonymous with the Beach Boys. They often performed on each others records, so the show included the Beach Boys' *Little Deuce Coupe*, *I Get Around*, and the recent *Kokomo* (ironically the name of this cafe). *Honolulu Lulu* (No. 11 in 1963) came complete with an eruption from the club's artificial volcano! 45 minutes into their performance came the song many people identify with the group since Berry's accident, *Dead Man's Curve* (No. 8 in 1964). This must be a difficult number for him to perform as it almost describes his accident three years before that tragedy. This was followed by a dance medley composed of five songs which were hits for others. The show ended with their only gold record, *Surf City*, and the Beach Boys' *Surfin' U.S.A.* On a number of the songs the band members took lead vocals. One notable performance was *Help Me Rhonda*, with keyboardist Gary Griffin singing lead. Only on *Sidewalk Surfin'* did the band falter; they each seemed in a different key.

While acts like the Beach Boys are touring to large amphitheaters, Jan and Dean took this chance to play at a small club. The audience of about 200, most not born during the "surfin' years," had a rare opportunity to see these legends up close and personal.

CD REVIEW
FANTASTIC BAGGYS
TELL 'EM I'M SURFIN'
BEST OF THE FANTASTIC BAGGYS

When is a Jan and Dean record not really a Jan and Dean record? When it's performed by P.F. Sloan and Steve Barri as the Fantastic Baggys. *Move Out, Little Mustang*, one of the bonus tracks on this disc, was included on Jan and Dean's LP, *Little Old Lady from Pasadena*, though they never sang on it. And no one noticed!

Sloan and Barri were unknown songwriters in L.A. when they got the opportunity to write for Jan and Dean. During their peak years, they also did backup vocals on Jan and Dean's albums. Sloan is the falsetto voice you often hear. They recorded one LP on their own, to latch on to the surf music craze, but never went on tour. That ten-track LP has just been reissued with 11 bonus tracks, including two cuts released only in South Africa (late starters in the surf music days), and some unreleased numbers, too.

The LP included their big hit, *Summer Means Fun*, and other surf and hot rod-related numbers. This was a quickly produced album they did for fun, and the fun shows. Among the numbers released only in South Africa is *Hot Rod, U.S.A.*, written by Bobby Darin and Terry Melcher (Melcher is Doris Day's son and, with Beach Boy Bruce Johnson, was half of Bruce and Terry). Like its surfin' equivalent, this song rhymes cities like Philly, P.A., Old L.A., and San Francisco Bay. The unreleased cuts include a cover of Carl Dobkin Jr.'s *My Heart Is an Open Book*, which seems out of place. The last track, (*Goes to Show*) *Just How Wrong You Can Be* (1966), shows the influence of the British Invasion, (this could be Peter and Gordon singing) and the serious direction Sloan's lyrics were taking (he also wrote Barry McGuire's hit, *Eve of Destruction*). Actually, there's an unlisted 22nd track, but it's just studio fun.

All the tracks on this disc have been remastered from the original three- and four-track master tapes, and they sound great. The book of liner notes recreates the original LP jacket showing four guys in the band. The small print on the back explained that the other two pictured were a "road drummer," and "a friend who hasn't had his picture taken in a long time." It's this sense of laid-back humor that permeates all of Sloan and Barri's songs, and, like a Jan and Dean album, can lift your spirits when it's cold and rainy outside.

—Steven I. Ramm

JAN AND DEAN NEWSLETTER

Done by: Jara and Kim

First issue

JARA & KIM NEWSLETTER FIRST ISSUE

A REVIEW OF JAN & DEAN

(Carla Vis is a Jan and Dean fan from Holland. She had regularly corresponded with Jara Beaubien about the guys, and earlier this year she made a trip to the United States and saw Jan & Dean in concert, and met them personally. This is a review she sent us of their concert.)

The whole theatre was jammed with people. Every seat was occupied and on every free space there was someone standing. When the lights in the theatre went out, and those lights on stage flashed on an enormous roar came from the crowd. You could faintly hear a guitar, and no one could stop the crowd anymore. The curtain went up and in front of our eyes was PAPADOORUNRUN, the band behind Jan & Dean.

They played two or three songs, to bring everybody in the right mood and then the time was right for Jan & Dean. While the audience was yelling as loud as possible, they came on stage. Jan was limping slightly, but looked good otherwise. They started with the "New Girl In School" and immediately had the audience, which included me in their grip. In all these years they were just as good as they had been and they hadn't lost any of their "radiation."

Around me were a couple of girls who seemed to be half hysterical while they were singing and dancing. The place looked like it was filled with madmen.

When "Baby Talk" started (Jan was grinning all over and obviously enjoying himself) Jan was nearly inaudible when he started singing papapapa...... His "Yeah" halfway through the song resulted in another wave of noise and turned out to be a real sensation. It was strange to hear this. Everybody seemed to wait for it. The whole song was built around these two sounds. That's the way the audience felt it. It's hard to describe, but Jan has got something. A certain kind of attraction. It's got nothing to do with his looks, but only with some strange kind of radiation. He's got what makes people a success on stage. It's that incredible thing called "charisma". Dean's personality is more attractive. He's open, friendly, and amiable.

It's no use talking about all of the songs one by one, they were all played reasonably good and some better. Everything and everybody worked together to make a success out of the concert. That as far as I'm concerned they succeeded completely is something that I don't have to emphasize anymore.

I was interested when I went to the concert, I was a fan when I came back. When later on Dean asked me if the concert had been worth it to make the trip from Holland to L.A. I could have hardly said "Yes" with more enthusiasm.

(Carla has since returned to Holland and has published a newsletter for Jan & Dean there, and it's helped, their popularity is growing more and more overseas. We'd like to take the time here to thank Carla for all of her help and support.)

JARA & KIM NEWSLETTER FIRST ISSUE

Hi there all of you Jan and Dean Fans!

After a lot of requests and tons of fan mail, here is our first Newsletter. Hope all of you will enjoy it as much as Kim and I have enjoyed putting it together.

Thru the next pages you'll find articles written about Jan and Dean, a review of Jan and Dean by a fan, an interview with Dean, and part one of "The Road Back From Deadman's Curve", parts 2, 3 & 4 will come out in further issues. This is the article from which the movie was based.

The newsletter will be printed four times a year at the cost of one dollar per issue. Enclosed in this issue is a blank order form for issue number two. Fill out this form and mail it back to us with your dollar.

You can also send us letters for the next newsletter. You can publicize for Jan and Dean Pen Pals, trade records, or if we have the space, you relate your experiences at Jan and Dean concerts and if you have met them in person you can tell us about the experience personally.

We really hope that you will like this newsletter. We'd also like you to tell us what you'd really like to know about the guys, and also tell us what you'd like to see more of in the up coming newsletters. Feedback always helps.

Bust Your Buns,

Jara & Kim

JARA & KIM NEWSLETTER FIRST ISSUE

Dean Torrance of the singing duo, Jan and Dean, and KUIC chief engineer and morning personality Bob Robertson appeared on stage

May Fair audience enjoys musicians

Benicia Herald 5-80

By PeggySue Wells

Singers Jan and Dean carried their audience into the realm of sunshine, surfing and hot rods Thursday night at the Dixon May Fair.

Highlighting the tenth Dixon May Fair was the concert performance by famed musicians Jan and Dean and their talented backup band, Papa Doo Run Run. Emceed by radio KUIC 95 FM personalities, the concert was held under the stars on the fair grounds.

Despite the cold temperature and brisk winds, a healthy crowd of all age groups sounded their enthusiasm and swayed to the strains of the typical '60's tunes.

San Jose natives, Papa Doo Run Run opened the performance, creating an atmosphere of fun in the summertime with such songs as California Cruisin' and Rocking in the Summer. The group featured cuts off their soon to be released new album including I Don't Believe It as well as classics like Wipe Out. Dressed in form fitting white jeans, Hawaiian print shirts and slick jackets, they portrayed that clean, beach-set image, trademark of Jan and Dean as well as associates, the Beach Boys.

Jan and Dean were welcomed on stage by an already warmed and anxious audience. The now seven musicians belted out such favorites as Little Deuce Coupe, California Girls and Help Me Rhonda. Jan's timing with his deep voiced bom-ba-boms was perfect and Dean provided that familiar high strain.

Both singers sported stylish surfer hair cuts and moved easily and comfortably on stage.

Towards the end of their fast paced performance, Jan soloed Deadman's Curve, a song he wrote and which was the title cut from a movie of the same name. The song is somewhat parallel to Jan's own experience in an auto accident and proved to be a moving moment for his attentive listeners.

Once more on the upswing, Jan, Dean and Papa Doo Run Run launched into more rock and roll, climaxing in a sing-a-long of popular Barbara Ann, a hit the Beach Boys made famous with back up from Jan and Dean. KUIC personalities joined the group on stage, lending their voices with those of the audience for the final number.

Old Hits, New Show

About 2,500 fairgoers attended the performance of Jan and Dean and Pappa Doo Run Run Thursday night at the Dixon May Fairgrounds. Dean Torrence, (above) took a break between sets to talk about the style of music he and his partner, Jan Berry, started with their first hit in 1958. Other musical groups that will perform at the fair today (Sunday) include Mark Naftalin's Rhythm and Blues Revue, Queen Ida and her good-time Zydeco band, the Golden State Jazz band, and Del Scorpion and the Stingers.

Vacaville Reporter 5-11-80

JARA & KIM NEWSLETTER FIRST ISSUE

Article from Rolling Stone Magazine   3-23-78

AMERICAN GRANDSTAND   Jan & Dean Ride the Waves   by   Dave Marsh

"A generation has been censored by TV," Marvin Kitman, the world's greatest television critic, wrote recently. Kitman was discussing ROCK FOLLIES, a British situation comedy which has had a brief airing in various parts of the country; it is, as Kitman points out, the only remotely authentic look at the rock scene that television has ever offered.

Television has a noted antipathy for rock. There is a reason for this, beyond the networks apparant hatred of anything less than stale Sonny Bono. Networks buy performance rights to all the songs in the known universe (ASCAP, BMI, SESAC) for an annual fee. But that just takes care of the song writers. To use a real recorded rock song, the networkd would have to enter into negotiations with the owner of the recording, something they don't find apparently worth their while---credibility rarely is. Thus NBC's cretinous crap house,"Whatever Happened To The Class of '65 ?", a series based on the premise that all sixties teenagers had swimming pools, is made even less credible by the fact that the version of California Girls that comes over the rich kids radios sounds like it was done by the same chorale that does the Herbal Essence comercials.

I have seen only one dramatic television show that has avoided that trap. "Deadman's Curve", CBS's February 3rd portrayal of the Jan & Dean story, was immediately striking because the theme song, as well as all of the shows incidental music was the real thing.

It wasn't only the music that clicked, DEADMAN'S CURVE was the best rock drama American television has ever presented, partly, of course, because it is almost the only one. Like ROCK FOLLIES, the show's authenticity was effective because it was so matter-of-fact. Rather than trumpeting the stylistic changes of the sixties--which ran from surfing costuming to psychedelic and back to casual-- these differences simply appeared, which is a lot closer to what happened in real life. When Jan Berry shows up at his birthday party no one says "Hey, neat Nehru jacket, Jan." No one even signed up Teddy Neeley or Sonny Bono as a guest star.

DEADMAN'S CURVE was based on a story which appeared in the Rolling Stone #169; that story detailed Jan Berry's car crash prophesied in the title song, and it's aftermath. And aside from that article, the only detailed commentary ever written about Jan & Dean, I beleive, was written by me, a 5000 word liner note to the 1971 anthology of their music, which was released as part of United Artists Legendary Masters Series. As Jan & Dean's only critical champion, I feel I have the right to claim that the show, for all it's high quality, missed a good deal of the point of the groups music.

According to the TV show, Jan Berry was a musical genius who thought him capable of doing everything himself. But the Jan and Dean songwriting credits, which always pair Berry with collarborator or three suggests otherwise. It is true that Berry produced most of the group's records himself, although in conductor Hal Blaine and "music director" Lou Adler, he had some very astute assistence. But it wasn't Jan & Dean's music that made them continually fascinating, it was their improbable satiric sense of humor. On one album the liner note refers to them as the LAUREL AND HARDY of the surf crowd; their hosting stunt for the TAMI show seems to support the claim. (As a result Dean showing Laurel and Hardy films in Jan's hospital room while Jan lies helpless in a coma is moving indeed.)

JARA & KIM NEWSLETTER FIRST ISSUE

It was my contention in 1971, and I see no reason to modify it, that Jan and Dean were the last authentically humerous rockers. California music has always been about the promise of fun, an elusive concept at best and one whose pursuit is often nothing but grim. (Witness the revitalized Beach Boys, who sell fun as mirthlessly as anyone in the Catskills). And unlike many modern day rock satirists as Flo and Eddie, Jan and Dean never telegraphed their humor; it was there in their hits, but hardly anyone caught on. Still, given our historical vantage point, it's now clear that only someone who thought that Brian Wilson really surfed could have believed that "There's two swinging honey's for every guy/ and all you've got to do is just wink your eye" was anything but a put on. Even "Deadman's Curve" for all it's later real-life resonance, was a satire of rock death songs like "Tell Laura I Love Her" and "Last Kiss".

Times have changed, but not much. In a way the real heirs of Jan and Dean are the Ramones, whose fans undoubtably think they are as committed to beating up women and sniffing glue as Jan and Dean were supposedly to surfing and hot-rodding. Still the cappella recitation of the opening line of "Surf City" by the actor who played Jan was the most moving I've heard in 1978. If it were really Jan Berry who recorded that - it certainly ought to have been - he ought to know that at least one of his old fans shed a tear for the old days, not because they were better, but just because they were more amusing.

THE END

GOSSIP GOSSIP GOSSIP GOSSIP GOSSIP GOSSIP GOSSIP GOSSIP GOSSIP GOSSIP GOSSIP GOSSIP
J&D J&D J&D J&D J&D J&D J&D J&D J&D J&D J&D J&D J&D J&D J&D J&D J&D J&D J&D
FLASH FLASH FLASH FLASH FLASH FLASH FLASH FLASH FLASH FLASH FLASH FLASH FLASH FLASH

Jan and Dean will be appearing at the Harrah's Lake Tahoe December 15th - 28th

The tour of Australia scheduled for Oct. 16th - Nov. 10th was cancelled.

Did you know that Dean has done album covers for Steve Martin, Beach Boys, Nilsson, Walter Egan, Linda Ronstadt and Nitty Gritty Dirt Band?

Did you know that Dean has been nominated for four Grammy's for his album covers and he has won one for an album titled "Pollution"?

Some of Jan's favorite musicians are Little River Band, The Doobies, Kiss and the Bay City Rollers! (Was he kidding? Only Capt. Jan knows for sure!)

Dean likes Steely Dan and ELO.

Here is a question to ponder..........
Who was that wild and crazy California guy with the blue eyes and curly hair that was reportedly discoing the night away last year in Tahoe? Will there be a repeat performance this year? Ah, it is a mystery! (One hint. It sure wasn't Dean the Boy Blunder!)

That's it for this column
Hope that you've enjoyed it

Jara and Kim

JARA & KIM NEWSLETTER FIRST ISSUE

OUR FIRST ANNUAL DEAN TORRENCE (SLIGHTLY OFF THE WALL) INTERVIEW   by Jara & Kim

This is our first interview with Dean and we'd like to thank him for answering our questions. Some of them are things that you, the fans have asked us and some of them came from our own warped minds. We figured he was probably awfully tired of the same run of the mill questions, so we invented a few slightly warped questions of our own, and as expected got a few slightly warped answers back. So be prepared, here we go.

Q: Why is the search for your middle name like finding the eighth wonder of the world?

A: (My middle name) is actually a zero.

Q: What kind of cookies do you like?

A: ANY KIND!

Q: What brand of tennis shoes do you prefer?

A: Tigers. (We should have figured that.)

Q: How would you incorporate Monty Python into your act with Jan?

A: In a cage.

Q: Why didn't you ever get married, or do you have any plans for that in the future Dean?

A: WHAT??

Q: What is your favorite color?

A: Gold.

Q: What kind of music do you like?

A: All kinds.

Q: Do you have any plans for overseas concerts?

A: Yes. (No other information is available as of yet, we'll keep you posted.)

Q: What kind of cars do you like?

A: Small ones.

Q: What do you like doing on your time off?

A: What time off??????

JARA & KIM NEWSLETTER FIRST ISSUE

Q: What is your favorite sport?

A: Football.

Q: What is your opinion of critics?

A: (They are) useless.

Q: What kind of advice would you give kids who want to start in the music field?

A: Know your craft as well as possible.

Q: Which areas do you prefer playing, the east coast or the west coast?

A: (I like) the midwest, south and west.

Q: We know the reason you haven't married is because you hadn't mastered the art of going steady, well it's been a year since you stated this in an interview, Do you have it mastered yet?

A: No.

Q: What is you favorite TV show?

A: General Hospital.

Q: Do you have a pet?

A: No.

Q: What brand of toilet paper do you use?

A: Some old fan letters. (He's just kidding kids. He actually uses some old Beach Boys fan letters).

Hope that all of you enjoyed this interview. Next newsletter we are going to try to pin Jan down for an interview. If you have any questions for the guys that you'd like to know, forward them to us and we'll try to ask them for you.

Jara and Kim

Printed in Surf City USA

Editing by: Kim

Interview of Dean done by: Jara

Pictures given by:
Dee and Jara

Our many thanks to:

Jan and Dean

The Torrences'

The Berrys'

and

All off the Jan & Dean fans

JARA & KIM NEWSLETTER FIRST ISSUE

JARA & KIM NEWSLETTER FIRST ISSUE

8D ST. PETERSBURG TIMES ■ MONDAY, JANUARY 2, 1978

personalities
BECK ON HOLLYWOOD

Jan Berry relives painful past

By MARILYN BECK

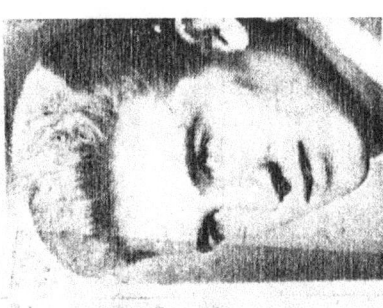

JAN BERRY ... eagerly waitin

HOLLYWOOD — No one is more eagerly awaiting CBS' broadcast of *Deadman's Curve*, the film story of the '60s pop idols Jan & Dean, that Jan Berry — whose near-fatal 1966 car crash put him in a coma for six months, put an end to the fame of Jan & Dean and to his almost-realized dream of becoming a doctor.

To Jan, the show (to be shown in theaters overseas) will serve as the chance to explain to the world why he faded into obscurity — and why he feels he's at last ready to pick up the pieces of his life.

Not that it has been easy for the 36-year-old Berry to relive his painful past while he watches his life unfold for the cameras. Some scenes, in fact, have been so powerful that producer Pat Rooney took pains to keep Jan off the set while they were shooting.

"But there was one time," reports Rooney, "when he came on the soundstage unnoticed. And there was actor Richard Hatch portraying Jan, sitting at the piano physically unable to translate the music in his head. He was just at the point where he was plunking at the keys, terribly frustrated — when all of a sudden we heard the real Jan burst into tears."

The real Jan Berry — whose right arm is still partially paralyzed, who walks with a pronounced limp, and whose sight and speech have been left impaired by the accident — has been recording for Ode Records the past few years and is working on an A&M album he hopes will be released in conjunction with *Deadman's Curve*.

He and Dean (who's also been recording on his own and operates Kittyhawk Graphics, an album design company) have no plans to formally reunite as a team — but they both hold high hopes that the CBS movie about their lives will bring about a new burst of interest in Jan Berry and Dean Torrence as individual entertainers.

JAN & DEAN and PAPA DOO RUN RUN AT STARS, PHILADELPHIA 1978

Stephen Starr Presents

STARS
2nd & Bainbridge 627-8033

TUES/MAY 1
THE BIG BONE BAND

WED/MAY 2
PAPA JOHN CREACH

THUR/MAY 3 WIOQ Concert Event
SUSAN

FRI/MAY 4
roye albrighton's
NEKTAR

SAT/MAY 5
JAMES COTTON
john cadillac blues band

MON/MAY 7
TONY WILLIAMS

THUR/MAY 10
CHARLIE HADEN/
DON PULLEN

FRI/MAY 11
JAN & DEAN
papa doo run run

THUR/MAY 17
HUGH MASAKELA

JUNE 14–16
THE PAT METHENY
GROUP TICKETS ON SALE

Ticket Outlets: Plastic Fantastic, Bryn Mawr; Record Revolution, Wilmington; Peaches, Northeast & Merchantville, N.J.; 3rd Street Jazz; Key Records, New Hope.

JAN & DEAN and PAPA DOO RUN RUN AT STARS, PHILADELPHIA 1978

JAN & DEAN VALLEY FORGE MUSIC FAIR 1981

Valley Forge Music Fair
DEVON, PA.
LEE GUBER & SHELLY GROSS PRESENT

SHA NA NA
special guest star
MARK MOZZARELLA
Thurs., Fri. (8 p.m.), Sat. (6:00 & 10:00 p.m.), Sun. (4:30 & 8:30 p.m.) $12.00

ST. PATRICK'S DAY FESTIVAL — **MON., MARCH 16**
DENNIS DAY
CARMEL QUINN
O'SULLIVAN'S IRISH FOLK DANCERS
Mon. (8 p.m.) $9.75

SUN., MARCH 22
OAK RIDGE BOYS
special guest star CON HUNLEY
Sun. (3 & 7:30 p.m.) $10.75

TUE., MARCH 24 thru SUN. MARCH 29
LIBERACE
Tues., Wed., Thurs. (8 p.m.), Fri. (2 p.m.), Sun. (3 p.m.) $13.75
Fri., Sat. (8 p.m.), Sun. (7:30 p.m.) $15.25

THURS., APRIL 9 thru SAT., APRIL 11
HARRY CHAPIN
Thurs., Fri., Sat. (8:00 p.m.) All Seats: $10.75

FRI., APRIL 24 & SAT., APRIL 25
DINAH SHORE
Inner Circle Tickets Being Held
Fri. (8:00 pm), Sat. (6:00 & 10:00) $12.75

FRI., MAY 15 thru SUN., MAY 17
JOHNNY CASH
Fri (8 p.m.), Sat. (5:30 & 9:30 p.m.), Sun. (3 & 7:30 p.m.) $10.75

TUES., MAY 19 & WED., MAY 20
AN EVENING WITH
LETTERMEN
Tues., Wed. (8 p.m.) $10.75

SAT., MAY 23 & SUN., MAY 24
LORETTA LYNN
special guest star to be announced
Sat. (5:30 & 9:30 p.m.), Sun. (3 & 7:30 p.m.) $10.75

FRI., JUNE 5 thru SUN., JUNE 7
ALAN KING
special guest star to be announced
Fri. (8:00 pm), Sat. (6:00 & 10:00) Sun. (7:30). All Seats. $12.50

MON., JUNE 15
JAMES GALWAY
CLEO LAINE
Mon. (8 p.m.) $15.00

WED., JUNE 17 thru SUN., JUNE 21
BOBBY VINTON
Wed., Thurs. (8:00 pm) $10.75
Fri. (8:00 pm), Sat. (6:00 & 10:00), Sun. (7:30) $11.75

TUES., JULY 7 thru SUN., JULY 12
FRANKIE LAINE   HELEN O'CONNELL
special guest star
HARRY JAMES AND HIS ORCHESTRA
Tues. (8 p.m.) $7.75, Wed., Thurs. (8 p.m.), Sun. (3 & 7:30 p.m.) $9.75
Fri. (8 p.m.), Sat. (5:30 & 9:30 p.m.) $10.75

MON., JULY 20 & TUES., JULY 21
JUDY COLLINS
Mon., Tues. (8 p.m.) $10.75

SAT., JULY 25
SMOKEY ROBINSON
Sat. (6:00 & 10:00 pm) $10.75

WED., JULY 22 & THURS., JULY 23
JAN & DEAN
Wed., Thurs. (8 p.m.) $9.75

FOR THE KIDS! MARCH 14 • 1:00 P.M.
THE PRINCE & THE PAUPER
APR. 15 & APR. 16 • 1:00 P.M.
ALICE IN WONDERLAND
$3.00 Individual
$2.00 Groups of 25 or more CALL (215) 879-8064
ALLEGRO PRODUCTIONS

CHARGE ON VISA or MC: (215) 296-9994
INFO: (215) 644-5000 • GROUPS: (215) 647-2307
MAIL ORD'RS write Valley Forge Music Fair, Devon, Pa. 19333. Send Check or Money order with self-addressed stamped envelope. Include $.50 handling charge. Please list alternate dates.
MUSIC FAIR ENTERPRISES INC.

JAN & DEAN VALLEY FORGE MUSIC FAIR 1981

The return of Jan Berry and Dean Torrance to the concert stage after an absence of nearly fourteen years is one of the most encouraging musical developments of the decade to date. Together with the backing Papa Doo Run Run band, Jan And Dean provided enthusiastic audiences across the country with a show that will prove them to once again be a major musical force to be reckoned with in the months to come.

JAN AND DEAN SUMMER TOUR 1980

BY MIKE McDOWELL

The Michigan stop of their tour brought them to the Meadowbrook Music Theatre on July 9, where a crowd of more than 8,000 people witnessed a superb show, combining such Jan And Dean classics as *The New Girl In School*, *Drag City*, and *Ride The Wild Surf* with an abundance of new originals, as well as a generous helping of such diverse covers as the Beach Boys' *Dance, Dance, Dance* and the Spencer Davis Group's *Gimme Some Lovin'*. The traditional on-stage dry humor was in full force, with Jan And Dean trading one-line gags in between numbers. Ever the showman, Dean attempted a demonstration of skateboard tricks (which was thwarted by the stage's carpet), but also proved himself to be a competent rhythm guitarist.

The sudden resurgence of Jan And Dean's popularity, has inspired several record companies to re-issue classic Jan And Dean material, a move that the duo is not entirely pleased with. The controversy centers around a recent Canadian package, *The Jan And Dean Story*, released on K-Tel records. "Making a deal with K-Tel was a big mistake in the first place," explained Dean Torrence. "K-Tel is simply the current incarnation of Roulette, a company making a living off of the hits of countless artists. Papa Doo Run Run and I re-cut some of the Jan And Dean hits for them in 1977. We deliberately did them as badly as we could, under the premise that nobody would ever think of releasing the material. But they did anyway." The K-Tel offering includes these re-recordings of the Liberty label Jan And Dean material, as well as some rare sides from their sessions for Dore records.

On the other hand, Blue Pacific records in Hollywood has released a superbly packaged two record set of some of the most in-demand Jan And Dean single releases, including *Hawaii, Fan Tan, Laurel And Hardy, Tijuana, Louisiana Man,* and *Love And Hate,* as well as alternate takes of *Ride The Wild Surf, From All Over The World,* and *Fun City.* The album comes documented with original release dates, matrix numbers, writers' credits, and rare photographs from Jan And Dean's Winter, 1966 tour program. All in all, a superbly done effort.

The best news of the tour is the imminent possibility of a new Jan And Dean single. "We've written a lot of new material," added Dean Torrence. "Jeff 'Skunk' Baxter, of the Doobie Brothers is mixing some tracks for us while we're on the road, and

he'll probably produce the session. If we don't get a satisfactory offer from any labels, we'll put it out ourselves." The A-side will probably be *Do It In The Dirt,* an up-tempo Papa Doo Run Run composition about motorbikes.

The remainder of the 1980 Summer tour takes them throughout the mid-west and Canada, after which the group returns to their California home base for a brief rest. The warm reception afforded them on this sold-out tour has erased any doubts the duo may have had about the success of such an endeavor, and their return to touring on a regular basis now seems certain. Perhaps, Jan Berry best sums up the feelings of the group as a whole towards this matter: *"I love it!"*

OPPOSITE PAGE: TOP—Jan And Dean. **BOTTOM**—Papa Doo Run Run's drummer during the drum solo of *Wipe Out.* **THIS PAGE: TOP LEFT**—Papa Doo Run Run rocks to *Do It In The Dirt.* **RIGHT**—Dean Torrance proved to be a competent rhythm guitarist during the Meadowbrook show. **ABOVE**—Papa Doo Run Run's bass player on stage at the Meadowbrook music theater.

PHOTOS BY DEANNE NICHOLS

www.ingramcontent.com/pod-product-compliance
Lightning Source LLC
Chambersburg PA
CBHW080449170426
43196CB00016B/2740